# International Arbitration Rules

## a comparative guide

*Edited by*
*Bridget Wheeler*
*MA (Cantab), Solicitor of the Supreme Court*

LLP

LLP Professional Publishing
2000

LLP Professional Publishing
(a trading division of Informa Publishing Group Ltd)
69-77 Paul Street
London EC2A 4LQ
Great Britain

EAST ASIA
LLP Asia
Sixth Floor, Hollywood Centre
233 Hollywood Road
Hong Kong



*British Library Cataloguing
in Publication Data
A catalogue record for this book
is available from the British Library*

ISBN 1 85978 523 9



Set in Adobe Minion
Printed and bound by Hobbs the Printers, Southampton

# Acknowledgements

The rules in this book have been reproduced with the kind permission of the following organisations:

**American Arbitration Association**

**China International Economic Trade Arbitration Commission (CIETAC)**

**International Chamber of Commerce**

*ICC Rules of Arbitration (1998) – ICC Rules of Conciliation (1998)*

ICC Publication No. 581 – ISBN 92.842.1239.1 (E)

Published in its official English version by the International Chamber of Commerce.



Available from: *The ICC International Court of Arbitration*, 38 Cours Albert 1er 75008, Paris, France or ICC United Kingdom, 14/15 Belgrave Square, London SW1X 8PS, United Kingdom.

**London Court of International Arbitration**

**Stockholm Chamber of Commerce**

**World Intellectual Property Organisation (WIPO)**

# Contents

CHAPTER 1

# Introduction

This book has its origins in a lecture trip I made shortly after the English 1996 Arbitration Act came into effect. I shared a platform in venues in the USA and New Zealand with arbitration experts from other countries. Whatever the subject matter of our respective papers in open forum session the question that most frequently arose was – if I have to have an arbitration, what are the benefits of the various institutions? What pitfalls may there be? And in spite of an attempt at objectivity, enthusiasm was generally expressed by panel members for those institutions with which they were most familiar.

In the course of these discussions, however, interesting snippets of information surfaced, one way or another, about special features of various institutions which took some of our audience (and panel) by surprise. For example, unless expressly stipulated to the contrary, the language of an international arbitration conducted under the Chinese CIETAC Rules will be Chinese (Article 75), the USA AAA effectively excludes the award of punitive damages (Article 28.5); CIETAC restricts appointments to members of its own panel.

It became a matter of interest to me to try and set out clearly how the rules varied and how they were similar. In doing this I saw it as primarily an aid to those concerned with the drafting of contracts, perhaps not themselves familiar with the arbitration process, as well as a useful *aide-mémoire* for the arbitration practitioner. To avoid requiring the draftsman to undertake a detailed review of all the rules, I attempted to break the arbitration process down into six logical parts and then to provide several headings within each part and a brief introduction to highlight practical points. The introductions included comments from the 1996 Arbitration Act so as to give a further, general, comparison with English ad hoc procedure and, to the extent that the l996 Act of laws UNCITRAL (which it does for the greater part) a feel for how UNCITRAL may differ.

There were huge difficulties. I used the ICC – the grandfather of all institutions – as my model, and whilst many of the provisions between institutions are similar (for example, all have procedures for ensuring arbitrator impartiality) sometimes there is no directly comparative provision. The ICC's exhaustive rules for procedure prior to the appointment of the Tribunal are not exactly mirrored elsewhere. The ICC, for example, can (and does) administer various stages of an arbitration itself in advance of the appointment of a Tribunal, and rules about the delivery of pleadings in other institutions (e.g., LCIA) find no directly comparative ICC provision. The ICC Request for arbitration stage (where typically a more general plea is made) is superficially similar but, in practice, a bespoke submission is later ordered pursuant to the Terms of Reference stage (Article 18) often long after the delivery of the Request. Terms of Reference are a unique ICC creature. I am afraid this edition will find duplication between sections, and perhaps inconsistency, the selection process being subjective. Perhaps the section of most interest to the commercial reader will be the final appendix – Appendix 3 – where a costs comparison is to be found.

This book does not attempt to extend its ambit beyond the simple wording of the rules of the various institutions. Most institutions permit the seat of the arbitration under their rules to be anywhere, world-wide. The impact of the local law is not part of this text, but obviously the attitude of the local courts where the arbitration is held, and indeed of the courts where it may be sought to be enforced are additional important considerations.

### The Big Six (and others)

The greater part of this text is directed to a direct comparison of the rules of the Big Six on a clause-by-clause basis. The present rules of the ICC have been chosen as the blueprint against which all the others are measured simply because it still probably represents by value of dispute the biggest arbitration institution in the world. Present research indicates that CIETAC is the fastest growing organisation. By way of introduction, however, a brief description of each of the Big Six and their main rivals is set out here. The "Big Six" are chosen not only in terms of size but – in the case of WIPO – which at present has not the volume of cases of the others for its overall importance, as its rules are in origin the most modern. In their second appendix at the end of the text are the present fee arrangements for the major institutions.

**International Chamber of Commerce ("ICC")**
*Headquarters:* 38 Cours Albert 1$^{er}$, 75008 Paris, France – Committees in over 50 countries.
*Date established:* 1919.
*Volume of arbitration p.a.:* Approximately 500 new cases p.a.
*Fast track process:* No.
*Specialist services:* Marine.
*Mediation services:* Yes
*Other comments:* Rules revised l998.

**London Court of International Arbitration ("LCIA")**
*Headquarters:* LCIA, The International Dispute Resolution Centre, 8 Breams Buildings, Chancery Lane, London, EC4A lHP.
*Date established:* 1892.
*Fast track process:* Not as such – expedited appointment process.
*Specialist services:* No.
*Mediation services:* Yes
*Other comments:* Rules revised 1998.

**American Arbitration Association ("AAA")**
*Headquarters:* American Arbitration Association, 335 Madison Avenue, 10th Floor, New York, NY 10017–4605, USA.
*Date established:* 1926.
*Fast track process:* No.
*Specialist services:* Big domestic capacity (60,000 cases p.a.) as well as international sector.
*Mediation services:* Yes.
*Other comments:* International rules revised 1997.

**China International Economic Trade Arbitration Commission ("CIETAC")**
*Headquarters:* Beijing.
*Date established:* 1954.
*Volume of arbitration p.a.:* In 1994, 829 new cases.
*Fast track process:* Yes.
*Mediation services:* Yes.
*Other comments:* Rules revised 1995.

**World Intellectual Property Organisation ("WIPO")**
*Headquarters:* Arbitration & Mediation Centre, World Intellectual Property Organisation, 34 Chenin des Colombettes, P O Box 18, 1211 Geneva 20, Switzerland.
*Date established:* 1994.
*Volume of arbitration p.a.:* Anticipating significant growth given boom in commerce.
*Fast track process:* Yes – expedited arbitration rules.
*Specialist services:* It is an intellectual property service.
*Mediation services:* Yes.
*Other comments:* An Inter-governmental organisation specialist agency of United Nations. 157 member states. Rules date from 1994.

**Stockholm – Chamber of Commerce**
*Headquarters:* Stockholm.
*Date established:* 1917.
*Fast track process:* Yes.
*Specialist services:* Yes – insurance.
*Mediation services:* Yes
*Other comments:* Rules revised 1999.

I conclude with setting out the observation of the panel members from my lecture tour and my own thoughts on the six institutions covered herein. First, the question "court or arbitration?" has to be addressed. The concern was that in an international contract each party would almost certainly be best served by and most comfortable with his local court (although on the whole, under the New York

Convention, arbitration awards are more freely enforceable world wide). That was unlikely to be an option in a hard fought negotiation. "Neutral" venue arbitration was therefore a logical fall back.

The ICC remains, I suspect, the "premier" choice, the oldest of the institutions, enjoying continued success as the choice of nations and companies with their most substantial disputes. If there is criticism that can be made it is that the administration is large, and various stages of the process can be slow – typically Tribunal selection, finalisation of Terms of Reference and scrutiny of awards. The quality of the awards is high and are cited as being expensive. That is not an altogether fair criticism. Cash flow can be seriously challenged as advances – to be in place is practice by the time of delivery of terms of reference – are calculated on a percentage of the amounts in issue. Draw down, however, is chiefly on the basis of an hourly rate, not out of line with the other institutions.

LCIA has enjoyed a resurgence over the last few years under energetic management, and its recent move to modern premises bodes well. The experience of this institution is that whilst it is smaller than the ICC in terms of the volume of arbitrations, it is growing. It has a good reputation for speed of response so far as the composition of tribunals is concerned (although it can still lag behind the ad hoc process where both parties are co-operative). The institution initially plays a low key supporting role once the Tribunal is in place. Whilst arbitrator rates are not dissimilar to those of the ICC, a slimline administration and shorter procedural schedule can usually result in a lower bill. A criticism levelled at it is that it still offers a very English style system.

AAA – The US Institution reorganised its international programme in New York a few years ago and its rules are clear and well drafted. There have in the past been concerns expressed of inconsistency with quality and it can be seen as very American in style. It has addressed the questions of quality by a continuing review of its pool or arbitrators. It is generally considered faster and less bureaucratic than the ICC.

WIPO – The rules are of particular interest as they are probably the most modern in origin. Whilst all the institutions have recent revisions to their rules, they are still based on pre-existing models. WIPO started with a clear slate and the rules read well. It is, however, not always a directly comparative institution, being specialist in the service it offers. It is highly regarded for its IP expertise and there has been significant activity regarding domain name disputes. Recently it has taken steps to broaden its on-line dispute resolution capabilities. It has, however, only a limited number of large arbitrations to date.

CIETAC is the fastest growing institution in the world and likely to remain so, in spite of concern (now probably resolved) that with the return of Hong Kong to China enforcement problems in Hong Kong under the New York Convention might arise. If there is concern it is lack of experience of the panel – although that said it includes illustrious western names as well as local arbitrators. There have been complaints of delay and of a lack of decisiveness. There is a perception that fees are relatively modest.

STOCKHOLM – One of the natural choices (along with Switzerland, Austria and London) where Eastern bloc countries are concerned. The new rules are simple and uncontroversial. Stockholm is well placed geographically as a venue. Concerns are: price, a relatively small pool of local lawyers with relevant existence to assist; and rules, which in the past have required arbitrations to run their entire course before complaints – such an excess of jurisdiction – can be resolved. Whilst an important centre it is probably the smallest (along with WIPO) of those reviewed here.

Finally, I have to acknowledge with continuing gratitude the guidance and help of my colleagues, William L. Craig and Gary Benton of Coudert Brothers, in the compilation of this text.

*Bridget Wheeler, November 2000*

CHAPTER 2

# Commencing the Arbitration

The UNCITRAL based English Arbitration Act 1996 deals with commencement at sections 12-14. The way in which arbitration is commenced is a matter on which the parties are free to agree, in default of which the proceedings are commenced when an arbitrator is named or designated, by service of a written notice by one party on the other requiring submission of the dispute to that party, or, where arbitrators are to be appointed by the parties, upon service of a written notice requiring the appointment of an arbitrator or agreement as to the identity of the arbitrator; if there is a provision in the arbitration agreement for appointment by a third party, proceedings commence with the written request to appoint by either party.

The ICC Rules provide at Article 4 for the submission of a Request for Arbitration (in a particular form) to the Secretariat, which in turn notifies the Claimant and Respondent. Article 5 calls for an Answer in a specific form to be provided, and Article 6 specifically refers to the ICC Rules current at the time of the "commencement of the arbitration proceedings" applying, a reference back to the time of making the request. The Secretariat is very aware of the importance, for example in cases where a time limit is imminent, of efficient logging of time of receipt; this can even be done out of office hours. Whilst hard copy requests are preferred, faxed requests will be accepted (and will be logged in to stop the time clock) so long as promptly followed by a hard copy.

The LCIA provides for commencement procedures at Article 1, by the sending of a request to the LCIA in a specific form. In rather more specific terms LCIA Article 1.2 identifies precisely the date of commencement of proceedings i.e. the date of receipt by the Registrar of the request.

AAA's International Arbitration rules provide at Article 2 the procedure for commencing arbitration. The Claimant is obliged to give a written notice (in a specific form) to the AAA administrator and at the same time to the Respondent, and the proceedings are deemed commenced on the date the administrator receives the notice.

CIETAC provides simply and succinctly at Article 13 that the arbitration proceedings shall commence from the date on which Notice of Arbitration is sent out by the Arbitration Commission with submissions. Article 14 specifies how the application to CIETAC for arbitration is to be made and Article 15 sets out the procedure the CIETAC Secretariat must adopt prior to sending ("immediately") the Notice to the Respondent.

WIPO provides at Articles 6-13 of Section II specific rules for commencing arbitrations. Article 7 specifies that the commencement date is "the date on which the Request for Arbitration [sent by the Claimant] is received by the Centre".

STOCKHOLM covers "initiation of proceedings" by Articles 5-15 (broadly); the arbitration is initiated by the Claimant filing a compliant request with the SCC Institute, and the date of commencement is the date on which the SCC receives the request.

Observations: There is considerable similarity with the way in which most of the institutions deal with the problem of commencement. It is (with the exception of CIETAC) when the *institution* receives the request. Provided that the institution is efficient at monitoring receipt this is a sensible way of stopping time and affords comfortable security to a claimant in danger of running out of time. It mirrors the court process in many countries. The CIETAC approach could prove problematic if but a short period of time remained before time expired as the clock only stops upon a responsive act by the CIETAC Secretariat. CIETAC is the fastest growing arbitration institution in the world, and to maintain its position it will be important for it to demonstrate speed and efficiency, in particular in turning around notifying claims within the date of receipt.

| ICC | LCIA | AAA | WIPO | CIETAC | STOCKHOLM |
|---|---|---|---|---|---|
| **1. Commencing arbitration: Request/Notice for Arbitration** | | | | | |
| **Article 4: Request for Arbitration**<br><br>**4(1)** A party wishing to have recourse to arbitration under these Rules shall submit its Request for Arbitration (the "Request") to the Secretariat, which shall notify the Claimant and Respondent of the receipt of the Request and the date of such receipt. | **Article 1: The Request for Arbitration**<br>**1.1** Any party wishing to commence an arbitration under these Rules ("the Claimant") shall send to the Registrar of the LCIA Court ("the Registrar") a written request for arbitration ("the Request"), containing or accompanied by: | **Notice of Arbitration and Statement of Claim Article 2**<br>**2.1.** The party initiating arbitration ("claimant") shall give written notice of arbitration to the administrator and at the same time to the party against whom a claim is being made ("respondent"). | **Article 6**<br>The Claimant shall transmit the Request for Arbitration to the Center and to the Respondent. | **Article 13:** The arbitration proceedings shall commence from the date on which the Notice of Arbitration is sent out by the Arbitration Commission or its Sub-Commissions.<br>**Article 14**<br>The Claimant shall satisfy the following requirements when submitting his Application for Arbitration: | **Article 5 Request for Arbitration**<br>Arbitration is initiated by the Claimant filing with the SCC Institute a Request for Arbitration which shall include: |
| **4(2)** The date on which the Request is received by the Secretariat shall, for all purposes, be deemed to be the date of the commencement of the arbitral proceedings. | **1.2** The date of receipt by the Registrar of the Request shall be treated as the date on which the arbitration has commenced for all purposes. The Request (including all accompanying documents) should be submitted to the Registrar in two copies where a sole arbitrator should be appointed, or, if the parties have agreed or the Claimant considers that three arbitrators should be appointed, in four copies. | **2.2.** Arbitral proceedings shall be deemed to commence on the date on which the administrator receives the notice of arbitration.<br>**2.3.a.** The notice for arbitration shall contain a statement of claim including the following:<br>a demand that the dispute be referred to arbitration; | **Article 7:** The date of commencement of the arbitration shall be the date on which the Request for Arbitration is received by the Center. | | **Article 8: Date of Commencement of the Arbitration**<br>The arbitration shall be deemed to have been commenced on the date on which the Request for Arbitration was received by the SCC Institute. |
| **2. Request/Notice to include description of parties and circumstances of dispute** | | | | | |
| **4(3)** The Request shall, inter alia, contain the following information:<br>**(a)** the name in full, description and address of each of the parties; | **1.1(a)** the names, addresses, telephone, facsimile, telex and e-mail numbers (if known) of the parties to the arbitration and of their legal representatives; | **2.3.b.** the names and addresses of the parties; | **Article 9**<br>The Request for Arbitration shall contain:<br>(i) a demand that the dispute be referred to arbitration under the WIPO Arbitration Rules;<br>(ii) the names, addresses and telephone, telex, telefax or other communication references of the parties and of the representative of the Claimant; | **Article 14**<br>The Claimant shall satisfy the following requirements when submitting his<br>Application for Arbitration:<br>(1) an Application for Arbitration in writing shall be submitted and the following shall be specified in the Application for Arbitration:<br>(a) the name and address of the Claimant and those of the Respondent, including the zip code, telephone number, telex number, fax number, cable number or other telecommunication means, if any; | **Article 5 Request for Arbitration**<br>Arbitration is initiated by the Claimant filing with the SCC Institute a Request for Arbitration which shall include:<br>(i) a statement of the names, addresses, telephone and facsimile numbers and e-mail addresses of the parties and their counsel; |
| **4(3)(b)** a description of the nature and circumstances of the dispute giving rise to the claims; | **1.1(c)** a brief statement describing the nature and circumstances of the dispute, and specifying the claims advanced by the Claimant against another party to the arbitration ("the Respondent"); | **2.3.f.** the relief or remedy sought and the amount claimed; and | (iv) a brief description of the nature and circumstances of the dispute, including an indication of the rights and property involved and the nature of any technology involved;<br>**Article 10**<br>The Request for Arbitration may also | (c) the facts of the case and the main points of dispute;<br>(d) the Claimant's claim and the facts and reasons on which his claim is based. The Application for Arbitration shall be signed and/or stamped by the Claimant and/or the | (ii) a summary of the dispute; |

| ICC | LCIA | AAA | WIPO | CIETAC | STOCKHOLM |
|---|---|---|---|---|---|
| | | | be accompanied by the Statement of Claim referred to in Article 41. | attorney authorized by the Claimant. **(2)** When an Application for Arbitration is submitted to the Arbitration Commission, the relevant documentary evidence on which the Claimant's claim is based shall accompany the Application for Arbitration. | |
| **3. Request/Notice to include description of relief sought** | | | | | |
| **4(3)(c)** a statement of the relief sought including, to the extent possible, an indication of any amount(s) claimed; | | | **9(v)** a statement of the relief sought and an indication, to the extent possible, of any amount claimed; | | **5(iii)** a preliminary statement of the relief sought by the Claimant; |
| **4. Request/Notice to include reference to arbitration agreement** | | | | | |
| **4(3)(d)** the relevant agreements and, in particular, the arbitration agreement; | **1.1(b)** a copy of the written arbitration clause or separate written arbitration agreement invoked by the Claimant ("the Arbitration Agreement"), together with a copy of the contractual documentation in which the arbitration clause is contained or in respect of which the arbitration arises; | **2.3(c)** a reference to the arbitration clause or agreement that is invoked;<br>**2.3(d)** a reference to any contract out of or in relation to which the dispute arises; | **9(iii)** a copy of the Arbitration Agreement and, if applicable, any separate choice-of-law clause; | **14(1)(b)** the arbitration agreement relied upon by the Claimant; | **5(iv)** a copy of the arbitration agreement or clause under which the dispute is to be settled; and |
| **5. Request/Notice to include details of intended Tribunal** | | | | | |
| **4(3)(e)** all relevant particulars concerning the number of arbitrators and their choice in accordance with the provisions of Articles 8, 9 and 10, and any nomination of an arbitrator required thereby; and | **1.1(d)** a statement of any matters (such as the seat or language(s) of the arbitration, or the number of arbitrators, or their qualifications or identities) on which the parties have already agreed in writing for the arbitration or in respect of which the Claimant wishes to make a proposal;<br>**1.1(e)** if the Arbitration Agreement calls for party nomination of arbitrators, the name, address, telephone, facsimile, telex and e-mail numbers (if known) of the Claimant's nominee; | **2.3.g.** may include proposals as to the means of designating and the number of arbitrators, the place of arbitration and the language(s) of the arbitration. | | | **5(v)** if applicable, a statement identifying the arbitrator appointed by the Claimant, including such arbitrator's address, telephone and facsimile numbers and e-mail address. |

| ICC | LCIA | AAA | WIPO | CIETAC | STOCKHOLM |
|---|---|---|---|---|---|
| **6. Request/Notice to include comments on venue, law and language of arbitration** | | | | | |
| **4(3)(f)** any comments as to the place of arbitration, the applicable rules of law and the language of the arbitration. | **1.1(d)** a statement of any matters (such as the seat or language(s) of the arbitration, or the number of arbitrators, or their qualifications or identities) on which the parties have already agreed in writing for the arbitration or in respect of which the Claimant wishes to make a proposal; | | **9(vi)** any appointment that is required by, or observations that the Claimant considers useful in connection with, Articles 14 to 20. | | |
| **7. Registration fees** | | | | | |
| **4(4)** Together with the Request, the Claimant shall submit the number of copies thereof required by Article 3(1) and shall make the advance payment on administrative expenses required by (Appendix III) ("Arbitration Costs and Fees") in force on the date the Request is submitted. In the event that the Claimant fails to comply with either of these requirements, the Secretariat may fix a time limit within which the Claimant must comply, failing which the file shall be closed without prejudice to the right of the Claimant to submit the same claims at a later date in another Request. | **1.1(f)** the fee prescribed in the Schedule of Costs (without which the Request shall be treated as not having been received by the Registrar and the arbitration as not having been commenced); | **33(1)** When a party files claims, the administrator may request the filing party to deposit appropriate amounts as an advance for the costs referred to in Article 31, paragraphs (a), (b) and (c). | **67(a)** The Request for Arbitration shall be subject to the payment to the Center of a registration fee, which shall belong to the International Bureau of WIPO. The amount of the registration fee shall be fixed in the Schedule of Fees applicable on the date on which the Request for Arbitration is received by the Center.<br>**67(b)** The registration fee shall not be refundable.<br>**67(c)** No action shall be taken by the Center on a Request for Arbitration until the registration fee has been paid.<br>**67(d)** If a Claimant fails, within 15 days after a second reminder in writing from the Center, to pay the registration fee, it shall be deemed to have withdrawn its Request for Arbitration. | **14(3)** The Claimant shall pay an arbitration fee in advance to the Arbitration Commission according to the Arbitration Fee Schedule of the Arbitration Commission. | **Article 6: Registration Fee**<br>**6(1)** At the same time as the Request for Arbitration is filed, the Claimant shall pay a Registration Fee. The amount of the fee is fixed in accordance with the SCC Institute's Regulations for Arbitration Costs in force on the date of the Request for Arbitration.<br>**6(2)** If the required Registration Fee is not paid when filing the Request for Arbitration, the SCC Institute will fix a period of time within which the Claimant must pay such fee.<br>**Article 7: Dismissal**<br>If it is clear that the SCC Institute lacks jurisdiction over the dispute or if the Registration Fee has not been paid in due time, the Claimant's Request for Arbitration shall be dismissed. |
| **8. Copies for other parties/institutions involved in Tribunal** | | | | | |
| **Article 3: Written notifications or communications; time limits**<br>**3(1)** All pleadings and other written communications submitted by any party, as well as all documents annexed thereto, shall be supplied in a number of copies sufficient to provide one copy for each party, plus one for each arbitrator, and one for | **1.1(g)** confirmation to the Registrar that copies of the Request (including all accompanying documents) have been or are being served simultaneously on all other parties to the arbitration by one or more means of service to be identified in such confirmation. | **2.4.** Upon receipt of the notice of arbitration, the administrator shall communicate with all parties with respect to the arbitration and shall acknowledge the commencement of the arbitration. | **Article 5**<br>**5(a)** Until the notification by the Center of the establishment of the Tribunal, any written statement, notice or other communication required or allowed under Articles 6 to 36 shall be submitted by a party to the Center and a copy thereof shall at the same time be transmit- | **Article 15:** After receipt of the Application for Arbitration and its attachments and when the secretariat of the Arbitration Commission, after examination, deems that the Claimant has not completed the formalities required for arbitration, the secretariat shall demand the Claimant to complete them, and | |

| ICC | LCIA | AAA | WIPO | CIETAC | STOCKHOLM |
|---|---|---|---|---|---|
| the Secretariat. A copy of any communication from the Arbitral Tribunal to the parties shall be sent to the Secretariat.<br>**3(2)** All notifications of communications from the Secretariat and the Arbitral Tribunal shall be made to the address or the last known address of the party or its representatives for whom the same or are intended, as notified either by the party in question or by the other party as appropriate. Such notification or communication may be made by delivery against receipt, registered post, courier, facsimile transmission, telex, telegram or any other means of telecommunication that provides a record of the sending thereof.<br>**3(3)** A notification or communication shall be deemed to have been effected on the day when it was received by the party itself or by its representative, or would have so been received if made in accordance with the preceding paragraph.<br>**4(5)** The Secretariat shall send a copy of the Request and the documents annexed thereto to the Respondent for its Answer to the Request once the Secretariat has sufficient copies of the Request and the required advance payment. | | | ted by that party to the other party.<br>**5(b)** Any written statement, notice or other communication so sent to the Center shall be sent in a number of copies equal to the number required to provide one copy for each envisaged arbitrator and one for the Center.<br>**5(c)** After the notification by the Center of the establishment of the Tribunal, any written statements, notices or other communications shall be submitted by a party directly to the Tribunal and a copy thereof shall at the same time be supplied by that party to the other party.<br>**5(d)** The Tribunal shall send to the Center a copy of each order or other decision that it makes.<br>**Article 8**<br>The Center shall inform the Claimant and the Respondent of the receipt by it of the Request for Arbitration and of the date of the commencement of the arbitration. | when the secretariat deems that the Claimant has completed the formalities, the secretariat shall immediately send to the Respondent a Notice of Arbitration together with one copy each of the Claimant's Application for Arbitration and its attachments as well as the Arbitration Rules, the Panel of Arbitrators and the Arbitration Fee Schedule of the Arbitration Commission, and shall simultaneously send to the Claimant one copy each of the Notice of Arbitration, the Arbitration Rules, the Panel of Arbitrators and Arbitration Fee Schedule. The secretariat of the Arbitration Commission, afte sending the Notice of Arbitration to the Claimant and Respondent, shall appoint one of its staff-members to take charge of procedural administration of the case.<br>**Article 20:** When submitting application for arbitration, written defense, statement of counterclaim, documentary evidence and other documents, the party/parties shall submit them in quintuplicate. If the number of the parties exceeds two, additional copies shall be submitted accordingly; if the number of arbitrator of the arbitration tribunal is one, two copies may be reduced. | |
| **9. Transmission to Respondent** | | | | | |
| | | | | **Article 15**: After receipt of the Application for Arbitration and its attachments and when the secretariat of the Arbitration Commission, after examination, deems that the Claimant has not completed the formalities required for arbitration, the secretariat shall demand the Claimant to complete them, and when the secretariat deems that the Claimant has completed the formalities, the secretariat shall immediately send to the Respondent a Notice of Arbitration together with one copy | **Article 10(4)** The SCC Institute shall communicate the Respondent's Reply to the Claimant. The Claimant shall be given an opportunity to comment on any objections and pleas advanced by the Respondent. |

| ICC | LCIA | AAA | WIPO | CIETAC | STOCKHOLM |
|---|---|---|---|---|---|
| | | | | each of the Claimant's Application for Arbitration and its attachments as well as the Arbitration Rules, the Panel of Arbitrators and the Arbitration Fee Schedule of the Arbitration Commission, and shall simultaneously send to the Claimant one copy each of the Notice of Arbitration, the Arbitration Rules, the Panel of Arbitrators and Arbitration Fee Schedule. The secretariat of the Arbitration Commission, after sending the Notice of Arbitration to the Claimant and Respondent, shall appoint one of its staff-members to take charge of procedural administration of the case. | |

## 10. Additional claims

| ICC | LCIA | AAA | WIPO | CIETAC | STOCKHOLM |
|---|---|---|---|---|---|
| **4(6)** When a party submits a Request in connection with a legal relationship in respect of which arbitration proceedings between the same parties are already pending under these Rules, the Court may, at the request of a party, decide to include the claims contained in the Request in the pending proceedings provided that the Terms of Reference have not yet been signed or approved by the Court. Once the Terms of Reference have been signed or approved by the Court, claims may only be included in the pending proceedings subject to the provisions of Article 19. | | | | | |

## 11. Answer/Response/Defence – time for, details of parties

| ICC | LCIA | AAA | WIPO | CIETAC | STOCKHOLM |
|---|---|---|---|---|---|
| **Article 5: Answer to the Request; counterclaims**<br>**5(1)** Within 30 days from the receipt of the Request from the Secretariat, the Respondent shall file an Answer (the "Answer") which shall, inter alia, contain the following information: | **2.1** Within 30 days of service of the Request on the Respondent, (or such lesser period fixed by the LCIA Court), the Respondent shall send to the Registrar a written response to the Request ("the Response"), containing or accompanied by: | **3.1.** Within 30 days after the commencement of the arbitration, a respondent shall submit a written statement of defense, responding to the issues raised in the notice of arbitration, to the claimant and any other parties, and to the administrator. | **Article 11:** Within 30 days from the date on which the Respondent receives the Request for Arbitration from the Claimant, the Respondent shall address to the Center and to the Claimant an Answer to the Request which shall contain comments on any of the elements in the Request | **Article 16:** The Claimant and the Respondent shall, within 20 days as from the date of receipt of the Notice of Arbitration, appoint an arbitrator from among the Panel of Arbitrators of the Arbitration Commission or authorize the Chairman of the Arbitration Commission to make | **Article 10: The Respondent's Reply**<br>(1) The Request for Arbitration shall be communicated by the SCC Institute to the Respondent. The Respondent shall be asked to submit a Reply to the SCC Institute. The Reply shall be submitted within the period of time determined by the |

| ICC | LCIA | AAA | WIPO | CIETAC | STOCKHOLM |
|---|---|---|---|---|---|
| **5(1)(a)** its name in full, description and address; | | | for Arbitration and may include indications of any counterclaim or setoff. | such appointment.<br>**Article 17:** The Respondent shall, within 45 days from the date of receipt of the Notice of Arbitration, submit his written defense and relevant documentary evidence to the secretariat of the Arbitration Commission. | SCC Institute and shall include: |
| **12. Answer to include description of circumstances of dispute and case on relief** | | | | | |
| **5(1)(b)** its comments as to the nature and circumstances of the dispute giving rise to the claims;<br>**5(1)(c)** its response to the relief sought; | **2.1(a)** confirmation or denial of all or part of the claims advanced by the Claimant in the Request; | | | | |
| **13. Defence** | | | | | |
| | | | **Article 12:** If the Claimant has filed a Statement of Claim with the Request for Arbitration pursuant to Article 10, the Answer to the Request may also be accompanied by the Statement of Defense referred to in Article 42. | | |
| **14. Answer to include comments on intended Tribunal, venue, law and language; counterclaims, formal procedure** | | | | | |
| **5(1)(d)** any comments concerning the number of arbitrators and their choice in light of the Claimant's proposals and in accordance with the provisions of Articles 8, 9 and 10, and any nomination of an arbitrator required thereby; and,<br>**5(1)(e)** any comments as to the place of arbitration, the applicable rules of law and the language of the arbitration.<br>**5(2)** The Secretariat may grant the Respondent an extension of the time for filing the Answer, provided the application for such an extension contains the Respondent's comments concerning the number of arbitrators and their choice, and where | **2.1(c)** comment in response to any statements contained in the Request, as called for under Article 1.1(d), on matters relating to the conduct of the arbitration;<br>**2.1(d)** if the Arbitration Agreement calls for party nomination of arbitrators, the name, address, telephone, facsimile, telex and e-mail numbers (if known) of the Respondent's nominee; and | **3.3.** A Respondent shall respond to the administrator, the claimant and other parties within 30 days after the commencement of the arbitration as to any proposals the Claimant may have made as to the number of arbitrators, the place of the arbitration or the language(s) of the arbitration, except to the extent that the parties have previously agreed as to these matters. | | **Article 16:** The Claimant and the Respondent shall, within 20 days as from the date of receipt of the Notice of Arbitration, appoint an arbitrator from among the Panel of Arbitrators of the Arbitration Commission or authorize the Chairman of the Arbitration Commission to make such appointment. | |

| ICC | LCIA | AAA | WIPO | CIETAC | STOCKHOLM |
|---|---|---|---|---|---|
| required by Articles 8, 9 and 10, the nomination of an arbitrator. If the Respondent fails to do so, the Court shall proceed in accordance with these Rules. | | | | | |
| **5(3)**. The Answer shall be supplied to the Secretariat in the number of copies specified by Article 3(1). | **2.2** The Response (including all accompanying documents) should be submitted to the Registrar in two copies, or if the parties have agreed or the Respondent considers that three arbitrators should be appointed, in four copies.<br>2.1(e) confirmation to the Registrar that copies of the Response (including all accompanying documents) have been or are being served simultaneously on all other parties to the arbitration by one or more means of service to be identified in such confirmation. | | | | |
| **5(4)**. A copy of the Answer and the documents annexed thereto shall be communicated by the Secretariat to the Claimant. | | | | | **10(4)** The SCC Institute shall communicate the Respondent's Reply to the Claimant. The Claimant shall be given an opportunity to comment on any objections and pleas advanced by the Respondent. |
| | **2.3** Failure to send a Response shall not preclude the Respondent from denying any claim or from advancing a counterclaim in the arbitration. However, if the Arbitration Agreement calls for party nomination of arbitrators, failure to send a Response or to nominate an arbitrator within time or at all shall constitute an irrevocable waiver of that party's opportunity to nominate an arbitrator. | **23.1.** If a party fails to file a statement of defense within the time established by the Tribunal without showing sufficient cause for such failure, as determined by the Tribunal, the Tribunal may proceed with the arbitration. | | | |
| **5(5)**. Any counterclaim(s) made by the Respondent shall be filed with its Answer and shall provide:<br>(**a**) a description of the nature and circumstances of the dispute giving rise to the counterclaim(s); and<br>(b) a statement of the relief sought and including, to the extent possible, an indication of any amount(s) counterclaimed. | **2.1(b)** a brief statement describing the nature and circumstances of any counterclaims advanced by the Respondent against the Claimant; | **3.2.** At the time a Respondent submits its Statement of Defense, a respondent may make counterclaims or assert setoffs as to any claim covered by the agreement to arbitrate, as to which the Claimant shall within 30 days submit a written statement of defense to the Respondent and any other parties and to the administrator. | | **Article 18** The Respondent shall, at the latest within 60 days from the date of receipt of the Notice of Arbitration, lodge with the secretariat of the Arbitration Commission his counterclaim in writing, if any. The arbitration tribunal may extend that time limit if it deems that there are justified reasons. When lodging a counterclaim, the Respondent must state in his written statement of counterclaim his specific claim, the facts and reasons upon which his | **10(3)** If the Respondent wishes to file a counterclaim or a set-off claim, a statement to that effect should be made in the Reply and should include the nature of the claim and a preliminary statement of the relief sought. The grounds for any counterclaim or set-off claim must be based on the arbitration agreement. [*Articles 21/22 are more detailed.*] |

| ICC | LCIA | AAA | WIPO | CIETAC | STOCKHOLM |
|---|---|---|---|---|---|
| | | | | claim is based, and attach to his written statement of counterclaim the relevant documentary evidence. | |
| **5(6).** The Claimant shall file a Reply to any counterclaim within 30 days from the date of receipt of the counterclaims communicated by the Secretariat. The Secretariat may grant the Claimant an extension of time for filing the Reply. | [*See also Article 15 in section 2.2 and 3.15 below.*] | | | | |
| | | | | | **Article 11 Amplification and Periods of Time**<br>**11(1)** The SCC Institute may request a party to expound upon any written comments to the SCC Institute. If the Claimant fails to comply with such a request, the SCC Institute may decide to dismiss the case. If the Respondent fails to comply with a request to expound upon a counterclaim, the counterclaim may be dismissed by the SCC Institute. Failure by the Respondent otherwise to comply with a request to expound upon a written statement shall not prevent the arbitral proceedings from continuing.<br>**11(2)** If the SCC Institute has requested a party to perform any act within a specified period of time, such period of time may be extended by the SCC Institute. |

CHAPTER 3

# The Arbitral Tribunal

The 1996 Act covers this at sections 15–32. It provides for local Court back up to replace arbitrations, a Court back-stop for default procedures for sole appointments, apportions liability jointly and severally to the parties for arbitrators' fees and expenses, confers mandatory immunity (except for the most serious of offences) on the Tribunal and for the first time in English law confers jurisdiction on the Tribunal to determine its own jurisdiction. (Sadly what it gives with one hand it takes away with the other reserving, on terms, a subsisting right to a rehearsing before the local Courts by Izov v. Baltic Shipping [1999] 1 All ER 476). The English law position remains that in default of agreement to more, the presumption will be of a sole arbitrator. Duties under the Act include the mandatory provision at section 33 "to act fairly and impartially as between the parties; and...to adopt procedures suitable to the circumstances of the particular case, avoid unnecessary delays and expenses so as to provide a fair means for the resolution of the matters falling to be determined".

The **ICC** covers the position in Articles 7–12. There is considerable emphasis on independence of the members of the Tribunal – and of certification of this formally. In terms of numbers Article 8 provides that unless the parties have agreed otherwise that the Tribunal will have one or three members, with a slight presumption to a sole. In practice the TCC will be guided by the parties' wishes in this respect, more substantial cases being considered more appropriate for a three man Tribunal. Multiple parties are dealt with at Article 10, challenges at Article 11, replacement at Article 12. The Tribunal is empowered to rule on matters of jurisdiction subject to an express right to the parties – if the ruling is that there is no arbitration agreement – to apply to the relevant Court (who presumably may reinstate the arbitration if they disagree with the arbitrators' findings). Duties are comprehensively set out variously throughout the rules and include a key duty "to act fairly and impartially and ensure that each party has a reasonable opportunity to be heard".

The **LCIA** covers the area in Articlc 5–12. It also imposes a positive obligation of independence, and includes a formal certification process (Article 5). The LCIA – in the absence of contra indications or party agreement – favours a sole appointment. Party appointments are respected subject to a (seldom involved) power of veto by the LCIA. Like the ICC the LCIA is alive to national sensitivities and sole arbitrators or chairmen may not ordinarily be of the same nationality as any of the parties (widely construed – including by reference to shareholders). Challenges are comprehensively covered in Article 10. Duties mirror the mission statement in section 33 of the 1996 Act (Article 14. 1).

**AAA** – The most relevant provisions of AAA rules are from Article 5 onwards. The warranty of independence has to be provided and absent party agreement or special circumstances, the presumption is to a sole arbitrator. National sensitivities are lower on the AAA's agenda although there is a provision to make appointments from a country other than that of the parties – but this is not mandatory (Article 6(4)). The AAA, alone of the institutions, omits to provide for special appointment procedures for multiparty disputes. Challenges are covered at Article 8 and following. Duties are most comprehensively set out throughout the rules, Article 16 mirroring the mission statement in the English Arbitration Act and the LCIA Rules.

**WIPO** – Follows the other institutions in requiring independence from its arbitrators and positive disclosure in this respect (Article 22). Party agreement or special circumstances apart, it has a presumption in favour of a sole arbitrator. It respects national sensitivities (subject to party autonomy) by providing for an arbitrator from a neutral country to be appointed (Article 20). It has comprehensive rules for multi-parties' appointments (Article 18) and for challenges (Article 24 and following). Duties are set out variously throughout the rules, and Article 38 reflects what are generally regarded as core duties – akin to section 33 of the 1996 Act.

**CIETAC** – Cietac's rules are slightly different in format. Articles 53 and 28 mirror the duty of impartiality and requirement of independence. The parties' freedom of choice is restricted to the CIETAC panel, although parties have freedom to appoint therefrom (Article 24), and the presumption is to a panel of three although there is provision for the appointment of a sole arbitrator (Article 25). There is no restriction on nationality. Multi-party arbitrations are provided for as are challenges (Article 29). Duties are succinctly set out, Article 53 being the "mission statement" provision. There is no provision concerning speed of the arbitration – but given a specific time limit (9 months) for publication of the award, from formation of the Tribunal, it is implicit.

**STOCKHOLM** – The key provisions are at Article 13 and following. Independence – as with all the institutions – is a formal requirement. The presumption (party agreement/circumstances apart) is to a three man Tribunal. Ordinarily arbitrators from a neutral venue are appointed. Multi-party arbitrations are provided for (Article 16), and there are comprehensive rules for challenges. Duties are succinct and by far the briefest of all the institutions.

All the institutions specifically empowered Tribunals themselves to adjudicate on their own authority – "Kompetenz–Kompetenz", a concept alien to English law prior to the 1996 which effectively introduced it. The ICC permits residual resort to Courts in the event of a negative ruling; the LCIA tends in the opposite direction (Article 23.4); CIETAC provides for the Peoples' Court to have precedence on the point. Other institutions do not deal with alternative routes in terms. The point is of considerable importance as an arbitration can be side tracked or held up by parallel Court proceedings in the absence of clear rules on the point. The question of the existence of or extent of the Tribunal's jurisdiction is one that is frequently taken – particularly by an unwilling Respondent. The ICC, LCIA, AAA and WIPO Rules probably cover the point in the most satisfactory manner.

| ICC | LCIA | AAA | WIPO | CIETAC | STOCKHOLM |
|---|---|---|---|---|---|
| **1. Pleas as to jurisdiction** | | | | | |
| **6(2)** If the Respondent does not file an Answer, as provided by Article 5, or if any party raises one or more pleas concerning the existence, validity or scope of the arbitration agreement, the Court may decide, without prejudice to the admissibility or merits of the plea or pleas, that the arbitration shall proceed if it is prima facie satisfied that an arbitration agreement under the Rules may exist. In such a case, any decision as to the jurisdiction of the Arbitral Tribunal shall be taken by the Arbitral Tribunal itself. If the Court is not so satisfied, the parties shall be notified that the arbitration cannot proceed. In such a case, any party retains the right to ask any Court having jurisdiction whether or not there is a binding arbitration agreement. | **23.1.** The Arbitral Tribunal shall have the power to rule on its own jurisdiction, including any objection to the initial or continuing existence, validity or effectiveness of the Arbitration Agreement. For that purpose, an arbitration clause which forms or was intended to form part of another agreement shall be treated as an arbitration agreement independent of that other agreement. A decision by the Arbitral Tribunal that such other agreement is non-existent, invalid or ineffective shall not entail ipso jure the non-existence, invalidity or ineffectiveness of the arbitration clause.<br>**23.2.** A plea by a Respondent that the Arbitral Tribunal does not have jurisdiction shall be treated as having been irrevocably waived unless it is raised not later than the Statement of Defence; and a like plea by a Respondent to Counterclaim shall be similarly treated unless it is raised no later than the Statement of Defence to Counterclaim. A plea that the Arbitral Tribunal is exceeding the scope of its authority shall be raised promptly after the Arbitral Tribunal has indicated its intention to decide on the matter alleged by any party to be beyond the scope of its authority, failing which such plea shall also be treated as having been waived irrevocably. In any case, the Arbitral Tribunal may nevertheless admit an untimely plea if it considers the delay justified in the particular circumstances.<br>23.3. The Arbitral Tribunal may determine the plea to its jurisdiction or authority in an award as to jurisdiction or later in an award on the merits, as it considers appropriate in the circumstances.<br>23.4. By agreeing to arbitration under these Rules, the parties shall be | **Pleas as to Jurisdiction: Article 15**<br>**15(1)** The tribunal shall have the power to rule on its own jurisdiction, including any objections with respect to the existence, scope or validity of the arbitration agreement.<br>**15(2)** The tribunal shall have the power to determine the existence or validity of a contract of which an arbitration clause forms a part. Such an arbitration clause shall be treated as an agreement independent of the other terms of the contract. A decision by the tribunal that the contract is null and void shall not for that reason alone render invalid the arbitration clause.<br>**15(3)** A party must object to the jurisdiction of the tribunal or to the arbitrability of a claim or counterclaim no later than the filing of the statement of defense, as provided in Article 3, to the claim or counterclaim that gives rise to the objection. The tribunal may rule on such objections as a preliminary matter or as part of the final award.<br>**16(2)** The tribunal, exercising its discretion, shall conduct the proceedings with a view to expediting the resolution of the dispute. It may conduct a preparatory conference with the parties for the purpose of organizing, scheduling and agreeing to procedures to expedite the subsequent proceedings. | **Article 36: Pleas as to the Jurisdiction of the Tribunal**<br>**36(a)** The Tribunal shall have the power to hear and determine objections to its own jurisdiction, including any objections with respect to form, existence, validity or scope of the Arbitration Agreement examined pursuant to Article 59(b).<br>**36(b)** The Tribunal shall have the power to determine the existence or validity of any contract of which the Arbitration Agreement forms part or to which it relates.<br>**36(c)** A plea that the Tribunal does not have jurisdiction shall be raised not later than in the Statement of Defense or, with respect to a counterclaim or a setoff, the Statement of Defense thereto, failing which any such plea shall be barred in the subsequent arbitral proceedings or before any court. A plea that the Tribunal is exceeding the scope of its authority shall be raised as soon as the matter alleged to be beyond the scope of its authority is raised during the arbitral proceedings. The Tribunal may, in either case, admit a later plea if it considers the delay justified.<br>**36(d)** The Tribunal may rule on a plea referred to in paragraph (c) as a preliminary question or, in its sole discretion, decide on such a plea in the final award.<br>**36(e)** A plea that the Tribunal lacks jurisdiction shall not preclude the Center from administering the arbitration. | **Article 4:** The Arbitration Commission has the power to decide on the existence and validity of an arbitration agreement and the jurisdiction over an arbitration case. If a party challenges the validity of the arbitration agreement and requests the Arbitration Commission to make a decision thereupon and the other party applies to the People's Court for a ruling, the Court's ruling shall prevail.<br>**Article 6:** Any objections to an arbitration agreement and/or jurisdiction over an arbitration case shall be raised before the first hearing conducted by the arbitration tribunal. Where a case is examined on the basis of documents only, the objections to jurisdiction should be raised before submission of the first substantive defense. | **Article 7: Dismissal**<br>If it is clear that the SCC Institute lacks jurisdiction over the dispute or if the Registration Fee has not been paid in due time, the Claimant's Request for Arbitration shall be dismissed.<br>**10(2)** If the Respondent wishes to raise any objection concerning the validity or applicability of the arbitration agreement, such objection shall be made in the Reply together with the grounds therefore.<br>**10(5)** Failure by the Respondent to submit a Reply shall not prevent the arbitration from proceeding pursuant to these Rules. |

| ICC | LCIA | AAA | WIPO | CIETAC | STOCKHOLM |
|---|---|---|---|---|---|
| | treated as having agreed not to apply to any state court or other judicial authority for any relief regarding the Arbitral Tribunal's jurisdiction or authority, except with the agreement in writing of all parties to the arbitration or the prior authorisation of the Arbitral Tribunal or following the latter's award ruling on the objection to its jurisdiction or authority. | | | | |
| **2. Failure by party to participate; effect** | | | | | |
| **6(3)** If any of the parties refuses or fails to take part in the arbitration or any stage thereof, the arbitration shall proceed notwithstanding such refusal or failure. | **15.8** If the Respondent fails to submit a Statement of Defence or the Claimant a Statement of Defence to Counterclaim, or if at any point any party fails to avail itself of the opportunity to present its case in the manner determined by Article 15.2 to **15.6** or directed by the Arbitral Tribunal, the Arbitral Tribunal may nevertheless proceed with the arbitration and make an award. | | | **Article 21:** The arbitration proceedings shall not be affected in case the Respondent fails to file his defense in writing or the Claimant fails to submit his written defense against the Respondent's counterclaim.<br>**Article 26:** If the Claimant or the Respondent fails to appoint or authorize the Chairman of the Arbitration Commission to appoint an arbitrator according to Article 16 of these Rules, the Chairman of the Arbitration Commission shall appoint an arbitrator for the Caimant or the Respondent.<br>**Article 42:** Should one of the parties fail to appear at the hearing, the arbitration tribunal may proceed with the hearing and make an award by default. | |
| **3. Independent life of arbitration clause** | | | | | |
| **6(4)** Unless otherwise agreed, the Arbitral Tribunal shall not cease to have jurisdiction by reason of any claim that the contract is null and void or allegation that it is non-existent provided that the Arbitral Tribunal upholds the validity of the arbitration agreement. The Arbitral Tribunal shall continue to have jurisdiction to determine the respective rights of the parties and to adjudicate upon their claims and pleas even though the contract itself may be | **Article 23: Jurisdiction of the Arbitral Tribunal.**<br>**23.1** The Arbitral Tribunal shall have the power to rule on its own jurisdiction, including any objection to the initial or continuing existence, validity or effectiveness of the Arbitration Agreement. For that purpose, an arbitration clause which forms or was intended to form part of another agreement shall be treated as an arbitration agreement independent of that other agreement. A | | | **Article 5:** An arbitration clause contained in a contract shall be regarded as existing independently and separately from the other clauses of the contract, and an arbitration agreement attached to a contract shall be treated as a part of the contract existing independently and separately from the other parts of the contract. The validity of an arbitration clause or an arbitration agreement shall not be affected by the modification, rescission, termination, invalidity, | |

| ICC | LCIA | AAA | WIPO | CIETAC | STOCKHOLM |
|---|---|---|---|---|---|
| non-existent or null and void. | decision by the Arbitral Tribunal that such other agreement is non-existent, invalid or ineffective shall not entail ipso jure the non-existence, invalidity or ineffectiveness of the arbitration clause. | | | revocation or non-existence of the contract. | |
| **4. Arbitrator's independence** | | | | | |
| **Article 7: General provisions**<br>**7.1.** Every arbitrator must be and remain independent of the parties involved in the arbitration. | **Article 5: Formation of the Arbitral Tribunal.**<br>**5.2** All arbitrators conducting an arbitration under these Rules shall be and remain at all times impartial and independent of the parties; and none shall act in the arbitration as advocates for any party. No arbitrator, whether before or after appointment, shall advise any party on the merits or outcome of the dispute. | **7.1.** Arbitrators acting under these rules shall be impartial and independent. Prior to accepting appointment, a prospective arbitrator shall disclose to the administrator any circumstance likely to give rise to justifiable doubts as to the arbitrator's impartiality or independence. If, at any stage during the arbitration, new circumstances arise that may give rise to such doubts, an arbitrator shall promptly disclose such circumstances to the parties and to the administrator. Upon receipt of such information from an arbitrator or a party, the administrator shall communicate it to the other parties and to the tribunal. | **22(a)** Each arbitrator shall be impartial and independent. | **17(1)** An arbitrator must be impartial and independent. | |
| **5. Arbitrator's continuing duty of disclosure in respect of independence; certificates of independence** | | | | | |
| **7(2)** Before appointment or confirmation, a prospective arbitrator shall sign a statement of independence and disclose in writing to the Secretariat any facts or circumstances which might be of such a nature as to call into question the arbitrator's independence in the eyes of the parties. The Secretariat shall provide such information to the parties in writing and fix a time limit for any comments from them.<br>**7(3)** An arbitrator shall immediately disclose in writing to the Secretariat and to the parties any facts or circumstances of a similar nature which may arise during the arbitration. | **5.3** Before appointment by the LCIA Court, each arbitrator shall furnish to the Registrar a written résumé of his past and present professional positions; he shall agree in writing upon fee rates conforming to the Schedule of Costs; and he shall sign a declaration to the effect that there are no circumstances known to him likely to give rise to any justified doubts as to his impartiality or independence, other than any circumstances disclosed by him in the declaration. Each arbitrator shall thereby also assume a continuing duty forthwith to disclose any such circumstances to the LCIA Court, to any other members of the Arbitral Tribunal and to | **7.1.** Arbitrators acting under these rules shall be impartial and independent. Prior to accepting appointment, a prospective arbitrator shall disclose to the administrator any circumstance likely to give rise to justifiable doubts as to the arbitrator's impartiality or independence. If, at any stage during the arbitration, new circumstances arise that may give rise to such doubts, an arbitrator shall promptly disclose such circumstances to the parties and to the administrator. Upon receipt of such information from an arbitrator or a party, the administrator shall communicate it to the other parties and to the tribunal. | **22(b)** Each prospective arbitrator shall, before accepting appointment, disclose to the parties, the Center and any other arbitrator who has already been appointed any circumstances that might give rise to justifiable doubt as to the arbitrator's impartiality or independence, or confirm in writing that no such circumstances exist.<br>**22(c)** If, at any stage during the arbitration, new circumstances arise that might give rise to justifiable doubt as to any arbitrator's impartiality or independence, the arbitrator shall promptly disclose such circumstances to the parties, the Center and the other arbitrators. | **Article 28** Any appointed arbitrator having a personal interest in the case shall himself disclose such circumstances to the Arbitration Commission and request a withdrawal from his office. | **17(2)** A person asked to accept an appointment as arbitrator must disclose any circumstances likely to give rise to justifiable doubts as to his impartiality and independence. If he is nevertheless appointed, he shall immediately, in a written statement, make the same disclosure to the parties and the other arbitrators.<br>**17(3)** An arbitrator who becomes aware of any circumstances which may disqualify him, must immediately, in writing, inform the parties and the other arbitrators thereof. |

| ICC | LCIA | AAA | WIPO | CIETAC | STOCKHOLM |
|---|---|---|---|---|---|
| | all the parties if such circumstances should arise after the date of such declaration and before the arbitration is concluded. | | | | |
| **6. Correspondence with Tribunal** | | | | | |
| | | **7.2.** No party or anyone acting on its behalf shall have any *ex parte* communication relating to the case with any arbitrator, or with any candidate for appointment as party-appointed arbitrator except to advise the candidate of the general nature of the controversy and of the anticipated proceedings and to discuss the candidate's qualifications, availability or independence in relation to the parties, or to discuss the suitability of candidates for selection as a third arbitrator where the parties or party-designated arbitrators are to participate in that selection. No party or anyone acting on its behalf shall have any *ex parte* communication relating to the case with any candidate for presiding arbitrator.<br>**16(4)** Documents or information supplied to the tribunal by one party shall at the same time be communicated by that party to the other party or parties. | **Article 21: Communication Between Parties and Candidates for Appointment as Arbitrator**<br>No party or anyone acting on its behalf shall have any *ex parte* communication with any candidate for appointment as arbitrator except to discuss the candidate's qualifications, availability or independence in relation to the parties.<br>**Article 45: Communication Between Parties and Tribunal**<br>Except as otherwise provided in these Rules or permitted by the Tribunal, no party or anyone acting on its behalf may have any *ex parte* communication with any arbitrator with respect to any matter of substance relating to the arbitration, it being understood that nothing in this paragraph shall prohibit *ex parte* communications which concern matters of a purely organizational nature, such as the physical facilities, place, date or time of the hearings. | | |
| **7. Finality of Court's decision on appointments** | | | | | |
| **7(4)** The decisions of the Court as to the appointment, confirmation, challenge or replacement of an arbitrator, shall be final and the reasons for such decisions shall not be communicated. | **5.5** The LCIA Court alone is empowered to appoint arbitrators. The LCIA Court will appoint arbitrators with due regard for any particular method or criteria of selection agreed in writing by the parties. In selecting arbitrators consideration will be given to the nature of the transaction, the nature and circumstances of the dispute, the nationality, location and languages of the parties and (if more than two) the number of parties. | | | | **Article 13 Appointment of Arbitrators and Place of Arbitration**<br>When the exchange of written submissions pursuant to Articles 5–11 has been concluded, the SCC Institute shall:<br>(i) decide the number of arbitrators, if not agreed by the parties;<br>(ii) when so required pursuant to Article 16, appoint a sole arbitrator or chairman of the Arbitral Tribunal and, if necessary, a co-arbitrator;<br>(iii) decide the Place of Arbitration, if not agreed upon by the parties; |

| ICC | LCIA | AAA | WIPO | CIETAC | STOCKHOLM |
|---|---|---|---|---|---|
| | | | | | and<br>(iv) fix the Advance on Costs pursuant to Article 14. |
| **8. The arbitrator's contract** | | | | | |
| **7(5)** By accepting to serve every arbitrator undertakes to carry out his responsibilities in accordance with these Rules.<br>**7(6)** Insofar as the parties have not provided otherwise, the Arbitral Tribunal shall be constituted in accordance with the provisions of Articles 8, 9 and 10. | | | **Article 23: Availability, Acceptance and Notification**<br>(a) Each arbitrator shall, by accepting appointment, be deemed to have undertaken to make available sufficient time to enable the arbitration to be conducted and completed expeditiously.<br>(b) Each prospective arbitrator shall accept appointment in writing and shall communicate such acceptance to the Center.<br>(c) The Center shall notify the parties of the establishment of the Tribunal. | | |
| **9. Number of arbitrators, default appointments** | | | | | |
| **Article 8: Number of arbitrators**<br>**8(1)** The disputes shall be decided by sole arbitrator or by three arbitrators.<br>**8(2)** Where the parties have not agreed upon the number of arbitrators, the Court shall appoint a sole arbitrator, save where it appears to the Court that the dispute is such as to warrant the appointment of three arbitrators. In such case, the Claimant shall nominate an arbitrator within a period of 15 days from the receipt of the notification of the decision of the Court, and the Respondent shall nominate an arbitrator within a period of 15 days from the receipt of the notification of the nomination made by the Claimant. | **5.4** The LCIA Court shall appoint the Arbitral Tribunal as soon as practicable after receipt by the Registrar of the Response or after the expiry of 30 days following service of the Request upon the Respondent if no Response is received by the Registrar (or such lesser period fixed by the LCIA Court). The LCIA Court may proceed with the formation of the Arbitral Tribunal notwithstanding that the Request is incomplete or the Response is missing, late or incomplete. A sole arbitrator shall be appointed unless the parties have agreed in writing otherwise, or unless the LCIA Court determines that in view of all the circumstances of the case a three-member tribunal is appropriate. | **Number of Arbitrators: Article 5**<br>If the parties have not agreed on the number of arbitrators, one arbitrator shall be appointed unless the administrator determines in its discretion that three arbitrators are appropriate because of the large size, complexity or other circumstances of the case. | **Article 14: Number of Arbitrators**<br>(a) The Tribunal shall consist of such number of arbitrators as has been agreed by the parties.<br>(b) Where the parties have not agreed on the number of arbitrators, the Tribunal shall consist of a sole arbitrator, except where the Center in its discretion determines that, in view of all the circumstances of the case, a Tribunal composed of three members is appropriate. | **Article 9:** The Arbitration Commission is composed of one Chairman, several Vice-Chairmen and a number of Commission members. The Chairman performs the functions and duties vested in him by these Rules and the Vice-Chairmen may perform the Chairman's functions and duties with the Chairman's authorization.<br>**Article 24.** Each of the parties shall appoint one arbitrator from among the Panel of Arbitrators of the Arbitration Commission or entrust the Chairman of the Arbitration Commission to make such appointment. The third arbitrator shall be jointly appointed by the parties or appointed by the Chairman of the Arbitration Commission upon the parties' joint authorization. In case the parties fail to jointly entrust the Chairman of the Arbitration Commission to appoint the third arbitrator within 20 days from the | **Article 16 Number of Arbitrators and Manner of their Appointment**<br>(1) The parties are free to determine the number of arbitrators. Where the parties have not agreed on the number of arbitrators, the Arbitral Tribunal shall consist of three arbitrators, unless the SCC Institute, taking into account, inter alia, the complexity of the case, the amount in dispute and other circumstances, decides that the dispute is to be settled by a sole arbitrator. |

| ICC | LCIA | AAA | WIPO | CIETAC | STOCKHOLM |
|---|---|---|---|---|---|
| | | | | date on which the Respondent receives the Notice of Arbitration, the third arbitrator shall be appointed by the Chairman of the Arbitration Commission. The third arbitrator shall act as the presiding arbitrator. The presiding arbitrator and the two appointed arbitrators shall jointly form an arbitration tribunal to jointly hear the case.<br>**Article 25**. Both parties may jointly appoint or jointly authorize the Chairman of the Arbitration Commission to appoint a sole arbitrator to form an arbitration tribunal to hear the case alone. If both parties have agreed on the appointment of a sole arbitrator to hear their case alone but have failed to agree on the choice of such a sole arbitrator within 20 days from the date on which the Respondent receives the Notice of Arbitration, the Chairman of the Arbitration Commission shall make such appointment. | |
| **10. Sole arbitrators** | | | | | |
| **8(3)** Where the parties have agreed that the dispute shall be settled by a sole arbitrator, they may, by agreement, nominate the sole arbitrator for confirmation. If the parties fail so to nominate a sole arbitrator within 30 days from the date when the Claimant's Request for Arbitration has been received by the other party, or within such additional time as may be allowed by the Secretariat, the sole arbitrator shall be appointed by the Court. | **5.4** The LCIA Court shall appoint the Arbitral Tribunal as soon as practicable after receipt by the Registrar of the Response or after the expiry of 30 days following service of the Request upon the Respondent if no Response is received by the Registrar (or such lesser period fixed by the LCIA Court). The LCIA Court may proceed with the formation of the Arbitral Tribunal notwithstanding that the Request is incomplete or the Response is missing, late or incomplete. A sole arbitrator shall be appointed unless the parties have agreed in writing otherwise, or unless the LCIA Court determines that in view of all the circumstances of the case a three-member tribunal is appropriate. | | **Article 16: Appointment of a Sole Arbitrator**<br>(a) Where a sole arbitrator is to be appointed and the parties have not agreed on a procedure of appointment, the sole arbitrator shall be appointed jointly by the parties.<br>(b) If the appointment of the sole arbitrator is not made within the period of time agreed upon by the parties or, in the absence of such an agreed period of time, within 30 days after the commencement of the arbitration, the sole arbitrator shall be appointed in accordance with Article 19. | **Article 16:** The Claimant and the Respondent shall, within 20 days as from the date of receipt of the Notice of Arbitration, appoint an arbitrator from among the Panel of Arbitrators of the Arbitration Commission or authorize the Chairman of the Arbitration Commission to make such appointment. | **16(5)** Where the dispute is to be decided by a sole arbitrator, the SCC Institute shall make the appointment, unless otherwise agreed by the parties. |

| ICC | LCIA | AAA | WIPO | CIETAC | STOCKHOLM |
|---|---|---|---|---|---|
| **11. Methodology for sole appointment** | | | | | |
| **9(3)** Where the Court is to appoint a sole arbitrator or the chairman of an Arbitral Tribunal, it shall make the appointment upon a proposal of a National Committee of the ICC that it considers to be appropriate. If the Court does not accept the proposal made, or if the National Committee fails to make the proposal requested within the time limit fixed by the Court, the Court may repeat its request or may request a proposal from another National Committee that it considers to be appropriate.<br>**9(4)** Where the Court considers that the circumstances so demand, it may choose the sole arbitrator or the chairman of the Arbitral Tribunal from a country where there is no National Committee, provided that neither of the parties objects within the time-limit fixed by the Court. | **5.4** The LCIA Court shall appoint the Arbitral Tribunal as soon as practicable after receipt by the Registrar of the Response or after the expiry of 30 days following service of the Request upon the Respondent if no Response is received by the Registrar (or such lesser period fixed by the LCIA Court). The LCIA Court may proceed with the formation of the Arbitral Tribunal notwithstanding that the Request is incomplete or the Response is missing, late or incomplete. A sole arbitrator shall be appointed unless the parties have agreed in writing otherwise, or unless the LCIA Court determines that in view of all the circumstances of the case a three-member tribunal is appropriate. | | | | |
| **12. Appointment of three arbitrators** | | | | | |
| **8(4)** Where the dispute is to be referred to three arbitrators, each party shall nominate in the Request and the Answer, respectively, one arbitrator for confirmation by the Court. If a party fails to nominate an arbitrator, the appointment shall be made by the Court. The third arbitrator, who will act as chairman of the Arbitral Tribunal, shall be appointed by the Court, unless the parties have agreed upon another procedure for such appointment, in which case the nomination will be subject to confirmation pursuant to Article 9. Should such procedure not result in a nomination within the time-limit fixed by the parties or the Court, the third arbitrator shall be appointed by the Court. | **5.6** In the case of a three-member Arbitral Tribunal, the chairman (who will not be a party-nominated arbitrator) shall be appointed by the LCIA Court. | | **Article 17: Appointment of Three Arbitrators**<br>(a) Where three arbitrators are to be appointed and the parties have not agreed upon a procedure of appointment, the arbitrators shall be appointed in accordance with this Article.<br>(b) The Claimant shall appoint an arbitrator in its Request for Arbitration. The Respondent shall appoint an arbitrator within 30 days from the date on which it receives the Request for Arbitration. The two arbitrators thus appointed shall, within 20 days after the appointment of the second arbitrator, appoint a third arbitrator, who shall be the presiding arbitrator.<br>(c) Notwithstanding paragraph (b), where three arbitrators are to be appointed as a result of the exercise | | **16(2)** Where the Arbitral Tribunal shall consist of more than one arbitrator, each party shall appoint an equal number of arbitrators. Where a party fails to appoint an arbitrator within the period of time stipulated by the SCC Institute, the SCC Institute shall make the appointment, unless otherwise agreed by the parties.<br>**16(4)** Where the Arbitral Tribunal is to consist of more than one arbitrator, the Chairman shall be appointed by the SCC Institute, unless otherwise agreed by the parties. |

| ICC | LCIA | AAA | WIPO | CIETAC | STOCKHOLM |
|---|---|---|---|---|---|
| | | | of the discretion of the Center under Article 14(b), the Claimant shall, by notice to the Center and to the Respondent, appoint an arbitrator within 15 days after the receipt by it of notification by the Center that the Tribunal is to be composed of three arbitrators. The Respondent shall appoint an arbitrator within 30 days after the receipt by it of the said notification. The two arbitrators thus appointed shall, within 20 days after the appointment of the second arbitrator, appoint a third arbitrator, who shall be the presiding arbitrator.<br>(d) If the appointment of any arbitrator is not made within the applicable period of time referred to in the preceding paragraphs, that arbitrator shall be appointed in accordance with Article 19. | | |
| **13. Considerations when making appointment** | | | | | |
| **Article 9: Appointment and confirmation of the arbitrators**<br>**9(1)** In confirming or appointing arbitrators, the Court shall consider the prospective arbitrator's nationality, residence and other relationships with the countries of which the parties or the other arbitrators are nationals and the prospective arbitrator's availability and ability to conduct the arbitration in accordance with these Rules. The same shall apply where the Secretary General confirms arbitrators pursuant to Article 9(2). | | | | | **Article 13 Appointment of Arbitrators and Place of Arbitration**<br>When the exchange of written submissions pursuant to Articles 5 - 11 has been concluded, the SCC Institute shall<br>(i) decide the number of arbitrators, if not agreed by the parties;<br>(ii) when so required pursuant to Article 16, appoint a sole arbitrator or chairman of the Arbitral Tribunal and, if necessary, a co-arbitrator;<br>(iii) decide the Place of Arbitration, if not agreed upon by the parties; and<br>(iv) fix the Advance on Costs pursuant to Article 14. |
| **14. Confirmation of party appointment** | | | | | |
| **9(2)** The Secretary General may confirm as co-arbitrators, sole arbitrators and chairmen of Arbitral Tribunals persons nominated by the parties or pursuant to their particu- | **5.3** The LCIA Court may refuse to appoint any such nominee if it determines that he is not suitable or independent or impartial.<br>**5.5** The LCIA Court alone is empow- | **6(1)** The parties may mutually agree upon any procedure for appointing arbitrators and shall inform the administrator as to such procedure.<br>6(2) The parties may mutually des- | **Article 15: Appointment Pursuant to Procedure Agreed Upon by the Parties**<br>(a) If the parties have agreed on a procedure of appointing the arbitra- | | |

| ICC | LCIA | AAA | WIPO | CIETAC | STOCKHOLM |
|---|---|---|---|---|---|
| lar agreements, provided they have filed a statement of independence without qualification or a qualified statement of independence has not given rise to objections. Such confirmation shall be reported to the Court at its next session. If the Secretary General considers that a co-arbitrator, sole arbitrator or chairman of an Arbitral Tribunal should not be confirmed, the matter shall be submitted to the Court. | ered to appoint arbitrators. The LCIA Court will appoint arbitrators with due regard for any particular method or criteria of selection agreed in writing by the parties. In selecting arbitrators consideration will be given to the nature of the transaction, the nature and circumstances of the dispute, the nationality, location and languages of the parties and (if more than two) the number of parties.<br>**7.1** If the parties have agreed that any arbitrator is to be appointed by one or more of them or by any third person, that agreement shall be treated as an agreement to nominate an arbitrator for all purposes. Such nominee may only be appointed by the LCIA Court as arbitrator subject to his prior compliance with Article | ignate arbitrators, with or without the assistance of the administrator. When such designations are made, the parties shall notify the administrator so that notice of the appointment can be communicated to the arbitrators, together with a copy of these rules. | tor or arbitrators other than as envisaged in Articles 16 to 20, that procedure shall be followed.<br>(b) If the Tribunal has not been established pursuant to such procedure within the period of time agreed upon by the parties or, in the absence of such an agreed period of time, within 45 days after the commencement of the arbitration, the Tribunal shall be established or completed, as the case may be, in accordance with Article 19. | | |

## 15. Nationality of arbitrator; circumstances when appointment may be made of an arbitrator from a country unrepresented by the institution

| ICC | LCIA | AAA | WIPO | CIETAC | STOCKHOLM |
|---|---|---|---|---|---|
| **9(5)** The sole arbitrator or the chairman of the Arbitral Tribunal shall be of a nationality other than those of the parties. However, in suitable circumstances and provided that neither of the parties objects within the time limit fixed by the Court, the sole arbitrator or the chairman of the Arbitral Tribunal may be chosen from a country of which any of the parties is a national. | **6.1** Where the parties are of different nationalities, a sole arbitrator or chairman of the Arbitral Tribunal shall not have the same nationality as any party unless the parties who are not of the same nationality as the proposed appointee all agree in writing otherwise.<br>**6.2** The nationality of parties shall be understood to include that of controlling shareholders or interests.<br>**6.3** For the purpose of this Article, a person who is a citizen of two or more states shall be treated as a national of each state; and citizens of the European Union shall be treated as nationals of its different Member States and shall not be treated as having the same nationality. | **6.4** In making such appointments, the administrator, after inviting consultation with the parties, shall endeavor to select suitable arbitrators. At the request of any party or on its own initiative, the administrator may appoint nationals of a country other than that of any of the parties. | **Article 20**<br>(a) An agreement of the parties concerning the nationality of arbitrators shall be respected.<br>(b) If the parties have not agreed on the nationality of the sole or presiding arbitrator, such arbitrator shall, in the absence of special circumstances such as the need to appoint a person having particular qualifications, be a national of a country other than the countries of the parties. | | **16(8)** If the parties are of different nationalities the SCC Institute shall appoint a sole arbitrator or a Chairman of a nationality other than of the parties, unless the parties have agreed differently or if otherwise deemed appropriate by the SCC Institute. |

| ICC | LCIA | AAA | WIPO | CIETAC | STOCKHOLM |
|---|---|---|---|---|---|
| **16. Party default appointments** | | | | | |
| **9(6)** Where the Court is to appoint an arbitrator on behalf of a party which has failed to nominate one, it shall make the appointment upon a proposal of the National Committee of the country of which that party is a national. If the Court does not accept the proposal made, or if the National Committee fails to make the proposal requested within the time-limit fixed by the Court, or if the country of which the said party is a national has no National Committee, the Court shall be at liberty to choose any person whom it regards as suitable. The Secretariat shall inform the National Committee, if one exists, of the country of which such person is a national | **7.2** Where the parties have howsoever agreed that the Respondent or any third person is to nominate an arbitrator and such nomination is not made within time or at all, the LCIA Court may appoint an arbitrator notwithstanding the absence of the nomination and without regard to any late nomination. Likewise, if the Request for Arbitration does not contain a nomination by the Claimant where the parties have howsoever agreed that the Claimant or a third person is to nominate an arbitrator, the LCIA Court may appoint an arbitrator notwithstanding the absence of the nomination and without regard to any late nomination. | **6(3)** If within 45 days after the commencement of the arbitration, all of the parties have not mutually agreed on a procedure for appointing the arbitrator(s) or have not mutually agreed on the designation of the arbitrator(s), the administrator shall, at the written request of any party, appoint the arbitrator(s) and designate the presiding arbitrator. If all of the parties have mutually agreed upon a procedure for appointing the arbitrator(s), but all appointments have not been made within the time limits provided in that procedure, the administrator shall, at the written request of any party, perform all functions provided for in that procedure that remain to be performed.<br>**6(4)** In making such appointments, the administrator, after inviting consultation with the parties, shall endeavor to select suitable arbitrators. At the request of any party or on its own initiative, the administrator may appoint nationals of a country other than that of any of the parties.<br>**6(5)** Unless the parties have agreed otherwise no later than 45 days after the commencement of the arbitration, if the notice of arbitration names two or more Claimants or two or more Respondents, the administrator shall appoint all the arbitrators. | **Article 19: Default Appointment**<br>(a) If a party has failed to appoint an arbitrator as required under Articles 15, 17 or 18, the Center shall, in lieu of that party, forthwith make the appointment.<br>(b) If the sole or presiding arbitrator has not been appointed as required under Articles 15, 16, 17 or 18, the appointment shall take place in accordance with the following procedure:<br>(i) The Center shall send to each party an identical list of candidates. The list shall comprise the names of at least three candidates in alphabetical order. The list shall include or be accompanied by a brief statement of each candidate's qualifications. If the parties have agreed on any particular qualifications, the list shall contain only the names of candidates that satisfy those qualifications.<br>(ii) Each party shall have the right to delete the name of any candidate or candidates to whose appointment it objects and shall number any remaining candidates in order of preference.<br>(iii) Each party shall return the marked list to the Center within 20 days after the date on which the list is received by it. Any party failing to return a marked list within that period of time shall be deemed to have assented to all candidates appearing on the list.<br>(iv) As soon as possible after receipt by it of the lists from the parties, or failing this, after the expiration of the period of time specified in the previous sub-paragraph, the Center shall, taking into account the preferences and objections expressed by the parties, invite a person from the list to be the sole | | **Article 13 Appointment of Arbitrators and Place of Arbitration**<br>When the exchange of written submissions pursuant to Articles 5–11 has been concluded, the SCC Institute shall<br>(i) decide the number of arbitrators, if not agreed by the parties;<br>(ii) when so required pursuant to Article 16, appoint a sole arbitrator or chairman of the Arbitral Tribunal and, if necessary, a co-arbitrator;<br>(iii) decide the Place of Arbitration, if not agreed upon by the parties; and<br>(iv) fix the Advance on Costs pursuant to Article 14. |

| ICC | LCIA | AAA | WIPO | CIETAC | STOCKHOLM |
|---|---|---|---|---|---|
| | | | or presiding arbitrator.<br>(v) If the lists which have been returned do not show a person who is acceptable as arbitrator to both parties, the Center shall be authorized to appoint the sole or presiding arbitrator. The Center shall similarly be authorized to do so if a person is not able or does not wish to accept the Center's invitation to be the sole or presiding arbitrator, or if there appear to be other reasons precluding that person from being the sole or presiding arbitrator, and there does not remain on the lists a person who is acceptable as arbitrator to both parties.<br>(c) Notwithstanding the provisions of paragraph (b), the Center shall be authorized to appoint the sole or presiding arbitrator if it determines in its discretion that the procedure described in that paragraph is not appropriate for the case. | | |
| **17. Multiple parties** | | | | | |
| **Article 10: Multiple parties**<br>**10(1)** Where there are multiple parties, whether as Claimant or as Respondent, and where the dispute is to be referred to three arbitrators, the multiple Claimants, jointly, and the multiple Respondents, jointly, shall nominate an arbitrator for confirmation pursuant to Article 9.<br>**10(2)** In the absence of such a joint nomination and where all parties are unable to agree to a method for the constitution of the Arbitral Tribunal, the Court may appoint each member of the Arbitral Tribunal and shall designate one of them to act as chairman. In such case, the Court shall be at liberty to choose any person whom it regards as suitable to act as arbitrator, applying Article 9 when it considers this appropriate. | **8.1** Where the Arbitration Agreement entitles each party howsoever to nominate an arbitrator, the parties to the dispute number more than two and such parties have not all agreed in writing that the disputant parties represent two separate sides for the formation of the Arbitral Tribunal as Claimant and Respondent respectively, the LCIA Court shall appoint the Arbitral Tribunal without regard to any party's nomination.<br>**8.2** In such circumstances, the Arbitration Agreement shall be treated for all purposes as a written agreement by the parties for the appointment of the Arbitral Tribunal by the LCIA Court.<br>**22.1(h)** to allow, only upon the application of a party, one or more third persons to be joined in the arbitration as a party provided any | | **Article 18: Appointment of Three Arbitrators in Case of Multiple Claimants or Respondents**<br>(a) Where<br>(i) three arbitrators are to be appointed,<br>(ii) the parties have not agreed on a procedure of appointment, and<br>(iii) the Request for Arbitration names more than one Claimant,<br>the Claimants shall make a joint appointment of an arbitrator in their Request for Arbitration. The appointment of the second arbitrator and the presiding arbitrator shall, subject to paragraph (b) of this Article, take place in accordance with Article 17(b), (c) or (d), as the case may be.<br>(b) Where<br>(i) three arbitrators are to be appointed,<br>(ii) the parties have not agreed on a | Article 27: When there are two or more Claimants and/or Respondents in an arbitration case, the Claimants' side and/or the Respondents' side each shall, through consultation, appoint or entrust the Chairman of the Arbitration Commission to appoint one arbitrator from among the Panel of Arbitrators of the Arbitration Commission. If the Claimants' side or the Respondents' side fails to make such appointment or entrustment within 20 days as from the date on which the Respondents' side receives the Notice of Arbitration, the appointment shall be made by the Chairman of the Arbitration Commission. | **16(3)** Where there are multiple parties on either side and the dispute is to be decided by more than one arbitrator, the multiple Claimants, jointly, and the multiple Respondents, jointly, shall appoint an equal number of arbitrators. If either side fails to make such joint appointment, the SCC Institute shall make the appointment for that side. If the circumstances so warrant the SCC Institute may appoint the entire Arbitral Tribunal, unless otherwise agreed by the parties. |

| ICC | LCIA | AAA | WIPO | CIETAC | STOCKHOLM |
|---|---|---|---|---|---|
| | such third person and the applicant party have consented thereto in writing, and thereafter to make a single final award, or separate awards, in respect of all parties so implicated in the arbitration; | | procedure of appointment, and<br>(iii) the Request for Arbitration names more than one Respondent, the Respondents shall jointly appoint an arbitrator. If, for whatever reason, the Respondents do not make a joint appointment of an arbitrator within 30 days after receiving the Request for Arbitration, any appointment of the arbitrator previously made by the Claimant or Claimants shall be considered void and two arbitrators shall be appointed by the Center. The two arbitrators thus appointed shall, within 30 days after the appointment of the second arbitrator, appoint a third arbitrator, who shall be the presiding arbitrator.<br>(c) Where<br>(i) three arbitrators are to be appointed,<br>(ii) the parties have agreed upon a procedure of appointment, and<br>(iii) the Request for Arbitration names more than one Claimant or more than one Respondent,<br>paragraphs (a) and (b) of this Article shall, notwithstanding Article 15(a), apply irrespective of any contractual provisions in the Arbitration Agreement with respect to the procedure of appointment, unless those provisions have expressly excluded the application of this Article. | | |

## 18. Challenges to arbitrators/revocation of authority by institution

| ICC | LCIA | AAA | WIPO | CIETAC | STOCKHOLM |
|---|---|---|---|---|---|
| **Article 11: Challenge of arbitrators**<br>**11(1)** A challenge of an arbitrator, whether for an alleged lack of independence or otherwise, shall be made by the submission to the Secretariat of a written statement specifying the facts and circumstances on which the challenge is based.<br>**11(3)** The Court shall decide on the admissibility, and, at the same time, if need be, on the merits of a chal- | **10.1** If either (a) any arbitrator gives written notice of his desire to resign as arbitrator to the LCIA Court, to be copied to the parties and the other arbitrators (if any) or (b) any arbitrator dies, falls seriously ill, refuses, or becomes unable or unfit to act, either upon challenge by a party or at the request of the remaining arbitrators, the LCIA Court may revoke that arbitrator's appointment and appoint another arbitrator. The | **8.1.** A party may challenge any arbitrator whenever circumstances exist that give rise to justifiable doubts as to the arbitrator's impartiality or independence. A party wishing to challenge an arbitrator shall send notice of the challenge to the administrator within 15 days after being notified of the appointment of the arbitrator or within 15 days after the circumstances giving rise to the challenge become known to that party. | **Article 24**<br>(a) Any arbitrator may be challenged by a party if circumstances exist that give rise to justifiable doubt as to the arbitrator's impartiality or independence.<br>(b) A party may challenge an arbitrator whom it has appointed or in whose appointment it concurred only for reasons of which it becomes aware after the appointment has been made. | **Article 29:** A party may make a request in writing to the Arbitration Commission for the removal of an appointed arbitrator from his office, if the party has justified reasons to suspect the impartiality and independence of the appointed arbitrator. In the request, the facts and reasons on which the request is based and evidence thereof must be given.<br>A challenge against an arbitrator for a removal from his office must be | **16(6)** Where an arbitrator appointed by a party dies, the party in question shall appoint another arbitrator. Where an arbitrator appointed by the SCC Institute dies, the SCC Institute shall appoint another arbitrator.<br>**18(1)** Where a party wishes to challenge an arbitrator that party shall send a written statement to the SCC Institute setting forth the reasons for the challenge. |

| ICC | LCIA | AAA | WIPO | CIETAC | STOCKHOLM |
|---|---|---|---|---|---|
| lenge after the Secretariat has afforded an opportunity for the arbitrator concerned, the other party or parties and any other members of the Arbitral Tribunal to comment in writing within a suitable period of time. Such comments shall be communicated to the parties and to the arbitrators. | LCIA Court shall decide upon the amount of fees and expenses to be paid for the former arbitrator's services (if any) as it may consider appropriate in all the circumstances.<br>**10.2** If any arbitrator acts in deliberate violation of the Arbitration Agreement (including these Rules) or does not act fairly and impartially as between the parties or does not conduct or participate in the arbitration proceedings with reasonable diligence, avoiding unnecessary delay or expense, that arbitrator may be considered unfit in the opinion of the LCIA Court.<br>**10.3** An arbitrator may also be challenged by any party if circumstances exist that give rise to justifiable doubts as to his impartiality or independence. A party may challenge an arbitrator it has nominated, or in whose appointment it has participated, only for reasons of which it becomes aware after the appointment has been made. | **8.2.** The challenge shall state in writing the reasons for the challenge.<br>**Article 9:** If the other party or parties do not agree to the challenge or the challenged arbitrator does not withdraw, the administrator in its sole discretion shall make the decision on the challenge. Replacement of an Arbitrator<br>**Article 10:** If an arbitrator withdraws after a challenge, or the administrator sustains the challenge, or the administrator determines that there are sufficient reasons to accept the resignation of an arbitrator, or an arbitrator dies, a substitute arbitrator shall be appointed pursuant to the provisions of Article 6, unless the parties otherwise agree. | **Article 25**<br>A party challenging an arbitrator shall send notice to the Center, the Tribunal and the other party, stating the reasons for the challenge, within 15 days after being notified of that arbitrator's appointment or after becoming aware of the circumstances that it considers give rise to justifiable doubt as to that arbitrator's impartiality or independence. | put forward in writing no later than the first oral hearing. If the grounds for the challege come out or are made known after the first oral hearing, the challenge may be raised after the first hearing but before the end of the last hearing.<br>**Article 30:** The Chairman of the Arbitration Commission shall decide on the challenge.<br>**Article 31:** If an arbitrator cannot perform his duty owing to withdrawal, demise, removal or other reasons, a substitute arbitrator shall be appointed in accordance with the procedure pursuant to which the original arbitrator was appointed. | **18(4)** The SCC Institute shall make the final decision on the challenge. If the SCC Institute finds an arbitrator disqualified, it shall remove the arbitrator. |

## 19. Procedure and time limits for challenges

| ICC | LCIA | AAA | WIPO | CIETAC | STOCKHOLM |
|---|---|---|---|---|---|
| **11(2)** For a challenge to be admissible, it must be sent by a party either within 30 days from receipt by that party of the notification of the appointment or confirmation of the arbitrator, or within 30 days from the date when the party making the challenge was informed of the facts and circumstances on which the challenge is based if such date is subsequent to the receipt of such notification.<br>**12(2)** An arbitrator shall also be replaced on the Court's own initiative when it decides that he is prevented *de jure* or *de facto* from fulfilling his functions, or that he is not fulfilling his functions in accordance with the Rules or within the prescribed time limits. | **10.4** A party who intends to challenge an arbitrator shall, within 15 days of the formation of the Arbitral Tribunal or (if later) after becoming aware of any circumstances referred to in Article 10.1, 10.2 or 10.3, send a written statement of the reasons for its challenge to the LCIA Court, the Arbitral Tribunal and all other parties. Unless the challenged arbitrator withdraws or all other parties agree to the challenge within 15 days of receipt of the written statement, the LCIA Court shall decide on the challenge. | | **Article 26:** When an arbitrator has been challenged by a party, the other party shall have the right to respond to the challenge and shall, if it exercises this right, send, within 15 days after receipt of the notice referred to in Article 25, a copy of its response to the Center, the party making the challenge and the arbitrators.<br>**Article 32:** At the request of a party or on its own motion, the Center may release an arbitrator from appointment as arbitrator if the arbitrator has become *de jure* or *de facto* unable to fulfil, or fails to fulfil, the duties of an arbitrator. In such a case, the parties shall be offered the opportunity to express their views thereon and the provisions of Articles 26 to 29 shall apply *mutatis mutandis.* | | **18(2)** Notification of a challenge must be made within 15 days as from the date on which the allegedly disqualifying circumstance became known to the party. Failure by a party to notify the SCC Institute of a challenge within the stipulated period of time will be considered a waiver of the right to initiate such a challenge.<br>**18(3)** The SCC Institute shall provide the parties and the arbitrators the opportunity to comment on the challenge.<br>**19(1)** Where an arbitrator is prevented from *de facto* fulfilling his duties or fails to perform his functions in an adequate manner, the SCC Institute shall remove the arbitrator.<br>**19(2)** Before removing an arbitrator, the SCC Institute shall solicit the |

| ICC | LCIA | AAA | WIPO | CIETAC | STOCKHOLM |
|---|---|---|---|---|---|
| | | | | | views of the parties and the arbitrators. |
| **20. Responses to challenges** | | | | | |
| **12(3)** When, on the basis of information that has come to its attention, the Court considers applying Article 12(2), it shall decide on the matter after the arbitrator concerned, the parties and any other members of the Arbitral Tribunal have had an opportunity to comment in writing within a suitable period of time. Such comments shall be communicated to the parties and to the arbitrators. | | | | | |
| **21. Withdrawal of arbitrator after challenge by agreement; replacement by agreement or upon resignation/incapacitation by natural causes** | | | | | |
| **12(1)** An arbitrator shall be replaced upon his death, upon the acceptance by the Court of the arbitrator's resignation, upon acceptance by the Court of a challenge or upon the request of all the parties. | **10.1** If either (a) any arbitrator gives written notice of his desire to resign as arbitrator to the LCIA Court, to be copied to the parties and the other arbitrators (if any) or (b) any arbitrator dies, falls seriously ill, refuses, or becomes unable or unfit to act, either upon challenge by a party or at the request of the remaining arbitrators, the LCIA Court may revoke that arbitrator's appointment and appoint another arbitrator. The LCIA Court shall decide upon the amount of fees and expenses to be paid for the former arbitrator's services (if any) as it may consider appropriate in all the circumstances. | **8(3)** Upon receipt of such a challenge, the administrator shall notify the other parties of the challenge. When an arbitrator has been challenged by one party, the other party or parties may agree to the acceptance of the challenge and, if there is agreement, the arbitrator shall withdraw. The challenged arbitrator may also withdraw from office in the absence of such agreement. In neither case does withdrawal imply acceptance of the validity of the grounds for the challenge.<br>**Article 10:** If an arbitrator withdraws after a challenge, or the administrator sustains the challenge, or the administrator determines that there are sufficient reasons to accept the resignation of an arbitrator, or an arbitrator dies, a substitute arbitrator shall be appointed pursuant to the provisions of Article 6, unless the parties otherwise agree. | **Article 28:** The other party may agree to the challenge or the arbitrator may voluntarily withdraw. In either case, the arbitrator shall be replaced without any implication that the grounds for the challenge are valid.<br>**Article 30: Release from Appointment**<br>At the arbitrator's own request, an arbitrator may be released from appointment as arbitrator either with the consent of the parties or by the Center.<br>**Article 31:** Irrespective of any request by the arbitrator, the parties may jointly release the arbitrator from appointment as arbitrator. The parties shall promptly notify the Center of such release.<br>**Article 32:** At the request of a party or on its own motion, the Center may release an arbitrator from appointment as arbitrator if the arbitrator has become *de jure* or *de facto* unable to fulfil, or fails to fulfil, the duties of an arbitrator. In such a case, | **Article 31:** If an arbitrator cannot perform his duty owing to withdrawal, demise, removal or other reasons, a substitute arbitrator shall be appointed in accordance with the procedure pursuant to which the original arbitrator was appointed. | **16(6)** Where an arbitrator appointed by a party dies, the party in question shall appoint another arbitrator. Where an arbitrator appointed by the SCC Institute dies, the SCC Institute shall appoint another arbitrator. |

| ICC | LCIA | AAA | WIPO | CIETAC | STOCKHOLM |
|---|---|---|---|---|---|
| | | | the parties shall be offered the opportunity to express their views thereon and the provisions of Articles 26 to 29 shall apply *mutatis mutandis.* | | |
| **22. Institution initiated replacements** | | | | | |
| **12(2)** An arbitrator shall also be replaced on the Court's own initiative when it decides that he is prevented de jure or de facto from fulfilling his functions, or that he is not fulfilling his functions in accordance with the Rules or within the prescribed time limits.<br>**12(3)** When, on the basis of information that has come to its attention, the Court considers applying Article 12(2), it shall decide on the matter after the arbitrator concerned, the parties and any other members of the Arbitral Tribunal have had an opportunity to comment in writing within a suitable period of time. Such comments shall be communicated to the parties and to the arbitrators. | | | **Article 29:** If the other party does not agree to the challenge and the challenged arbitrator does not withdraw, the decision on the challenge shall be made by the Center in accordance with its internal procedures. Such a decision is of an administrative nature and shall be final. The Center shall not be required to state reasons for its decision. | | **Article 19: Removal of Arbitrator**<br>**19(1)** Where an arbitrator is prevented from *de facto* fulfilling his duties or fails to perform his functions in an adequate manner, the SCC Institute shall remove the arbitrator.<br>**19(2)** Before removing an arbitrator, the SCC Institute shall solicit the views of the parties and the arbitrators. |
| **23. Procedural impact of withdrawals/replacement; discretions; past proceedings** | | | | | |
| **12(4)** When an arbitrator is to be replaced, the Court has discretion to decide whether or not to follow the original nominating process. Once reconstituted, and after having invited the parties to comment, the Arbitral Tribunal shall determine if and to what extent prior proceedings shall be repeated before the reconstituted Arbitral Tribunal. | **11.1** In the event that the LCIA Court determines that any nominee is not suitable or independent or impartial or if an appointed arbitrator is to be replaced for any reason, the LCIA Court shall have a complete discretion to decide whether or not to follow the original nominating process.<br>**11.2** If the LCIA Court should so decide, any opportunity given to a party to make a re-nomination shall be waived if not exercised within 15 days (or such lesser time as the LCIA Court may fix), after which the LCIA Court shall appoint the replacement arbitrator. | **11(2)** If a substitute arbitrator is appointed under either Article 10 or Article 11, the tribunal shall determine at its sole discretion whether all or part of any prior hearings shall be repeated. | **Article 27:** The Tribunal may, in its discretion, suspend or continue the arbitral proceedings during the pendency of the challenge.<br>**Article 33**<br>(a) Whenever necessary, a substitute arbitrator shall be appointed pursuant to the procedure provided for in Articles 15 to 19 that was applicable to the appointment of the arbitrator being replaced.<br>(b) In the event that an arbitrator appointed by a party has either been successfully challenged on grounds which were known or should have been known to that party at the time of appointment, or has been released from appointment as arbitrator in | | **25(2)** If an arbitrator is replaced in the course of the proceedings, the newly composed Arbitral Tribunal shall decide whether and to what extent a previously held oral hearing is to be repeated. |

| ICC | LCIA | AAA | WIPO | CIETAC | STOCKHOLM |
|---|---|---|---|---|---|
| | | | accordance with Article 32, the Center shall have the discretion not to permit that party to make a new appointment. If it chooses to exercise this discretion, the Center shall make the substitute appointment.<br>(c) Pending the replacement, the arbitral proceedings shall be suspended, unless otherwise agreed by the parties.<br>**Article 34:** Whenever a substitute arbitrator is appointed, the Tribunal shall, having regard to any observations of the parties, determine in its sole discretion whether all or part of any prior hearings are to be repeated. | | |
| **24. Power/liberty on majority to proceed alone** | | | | | |
| **12(5)** Subsequent to the closing of the proceedings, instead of replacing an arbitrator who has died or been removed by the Court pursuant to Articles 12(1) and 12(2), the Court may decide, when it considers it appropriate, that the remaining arbitrators shall continue the arbitration. In making such determination, the Court shall take into account the views of the remaining arbitrators and of the parties and such other matters that it considers appropriate in the circumstances. | **12.1** If any arbitrator on a three-member Arbitral Tribunal refuses or persistently fails to participate in its deliberations, the two other arbitrators shall have the power, upon their written notice of such refusal or failure to the LCIA Court, the parties and the third arbitrator, to continue the arbitration (including the making of any decision, ruling or award), notwithstanding the absence of the third arbitrator.<br>**12.2** In determining whether to continue the arbitration, the two other arbitrators shall take into account the stage of the arbitration, any explanation made by the third arbitrator for his non-participation and such other matters as they consider appropriate in the circumstances of the case. The reasons for such determination shall be stated in any award, order or other decision made by the two arbitrators without the participation of the third arbitrator.<br>**12.3** In the event that the two other arbitrators determine at any time not to continue the arbitration without the participation of the third arbitrator missing from their deliberations, the two arbitrators shall notify in | **11(1)** If an arbitrator on a three-person tribunal fails to participate in the arbitration for reasons other than those identified in Article 10, the two other arbitrators shall have the power in their sole discretion to continue the arbitration and to make any decision, ruling or award, notwithstanding the failure of the third arbitrator to participate. In determining whether to continue the arbitration or to render any decision, ruling or award without the participation of an arbitrator, the two other arbitrators shall take into account the stage of the arbitration, the reason, if any, expressed by the third arbitrator for such nonparticipation, and such other matters as they consider appropriate in the circumstances of the case. In the event that the two other arbitrators determine not to continue the arbitration without the participation of the third arbitrator, the administrator on proof satisfactory to it shall declare the office vacant, and a substitute arbitrator shall be appointed pursuant to the provisions of Article 6, unless the parties otherwise agree. | **35(a)** If an arbitrator on a three-person Tribunal, though duly notified and without good cause, fails to participate in the work of the Tribunal, the two other arbitrators shall, unless a party has made an application under Article 32, have the power in their sole discretion to continue the arbitration and to make any award, order or other decision, notwithstanding the failure of the third arbitrator to participate. In determining whether to continue the arbitration or to render any award, order or other decision without the participation of an arbitrator, the two other arbitrators shall take into account the stage of the arbitration, the reason, if any, expressed by the third arbitrator for such non-participation, and such other matters as they consider appropriate in the circumstances of the case.<br>**35(b)** In the event that the two other arbitrators determine not to continue the arbitration without the participation of a third arbitrator, the Center shall, on proof satisfactory to it of the failure of the arbitrator to participate in the work of the Tribunal, declare the office vacant, | | **16(7)** Where an arbitrator resigns or is removed, the SCC Institute shall appoint another arbitrator. If the arbitrator had been appointed by a party, the SCC Institute shall solicit the views of the appointing party. Where the Arbitral Tribunal consists of three or more arbitrators, the SCC Institute may decide that the remaining arbitrators shall proceed with the case. Prior to making such a decision, the views of the parties and the arbitrators shall be solicited. |

| ICC | LCIA | AAA | WIPO | CIETAC | STOCKHOLM |
|---|---|---|---|---|---|
| | writing the parties and the LCIA Court of such determination; and in that event, the two arbitrators or any party may refer the matter to the LCIA Court for the revocation of that third arbitrator's appointment and his replacement under Article 10. | | and a substitute arbitrator shall be appointed by the Center in the exercise of the discretion defined in Article 33, unless the parties agree otherwise. | | |
| **25. Confidentiality** | | | | | |
| | **Article 30: Confidentiality**<br>**30.1** Unless the parties expressly agree in writing to the contrary, the parties undertake as a general principle to keep confidential all awards in their arbitration, together with all materials in the proceedings created for the purpose of the arbitration and all other documents produced by another party in the proceedings not otherwise in the public domain – save and to the extent that disclosure may be required of a party by legal duty, to protect or pursue a legal right or to enforce or challenge an award in *bona fide* legal proceedings before a state court or other judicial authority.<br>**30.2** The deliberations of the Arbitral Tribunal are likewise confidential to its members, save and to the extent that disclosure of an arbitrator's refusal to participate in the arbitration is required of the other members of the Arbitral Tribunal under Articles 10, 12 and 26.<br>**30.3** The LCIA Court does not publish any award or any part of an award without the prior written consent of all parties and the Arbitral Tribunal. | **27.4.** An award may be made public only with the consent of all parties or as required by law.<br>**Confidentiality: Article 34**<br>Confidential information disclosed during the proceedings by the parties or by witnesses shall not be divulged by an arbitrator or by the administrator. Unless otherwise agreed by the parties, or required by applicable law, the members of the Tribunal and the administrator shall keep confidential all matters relating to the arbitration or the award. | | **Article 32:** The Arbitration Tribunal shall hold oral hearings when examining a case. At the request of the parties or with their consent, oral hearings may be omitted if the arbitration tribunal also deems that oral hearings are unnecessary, and then the Arbitration Tribunal may examine the case and make an award on the basis of documents only.<br>**Article 37:** When a case is heard in closed session, the parties, their attorneys, witnesses, arbitrators, experts consulted by the arbitration tribunal, appraisers appointed by the arbitration tribunal and the relevant staff-members of the secretariat of the Arbitration Commission shall not disclose to outsiders the substantive or procedural matters of the case. | **Article 9: Procedures of the SCC Institute**<br>The SCC Institute shall maintain the confidentiality of the arbitration and shall deal with the arbitration in an impartial, practical and expeditious manner.<br>**25(2)** If an arbitrator is replaced in the course of the proceedings, the newly composed Arbitral Tribunal shall decide whether and to what extent a previously held oral hearing is to be repeated. |
| **26. Arbitrators' duties** | | | | | |
| **7(1)** Every arbitrator must be and remain independent of the parties involved in the arbitration.<br>**7(2)** Before appointment or confirmation, a prospective arbitrator shall | **5.2** All arbitrators conducting an arbitration under these Rules shall be and remain at all times impartial and independent of the parties; and none shall act in the arbitration as advo- | **7(1)** Arbitrators acting under these rules shall be impartial and independent. Prior to accepting appointment, a prospective arbitrator shall disclose to the administrator any cir- | **22(a)** Each arbitrator shall be impartial and independent.<br>**23(a)** Each arbitrator shall, by accepting appointment, be deemed to have undertaken to make available | **Article 28:** Any appointed arbitrator having a personal interest in the case shall himself disclose such circumstances to the Arbitration Commission and request a withdrawal | **17(1)** An arbitrator must be impartial and independent.<br>**20(3)** The Arbitral Tribunal shall maintain the confidentiality of the arbitration and conduct each case in |

| ICC | LCIA | AAA | WIPO | CIETAC | STOCKHOLM |
|---|---|---|---|---|---|
| sign a statement of independence and disclose in writing to the Secretariat any facts or circumstances which might be of such a nature as to call into question the arbitrator's independence in the eyes of the parties. The Secretariat shall provide such information to the parties in writing and fix a time limit for any comments from them.<br>**7(3)** An arbitrator shall immediately disclose in writing to the Secretariat and to the parties any facts or circumstances of a similar nature which may arise during the arbitration.<br>**7(5)** By accepting to serve every arbitrator undertakes to carry out his responsibilities in accordance with these Rules.<br>**8(1)** The disputes shall be decided by sole arbitrator or by three arbitrators.<br>**15(2)** In all cases, the Arbitral Tribunal shall act fairly and impartially and ensure that each party has a reasonable opportunity to present its case.<br>**17(2)** In all cases, the Arbitral Tribunal shall take account of the provisions of the contract and the relevant trade usages.<br>**18(1)** As soon as it has received the file from the Secretariat, the Arbitral Tribunal shall draw up, on the basis of documents or in the presence of the parties and in the light of their most recent submissions, a document defining its Terms of Reference. This document shall include the following particulars:<br>(a) the full names and description of the parties;<br>(b) the addresses of the parties to which notifications and communications arising in the course of the arbitration may be made;<br>(c) a summary of the parties' respective claims and of the relief sought by each party with an indication to the extent possible of the amounts claimed or counterclaimed; | cates for any party. No arbitrator, whether before or after appointment, shall advise any party on the merits or outcome of the dispute.<br>**5.3** Before appointment by the LCIA Court, each arbitrator shall furnish to the Registrar a written résumé of his past and present professional positions; he shall agree in writing upon fee rates conforming to the Schedule of Costs; and he shall sign a declaration to the effect that there are no circumstances known to him likely to give rise to any justified doubts as to his impartiality or ndependence, other than any circumstances disclosed by him in the declaration. Each arbitrator shall thereby also assume a continuing duty forthwith to disclose any such circumstances to the LCIA Court, to any other members of the Arbitral Tribunal and to all the parties if such circumstances should arise after the date of such declaration and before the arbitration is concluded.<br>**14.1** The parties may agree on the conduct of their arbitral proceedings and they are encouraged to do so, consistent with the Arbitral Tribunal's general duties at all times:<br>(i) to act fairly and impartially as between all parties, giving each a reasonable opportunity of putting its case and dealing with that of its opponent; and<br>(ii) to adopt procedures suitable to the circumstances of the arbitration, avoiding unnecessary delay or expense, so as to provide a fair and efficient means for the final resolution of the parties' dispute.<br>Such agreements shall be made by the parties in writing or recorded in writing by the Arbitral Tribunal at the request of and with the authority of the parties.<br>**14.2** Unless otherwise agreed by the parties under Article 14.1, the Arbitral Tribunal shall have the widest discretion to discharge its | cumstance likely to give rise to justifiable doubts as to the arbitrator's impartiality or independence. If, at any stage during the arbitration, new circumstances arise that may give rise to such doubts, an arbitrator shall promptly disclose such circumstances to the parties and to the administrator. Upon receipt of such information from an arbitrator or a party, the administrator shall communicate it to the other parties and to the tribunal.<br>**16(1)** Subject to these rules, the Tribunal may conduct the arbitration in whatever manner it considers appropriate, provided that the parties are treated with equality and that each party has the right to be heard and is given a fair opportunity to present its case.<br>**16(2)** The Tribunal, exercising its discretion, shall conduct the proceedings with a view to expediting the resolution of the dispute. It may conduct a preparatory conference with the parties for the purpose of organizing, scheduling and agreeing to procedures to expedite the subsequent proceedings.<br>**20(1)** The Tribunal shall give the parties at least 30 days' advance notice of the date, time and place of the initial oral hearing. The Tribunal shall give reasonable notice of subsequent hearings.<br>**20(6)** The Tribunal shall determine the admissibility, relevance, materiality and weight of the evidence offered by any party. The Tribunal shall take into account applicable principles of legal privilege, such as those involving the confidentiality of communications between a lawyer and client.<br>**27(1)** Awards shall be made in writing, promptly by the Tribunal, and shall be final and binding on the parties. The parties undertake to carry out any such award without delay.<br>**27(2)** The Tribunal shall state the | sufficient time to enable the arbitration to be conducted and completed expeditiously.<br>**Article 38: General Powers of the Tribunal**<br>(a) Subject to Article 3, the Tribunal may conduct the arbitration in such manner as it considers appropriate.<br>(b) In all cases, the Tribunal shall ensure that the parties are treated with equality and that each party is given a fair opportunity to present its case.<br>(c) The Tribunal shall ensure that the arbitral procedure takes place with due expedition. It may, at the request of a party or on its own motion, extend in exceptional cases a period of time fixed by these Rules, by itself or agreed to by the parties. In urgent cases, such an extension may be granted by the presiding arbitrator alone.<br>**48(a)** The Tribunal shall determine the admissibility, relevance, materiality and weight of evidence.<br>**59(a)** The Tribunal shall decide the substance of the dispute in accordance with the law or rules of law chosen by the parties. Any designation of the law of a given State shall be construed, unless otherwise expressed, as directly referring to the substantive law of that State and not to its conflict of laws rules. Failing a choice by the parties, the Tribunal shall apply the law or rules of law that it determines to be appropriate. In all cases, the Tribunal shall decide having due regard to the terms of any relevant contract and taking into account applicable trade usages. The Tribunal may decide as amiable compositeur or *ex aequo et bono* only if the parties have expressly authorized it to do so.<br>**76(a)** Unless the parties agree otherwise, the Center and the arbitrator shall maintain the confidentiality of the arbitration, the award and, to the | from his office.<br>**Article 52:** The Arbitration Tribunal shall render an arbitral award within 9 months as from the date on which the arbitration tribunal is formed. The Secretary-General of the Arbitration Commission may extend this time limit at the request of the Arbitration Tribunal if the Secretary-General of the Arbitration Commission considers that it is really necessary and the reasons for extension are truly justified.<br>**Article 53:** The Arbitration Tribunal shall independently and impartially make its arbitral award on the basis of the facts, in accordance with the law and the terms of the contracts, with reference to international practices and in compliance with the principle of fairness and reasonableness.<br>**Article 54:** Where a case is heard by an Arbitration Tribunal composed of three arbitrators, the arbitral award shall be decided by the majority of the arbitrators and the minority opinion may be written in the record and docketed into the file. When the Arbitration Tribunal cannot attain a majority opinion, the arbitral award shall be decided in accordance with the presiding arbitrator's opinion.<br>**Article 55:** The Arbitration Tribunal shall state in the arbitral award the claims, the facts of the dispute, the reasons on which the arbitral award is based, the result of the arbitral award, the allocation of the arbitration costs, the date on which and the place at which the arbitral award is made. The facts of the dispute and the reasons on which the arbitral award is based may not be stated in the arbitral award if the parties have agreed not to state them in the arbitral award, or the arbitral award is made in accordance with the contents of the settlement agreement reached between the parties. | an impartial, practical and expeditious manner, giving each party sufficient opportunity to present its case.<br>**Article 33: Time for Rendering an Award**<br>An Award shall be rendered not later than six months as from the date when the case was referred to the Arbitral Tribunal. The SCC Institute may extend the period of time for rendering an Award. |

| ICC | LCIA | AAA | WIPO | CIETAC | STOCKHOLM |
|---|---|---|---|---|---|
| (d) unless the Arbitral Tribunal considers it inappropriate, a list of issues to be determined;<br>(e) the full names, descriptions and addresses of the arbitrators;<br>(f) the place of the arbitration; and<br>(g) particulars of the applicable procedural rules and, if such is the case, reference to the power conferred upon the Arbitral Tribunal to act as *amiable compositeur* or to decide *ex aequo et bono.*<br>**20(1)** The Arbitral Tribunal shall proceed within as short a time as possible to establish the facts of case by all appropriate means.<br>**20(2)** After study of the written submissions of the parties and of all documents relied upon, the Arbitral Tribunal shall hear the parties together in person if any of them so requests or failing such a request, it may of its own motion decide to hear them.<br>**35. General Rule**<br>In all matters not expressly provided for in these Rules, the court and the Arbitral Tribunal shall act in the spirit of these Rules and shall make every effort to make sure that the Award is enforceable at law. | duties allowed under such law(s) or rules of law as the Arbitral Tribunal may determine to be applicable; and at all times the parties shall do everything necessary for the fair, efficient and expeditious conduct of the arbitration.<br>**26.1** The Arbitral Tribunal shall make its award in writing and, unless all parties agree in writing otherwise, shall state the reasons upon which its award is based. The award shall also state the date when the award is made and the seat of the arbitration; and it shall be signed by the Arbitral Tribunal or those of its members assenting to it.<br>**26.3** Where there are three arbitrators and the Arbitral Tribunal fails to agree on any issue, the arbitrators shall decide that issue by a majority. Failing a majority decision on any issue, the chairman of the Arbitral Tribunal shall decide that issue. | reasons upon which the award is based, unless the parties have agreed that no reasons need be given.<br>**27(3)** The award shall contain the date and the place where the award was made, which shall be the place designated pursuant to Article 13.<br>**28(1)** The Tribunal shall apply the substantive law(s) or rules of law designated by the parties as applicable to the dispute. Failing such a designation by the parties, the Tribunal shall apply such law(s) or rules of law as it determines to be appropriate.<br>**28(2)** In arbitrations involving the application of contracts, the Tribunal shall decide in accordance with the terms of the contract and shall take into account usages of the trade applicable to the contract.<br>**Article 31: Costs**<br>The Tribunal shall fix the costs of arbitration in its award.<br>**Article 34: Confidentiality**<br>Confidential information disclosed during the proceedings by the parties or by witnesses shall not be divulged by an arbitrator or by the administrator. Unless otherwise agreed by the parties, or required by applicable law, the members of the Tribunal and the administrator shall keep confidential all matters relating to the arbitration or the award.<br>**Article 36: Interpretation of Rules**<br>The Tribunal shall interpret and apply these rules insofar as they relate to its powers and duties. | extent that they describe information that is not in the public domain, any documentary or other evidence disclosed during the arbitration, except to the extent necessary in connection with a court action relating to the award, or as otherwise required by law. | | |

CHAPTER 4

# Proceedings

The conduct of the proceedings, under the 1996 Act, is a matter over which the parties have considerable influence if they so wish, otherwise the Tribunal – subject to its overriding obligations – will have control. Most of the institutions rules afford the parties varying degrees of control over how proceedings are run.

The ICC rules observe any agreement made by the parties as to the place of the arbitration (which may be important if local Court assistance is contemplated), but otherwise the Court will fix the venue. Similar rules apply to the location of hearings. The ICC expressly imposes its rules as the procedural rules of the arbitration (Article 15) or supplementary rules agreed by the parties/Tribunal. The ICC rules entitles the parties to a hearing (Article 20(2)) – although whether this extends to procedural matters is doubtful. The corollory is that in certain cases – unless parties or the Tribunal so require – the arbitration may be conducted on written submissions and supporting documents alone. The Tribunal will apply the parties' chosen substantive law, in default of which the Tribunal will determine the law (Article 17). In common with virtually every system the Tribunal will act as amiable compositeur only with the parties' express agreement. The ICC has a unique creative – the Terms of Reference (Article 18). These have been criticised as creating an unnecessary procedural hurdle. The terms are imposed to define issues and tasks. Whilst the ICC rules do not of themselves contain a detailed timetable for the exchange of submissions (apart from the basic information to be set out in the Request and Answer), one function of the Terms of Reference is to order exchanges and otherwise set bespoke timetables for the conduct of the specific proceedings. The flexibility of this approach is sensible (it avoids the one size fits all approach of other institutions) but can and does hold up matters whilst terms are "negotiated". The ICC is alone in making special provisions for the inclusions of new claims; it has similar liberties for amendments to the other institutions. The rules concerning evidence are short in general and this is because for timetabling and practical purposes these will be addressed at the Terms of Reference stage.

The **ICC** – in common with all institutions (and the English Act) – entitles the Tribunal, in consultation with the parties, to appoint its own experts. There are powers for interim and conservatory measures and permission to seek judicial assistance in appropriate circumstances limited rules for the expedition of proceedings exist. Hearings are classically short. Whilst the rules permit requests for security for costs, in practice these are rarely awarded.

The **LCIA** is similar in many respects. Notable differences are that in default of agreement as to the place of arbitration it will be London (Article 16) unless, on the parties' application, a case is made out for an alternative venue. A detailed timetable (largely mirroring the English Courts' timetable) for exchange of submissions is set out (see Article 5), although in practice this tends not to be rigidly enforced but to be operated accordingly to the dictates of the particular case. Hearings "on the merits of the disputes" are an entitlement. Detailed rules are prescribed for evidence. There are wide powers in respect of interim and conservatory measures. These include a power to award security for costs, not infrequently invoked (and the subject matter of bitter criticism from some parties). Hearings tend to be long and the cross examination process more prolonged, although this varies between Tribunals.

**AAA** – Distinguishing features of AAA include in default of agreement, on an interim basis, the administration determines place of arbitration; oral hearings are positively contemplated (Article 20.1); whilst there are widespread interim/conservatory measures judicial assistance is not excluded.

**WIPO** – Special features of WIPO include a decision on the place of arbitration (in default of agreement) by the Centre. A preparatory conference to make specific bespoke directions is provided for (Article 47). The Tribunal may refuse the appearance of witnesses (on grounds of redundancy or otherwise); Article 47 notwithstanding, a general timetable for the various stages of the hearing is prescribed (Articles 41, 42 and 43). Hearings are obligatory on request. Interim measures are broadly drafted and include specific provisions for security for costs, they are also tailored to intellectual property matters. Party representatives must have sufficient time available to enable expeditious arbitrations – holidays/work load are not good excuses. There is a separate set of rules for expedited hearings.

**CIETAC** – Beijing is the default place of arbitration absent agreement or good reasons to the contrary. See also Article 12 as to the option to elect a specific commission to conduct the arbitration. Article 75 provides that Chinese is the official language – unless otherwise agreed. Oral hearings are to be held (Article 32) but the parties may request they be omitted. Party representatives must hold valid powers of attorney – the only organisation to impose this formal requirement. Interim measures are dealt with at Article 34 and are exercised through the local Peoples' Court. There is no provision for (or against) extra territorial measures.

**STOCKHOLM** – The Stockholm rules follow a traditional pattern, giving the Tribunal wide powers to decide questions of locality and procedure (absent party agreement) with regard to the specific facts and with almost no default procedures. Evidence may be refused if "irrelevant, non-essential or if proof can be established by other [more convenientlless expensive] means". Hearings are provided for and judicial assistance is not excluded. There is no provision for security for costs.

| ICC | LCIA | AAA | WIPO | CIETAC | STOCKHOLM |
|---|---|---|---|---|---|
| **1. Effect of arbitration agreement** | | | | | |
| **Article 6: Effect of the arbitration agreement**<br>**6(1)** Where the parties have agreed to submit to arbitration under the Rules, they shall be deemed to have submitted *ipso facto* to the Rules in effect on the date of commencement of the arbitration proceedings unless they have agreed to submit to the Rules in effect on the date of their arbitration agreement. | **Preamble:** Where any agreement, submission or reference provides in writing and in whatsoever manner for arbitration under the rules of the LCIA or by the Court of the LCIA ("the LCIA Court"), the parties shall be taken to have agreed in writing that the arbitration shall be conducted in accordance with the following rules ("the Rules") or such amended rules as the LCIA may have adopted hereafter to take effect before the commencement of the arbitration. The Rules include the Schedule of Costs in effect at the commencement of the arbitration, as separately amended from time to time by the LCIA Court. | | | **Article 7:** Once the parties agree to submit their dispute to the Arbitration Commission for arbitration, it shall be deemed that they have agreed to conduct the arbitration under these Rules. In case the parties have agreed otherwise which is also agreed by the Arbitration Commission, the parties agreement shall prevail.<br>**Article 3:** The Arbitration Commission takes cognizance of cases in accordance with an arbitration agreement between the parties concluded before or after the occurrence of the dispute to refer their dispute to the Arbitration Commission for arbitration and upon the written application by one of the parties.<br>An arbitration agreement means an arbitration clause stipulated by the parties in their contract or a written agreement concluded by the parties in other forms to submit their dispute for arbitration. | |
| **2. Passing the file to the Tribunal** | | | | | |
| **Article 13: Transmission of the file to the Arbitral Tribunal**<br>The Secretariat shall transmit the file to the Arbitral Tribunal as soon as it has been constituted, provided the advances on costs requested by the Secretariat at this stage has been paid. | **Article 13: Communications between Parties and the Arbitral Tribunal**<br>**13.1** Until the Arbitral Tribunal is formed, all communications between parties and arbitrators shall be made through the Registrar.<br>**13.2** Thereafter, unless and until the Arbitral Tribunal directs that communications shall take place directly between the Arbitral Tribunal and the parties (with simultaneous copies to the Registrar), all written communications between the parties and the Arbitral Tribunal shall continue to be made through the Registrar.<br>**13.3** Where the Registrar sends any written communication to one party on behalf of the Arbitral Tribunal, he | | **5(a)** Until the notification by the Center of the establishment of the Tribunal, any written statement, notice or other communication required or allowed under Articles 6 to 36 shall be submitted by a party to the Center and a copy thereof shall at the same time be transmitted by that party to the other party.<br>**Article 37:** The Center shall transmit the file to each arbitrator as soon as the arbitrator is appointed. | | **Article 15: Referral of a Case to the Arbitral Tribunal**<br>When the Arbitral Tribunal has been appointed and the Advance on Costs has been paid, the SCC Institute shall refer the case to the Arbitral Tribunal. |

| ICC | LCIA | AAA | WIPO | CIETAC | STOCKHOLM |
|---|---|---|---|---|---|
| | shall send a copy to each of the other parties. Where any party sends to the Registrar any communication (including Written Statements and Documents under Article 15), it shall include a copy for each arbitrator; and it shall also send copies direct to all other parties and confirm to the Registrar in writing that it has done or is doing so. | | | | |
| **3. Place of arbitration** | | | | | |
| **Article 14: Place of the Arbitration**<br>**14(1)** The place of the arbitration shall be fixed by the Court unless agreed upon by the parties. | **16.1** The parties may agree in writing the seat (or legal place) of their arbitration. Failing such a choice, the seat of arbitration shall be London, unless and until the LCIA Court determines in view of all the circumstances, and after having given the parties an opportunity to make written comment, that another seat is more appropriate. | **Place of Arbitration Article 13**<br>1. If the parties disagree as to the place of arbitration, the administrator may initially determine the place of arbitration, subject to the power of the tribunal to determine finally the place of arbitration within 60 days after its constitution. All such determinations shall be made having regard for the contentions of the parties and the circumstances of the arbitration. | **Article 39: Place of Arbitration**<br>(a) Unless otherwise agreed by the parties, the place of arbitration shall be decided by the Center, taking into consideration any observations of the parties and the circumstances of the arbitration.<br>(b) The Tribunal may, after consultation with the parties, conduct hearings at any place that it considers appropriate. It may deliberate wherever it deems appropriate.<br>(c) The award shall be deemed to have been made at the place of arbitration. | **Article 12:** The Parties may agree to have their dispute submitted for arbitration conducted by the Arbitration Commission in Beijing or by its Shenzhen Sub-Commission in Shenzhen or by its Shanghai Sub-Commission in Shanghai.<br>In the absence of such an agreement, the Claimant may opt to have the arbitration conducted by the Arbitration Commission in Beijing or by its Shenzhen Sub-Commission in Shenzhen or by its Shanghai Sub-Commission in Shanghai.<br>When exercising such option, the option first made shall prevail. If a dispute arises over the option, it shall be decided by the Arbitration Commission.<br>**Article 35:** In case the parties have agreed the place of arbitration, the hearing of the case shall be conducted in the place of arbitration. Unless otherwise agreed by the parties, the cases taken cognizance of by the Arbitration Commission shall be heard in Beijing, or in other places with the approval of the Secretary-General of the Arbitration Commission. The cases taken cognizance of by a Sub-Commission of the Arbitration Commission shall be heard in the place where the Sub-Commission is located, or in other places with the approval of the Secretary-General of the Sub-Commission. | |

| ICC | LCIA | AAA | WIPO | CIETAC | STOCKHOLM |
|---|---|---|---|---|---|
| **4. Place of hearings** | | | | | |
| **14(2)** The Arbitral Tribunal may, after consultation with the parties, conduct hearings and meetings at any location it considers appropriate unless otherwise agreed by the parties. | **16.2** The Arbitral Tribunal may hold hearings, meetings and deliberations at any convenient geographical place in its discretion; and if elsewhere than the seat of the arbitration, the arbitration shall be treated as an arbitration conducted at the seat of the arbitration and any award as an award made at the seat of the arbitration for all purposes. | **13(2)** The Tribunal may hold conferences or hear witnesses or inspect property or documents at any place it deems appropriate. The parties shall be given sufficient written notice to enable them to be present at any such proceedings. | | | **20(4)** The Arbitral Tribunal may, after consultation with the parties, decide to conduct hearings at a location other than the Place of Arbitration. |
| **5. Place of Tribunal's deliberations** | | | | | |
| **14(3)** The Arbitral Tribunal may deliberate at any location it considers appropriate. | **16.2** The Arbitral Tribunal may hold hearings, meetings and deliberations at any convenient geographical place in its discretion; and if elsewhere than the seat of the arbitration, the arbitration shall be treated as an arbitration conducted at the seat of the arbitration and any award as an award made at the seat of the arbitration for all purposes. | | | | |
| **6. Procedural rules applying** | | | | | |
| **Article 15: Rules governing the proceedings**<br>**15(1)** The proceedings before the Arbitral Tribunal shall be governed by these Rules, and where these Rules are silent, any rules which the parties or, failing them, the Arbitral Tribunal, may settle, whether or not reference is thereby made to the rules of procedure of a national law to be applied to the arbitration. | **14.1** The parties may agree on the conduct of their arbitral proceedings and they are encouraged to do so, consistent with the Arbitral Tribunal's general duties at all times.<br>**14.2** Unless otherwise agreed by the parties under Article 14.1, the Arbitral Tribunal shall have the widest discretion to discharge its duties allowed under such law(s) or rules of law as the Arbitral Tribunal may determine to be applicable; and at all times the parties shall do everything necessary for the fair, efficient and expeditious conduct of the arbitration.<br>**14.3** In the case of a three-member Arbitral Tribunal the chairman may, with the prior consent of the other two arbitrators, make procedural rulings alone. | **20.6.** The Tribunal shall determine the admissibility, relevance, materiality and weight of the evidence offered by any party. The Tribunal shall take into account applicable principles of legal privilege, such as those involving the confidentiality of communications between a lawyer and client.<br>**Interpretation of Rules: Article 36**<br>The Tribunal shall interpret and apply these rules insofar as they relate to its powers and duties.<br>The administrator shall interpret and apply all other rules. | **Article 3(a)** These Rules shall govern the arbitration, except that, where any of these Rules is in conflict with a provision of the law applicable to the arbitration from which the parties cannot derogate, that provision shall prevail.<br>**38(a)** Subject to Article 3, the Tribunal may conduct the arbitration in such manner as it considers appropriate. | **Article 81:** The power to interpret these Rules is vested in the Arbitration Commission. | **Article 20: Procedures of the Arbitral Tribunal**<br>**20(1)** The manner of conducting the proceedings is to be determined by the Arbitral Tribunal in compliance with the conditions set down in the arbitration agreement and these Rules, with due account taken to the wishes of the parties.<br>**20(2)** The Arbitral Tribunal may decide that the Chairman alone may make procedural rulings.<br>**20(3)** The Arbitral Tribunal shall maintain the confidentiality of the arbitration and conduct each case in an impartial, practical and expeditious manner, giving each party sufficient opportunity to present its case.<br>**20(4)** The Arbitral Tribunal may, |

| ICC | LCIA | AAA | WIPO | CIETAC | STOCKHOLM |
|---|---|---|---|---|---|
| | | | | | after consultation with the parties, decide to conduct hearings at a location other than the Place of Arbitration.<br>**20(5)** Article 12 shall apply with respect to communications from the Arbitral Tribunal. |

## 7. Duty of Tribunal to give opportunity to be heard/fairness

| ICC | LCIA | AAA | WIPO | CIETAC | STOCKHOLM |
|---|---|---|---|---|---|
| **15(2)** In all cases, the Arbitral Tribunal shall act fairly and impartially and ensure that each party has a reasonable opportunity to present its case.<br>**20(1)** The Arbitral Tribunal shall proceed within as short a time as possible to establish the facts of case by all appropriate means. | **14.1** The parties may agree on the conduct of their arbitral proceedings and they are encouraged to do so, consistent with the Arbitral Tribunal's general duties at all times:<br>(i) to act fairly and impartially as between all parties, giving each a reasonable opportunity of putting its case and dealing with that of its opponent; and<br>(ii) to adopt procedures suitable to the circumstances of the arbitration, avoiding unnecessary delay or expense, so as to provide a fair and efficient means for the final resolution of the parties' dispute.<br>Such agreements shall be made by the parties in writing or recorded in writing by the Arbitral Tribunal at the request of and with the authority of the parties. | **16.1.** Subject to these rules, the Tribunal may conduct the arbitration in whatever manner it considers appropriate, provided that the parties are treated with equality and that each party has the right to be heard and is given a fair opportunity to present its case. | **38(b)** In all cases, the Tribunal shall ensure that the parties are treated with equality and that each party is given a fair opportunity to present its case.<br>**38(c)** The Tribunal shall ensure that the arbitral procedure takes place with due expedition. It may, at the request of a party or on its own motion, extend in exceptional cases a period of time fixed by these Rules, by itself or agreed to by the parties. In urgent cases, such an extension may be granted by the presiding arbitrator alone. | | |

## 8. Language of arbitration

| ICC | LCIA | AAA | WIPO | CIETAC | STOCKHOLM |
|---|---|---|---|---|---|
| **Article 16: Language of the arbitration**<br>**16(1)** In the absence of an agreement by the parties, the Arbitral Tribunal shall determine the language or languages of the arbitration, due regard being given to all relevant circumstances, including the language of the contract. | **Article 17: Language of Arbitration**<br>**17.1** The initial language of the arbitration shall be the language of the Arbitration Agreement, unless the parties have agreed in writing otherwise and providing always that a non-participating or defaulting party shall have no cause for complaint if communications to and from the Registrar and the arbitration proceedings are conducted in English.<br>**17.2** In the event that the Arbitration Agreement is written in more than one language, the LCIA Court may, | **Language: Article 14**<br>If the parties have not agreed otherwise, the language(s) of the arbitration shall be that of the documents containing the arbitration agreement, subject to the power of the Tribunal to determine otherwise based upon the contentions of the parties and the circumstances of the arbitration. The Tribunal may order that any documents delivered in another language shall be accompanied by a translation into the language(s) of the arbitration. | **Article 40: Language of Arbitration**<br>(a) Unless otherwise agreed by the parties, the language of the arbitration shall be the language of the Arbitration Agreement, subject to the power of the Tribunal to determine otherwise, having regard to any observations of the parties and the circumstances of the arbitration.<br>(b) The Tribunal may order that any documents submitted in languages other than the language of arbitration be accompanied by a translation in whole or in part into the language of arbitration. | **Article 75**: The Chinese language is the official language of the Arbitration Commission. If the parties have agreed otherwise, their agreement shall prevail. | **Article 23: Language**<br>Unless the parties have agreed in the arbitration agreement on the language or languages to be used in the proceedings, the Arbitral Tribunal shall, after consultation with the parties, make such decision. |

| ICC | LCIA | AAA | WIPO | CIETAC | STOCKHOLM |
|---|---|---|---|---|---|
| | unless the Arbitration Agreement provides that the arbitration proceedings shall be conducted in more than one language, decide which of those languages shall be the initial language of the arbitration.<br>**17.3** Upon the formation of the Arbitral Tribunal and unless the parties have agreed upon the language or languages of the arbitration, the Arbitration Tribunal shall decide upon the language(s) of the arbitration, after giving the parties an opportunity to make written comment and taking into account the initial language of the arbitration and any other matter it may consider appropriate in all the circumstances of the case.<br>**17.4** If any document is expressed in a language other than the language(s) of the arbitration and no translation of such document is submitted by the party relying upon the document, the Arbitral Tribunal or (if the Arbitral Tribunal has not been formed) the LCIA Court may order that party to submit a translation in a form to be determined by the Arbitral Tribunal or the LCIA Court, as the case may be. | | | | |

## 9. The substantive law

| ICC | LCIA | AAA | WIPO | CIETAC | STOCKHOLM |
|---|---|---|---|---|---|
| **Article 17: Applicable Rules of Law**<br>**17(1)** The parties shall be free to agree upon the rules of law to be applied by the Arbitral Tribunal to the merits of the dispute. In the absence of any such agreement, the Arbitral Tribunal shall apply the rules of law which it determines to be appropriate.<br>**17(2)** In all cases, the Arbitral Tribunal shall take account of the provisions of the contract and relevant trade usages. | **16.3** The law applicable to the arbitration (if any) shall be the arbitration law of the seat of arbitration, unless and to the extent that the parties have expressly agreed in writing on the application of another arbitration law and such agreement is not prohibited by the law of the arbitral seat.<br>**22.1(f)** To decide whether or not to apply any strict rules of evidence (or any other rules) as to the admissibility, relevance or weight of any material tendered by a party on any matter of fact or expert opinion; and to determine the time, manner and | **28.1.** The Tribunal shall apply the substantive law(s) or rules of law designated by the parties as applicable to the dispute. Failing such a designation by the parties, the Tribunal shall apply such law(s) or rules of law as it determines to be appropriate.<br>**28.2.** In arbitrations involving the application of contracts, the Tribunal shall decide in accordance with the terms of the contract and shall take into account usages of the trade applicable to the contract. | **3(b)** The law applicable to the arbitration shall be determined in accordance with Article 59(b).<br>**Article 59: Laws Applicable to the Substance of the Dispute, the Arbitration and the Arbitration Agreement**<br>(a) The Tribunal shall decide the substance of the dispute in accordance with the law or rules of law chosen by the parties. Any designation of the law of a given State shall be construed, unless otherwise expressed, as directly referring to the substantive law of that State and not to its conflict of laws rules. Failing a | | **Article 24: Applicable Law**<br>(1) The Arbitral Tribunal shall decide the merits of the dispute on the basis of the law or rules of law agreed by the parties. In the absence of such an agreement, the Arbitral Tribunal shall apply the law or rules of law which it considers to be most appropriate. |

| ICC | LCIA | AAA | WIPO | CIETAC | STOCKHOLM |
|---|---|---|---|---|---|
| | form in which such material should be exchanged between the parties and presented to the Arbitral Tribunal; **22.3** The Arbitral Tribunal shall decide the parties' dispute in accordance with the law(s) or rules of law chosen by the parties as applicable to the merits of their dispute. If and to the extent that the Arbitral Tribunal determines that the parties have made no such choice, the Arbitral Tribunal shall apply the law(s) or rules of law which it considers appropriate. | | choice by the parties, the Tribunal shall apply the law or rules of law that it determines to be appropriate. In all cases, the Tribunal shall decide having due regard to the terms of any relevant contract and taking into account applicable trade usages. The Tribunal may decide as amiable compositeur or *ex aequo et bono* only if the parties have expressly authorized it to do so.<br>(b) The law applicable to the arbitration shall be the arbitration law of the place of arbitration, unless the parties have expressly agreed on the application of another arbitration law and such agreement is permitted by the law of the place of arbitration.<br>(c) An Arbitration Agreement shall be regarded as effective if it conforms to the requirements concerning form, existence, validity and scope of either the law or rules of law applicable in accordance with paragraph (a), or the law applicable in accordance with paragraph (b). | | |
| **10. Amiable compositeur/ex aequo et bono** | | | | | |
| **17(3)** The Arbitral Tribunal shall assume the powers of an amiable compositeur or decide *ex aequo et bono* only if the parties have agreed to give it such powers. | **22.4** The Arbitral Tribunal shall only apply to the merits of the dispute principles deriving from "*ex aequo et bono*", "amiable composition" or "honourable engagement" where the parties have so agreed expressly in writing. | **28.3.** The tribunal shall not decide as amiable compositeur or *ex aequo et bono* unless the parties have expressly authorized it to do so. | | | **24(3)** The Arbitral Tribunal shall decide the dispute *ex aequo et bono* or as amiable compositeur only if the parties have expressly authorized it to do so. |
| **11. Application of rules of conflicts of law** | | | | | |
| | **22.1(g)** to order the correction of any contract between the parties or the Arbitration Agreement, but only to the extent required to rectify any mistake which the Arbitral Tribunal determines to be common to the parties and then only if and to the extent to which the law(s) or rules of law applicable to the contract or Arbitration Agreement permit such correction; and | | | | **24(2)** Any designation made by the parties of the law of a given state shall be construed as directly referring to the substantive law of that state and not to its conflict of laws rules. |

| ICC | LCIA | AAA | WIPO | CIETAC | STOCKHOLM |
|---|---|---|---|---|---|
| **12. Terms of reference** | | | | | |
| **Article 18: Terms of Reference; Procedural Timetable**<br>18(1) As soon as it has received the file from the Secretariat, the Arbitral Tribunal shall draw up, on the basis of documents or in the presence of the parties and in the light of their most recent submissions, a document defining its Terms of Reference. This document shall include the following particulars:<br>(a) the full names and description of the parties;<br>(b) the addresses of the parties to which notifications and communications arising in the course of the arbitration may be made;<br>(c) a summary of the parties' respective claims and of the relief sought by each party, with an indication to the extent possible of the amounts claimed or counterclaimed;<br>(d) unless the Arbitral Tribunal considers it inappropriate, a list of issues to be determined;<br>(e) the full names, descriptions and addresses of the arbitrators;<br>(f) the place of the arbitration; and<br>(g) particulars of the applicable procedural rules and, if such is the case, reference to the power conferred upon the Arbitral Tribunal to act as *amiable compositeur* or to decide *ex aequo et bono.*<br>18(2) The Terms of Reference shall be signed by the parties and the Arbitral Tribunal. Within two months of the date when the file has been transmitted to it, the Arbitral Tribunal shall transmit to the Court the Terms of Reference signed by it and by the parties. The Court may extend this time limit, pursuant to a reasoned request from the Arbitral Tribunal or on its own initiative, if it decides it is necessary to do so.<br>18(3) If any of the parties refuses to take part in the drawing up of the | **14.1** The parties may agree on the conduct of their arbitral proceedings and they are encouraged to do so, consistent with the Arbitral Tribunal's general duties at all times:<br>(i) to act fairly and impartially as between all parties, giving each a reasonable opportunity of putting its case and dealing with that of its opponent; and<br>(ii) to adopt procedures suitable to the circumstances of the arbitration, avoiding unnecessary delay or expense, so as to provide a fair and efficient means for the final resolution of the parties' dispute.<br>Such agreements shall be made by the parties in writing or recorded in writing by the Arbitral Tribunal at the request of and with the authority of the parties.<br>**14.2** Unless otherwise agreed by the parties under Article 14.1, the Arbitral Tribunal shall have the widest discretion to discharge its duties allowed under such law(s) or rules of law as the Arbitral Tribunal may determine to be applicable; and at all times the parties shall do everything necessary for the fair, efficient and expeditious conduct of the arbitration.<br>**14.3** In the case of a three-member Arbitral Tribunal the chairman may, with the prior consent of the other two arbitrators, make procedural rulings alone. | | **Article 47:** The Tribunal may, in general following the submission of the Statement of Defense, conduct a preparatory conference with the parties for the purpose of organizing and scheduling the subsequent proceedings. | | |

| ICC | LCIA | AAA | WIPO | CIETAC | STOCKHOLM |
|---|---|---|---|---|---|
| Terms of Reference or to sign the same, they shall be submitted to the Court for approval. When the Terms of Reference are signed in accordance with Article 18(2) or approved by the Court, the arbitration shall proceed.<br>**18(4)** When drawing up the Terms of Reference, or as soon as possible thereafter, the Arbitral Tribunal, after having consulted the parties, shall establish in a separate document a provisional timetable that it intends to follow for the conduct of the arbitration and shall communicate it to the Court and the parties. Any subsequent modifications of the provisional timetable shall be communicated to the Court and the parties. | | | | | |
| **13. New claims** | | | | | |
| **Article 19: New claims**<br>After the Terms of Reference have been signed or approved by the Court, no party shall make new claims or counter claims which fall outside the limits of the Terms of Reference unless it has been authorized to do so by the Arbitral Tribunal, which shall consider the nature of such new claims or counterclaims, the stage of the arbitration and other relevant circumstances. | | | | | |
| **14. Submission of witness statements and documents** | | | | | |
| | **Article 15: Submission of Written Statements and Documents**<br>**15.1** Unless the parties have agreed otherwise under Article 14.1 or the Arbitral Tribunal should determine differently, the written stage of the proceedings shall be as set out below.<br>**15.2** Within 30 days of receipt of written notification from the Registrar of the formation of the Arbitral Tribunal, the Claimant shall send to the Registrar a Statement of | **Further Written Statements: Article 17**<br>**17.1.** The tribunal may decide whether the parties shall present any written statements in addition to statements of claims and counterclaims and statements of defense, and it shall fix the periods of time for submitting any such statements.<br>**17.2.** The periods of time fixed by the tribunal for the communication of such written statements should not | **Article 54: Witnesses**<br>(a) Before any hearing, the Tribunal may require either party to give notice of the identity of witnesses it wishes to call, as well as of the subject matter of their testimony and its relevance to the issues.<br>(b) The Tribunal has discretion, on the grounds of redundance and irrelevance, to limit or refuse the appearance of any witness, whether witness of fact or expert witness. | | |

| ICC | LCIA | AAA | WIPO | CIETAC | STOCKHOLM |
|---|---|---|---|---|---|
| | Case setting out in sufficient detail the facts and any contentions of law on which it relies, together with the relief claimed against all other parties, save and insofar as such matters have not been set out in its Request.<br>15.3 Within 30 days of receipt of the Statement of Case or written notice from the Claimant that it elects to treat the Request as its Statement of Case, the Respondent shall send to the Registrar a Statement of Defence setting out in sufficient detail which of the facts and contentions of law in the Statement of Case or Request (as the case may be) it admits or denies, on what grounds and on what other facts and contentions of law it relies. Any counterclaims shall be submitted with the Statement of Defence in the same manner as claims are to be set out in the Statement of Case. | exceed 45 days. However, the tribunal may extend such time limits if it considers such an extension justified.<br>**Notices: Article 18**<br>**18.1.** Unless otherwise agreed by the parties or ordered by the tribunal, all notices statements and written communications may be served on a party by air mail, air courier, facsimile transmission, telex, telegram, or other written forms of electronic communication addressed to the party or its representative at its last known address or by personal service.<br>**18.2.** For the purpose of calculating a period of time under these rules, such period shall begin to run on the day following the day when a notice, statement or written communication is received. If the last day of such period is an official holiday at the place received, the period is extended until the first business day which follows. Official holidays occurring during the running of the period of time are included in calculating the period. | (c) Any witness who gives oral evidence may be questioned, under the control of the Tribunal, by each of the parties. The Tribunal may put questions at any stage of the examination of the witnesses.<br>(d) The testimony of witnesses may, either at the choice of a party or as directed by the Tribunal, be submitted in written form, whether by way of signed statements, sworn affidavits or otherwise, in which case the Tribunal may make the admissibility of the testimony conditional upon the witnesses being made available for oral testimony.<br>(e) A party shall be responsible for the practical arrangements, cost and availability of any witness it calls.<br>(f) The Tribunal shall determine whether any witness shall retire during any part of the proceedings, particularly during the testimony of other witnesses. | | |
| **15. Claims, defences, counterclaims, replies, form and timing** | | | | | |
| [*No specific provision is made for a statement of claim, defence etc. except as implicitly anticipated by Article 18 on Terms of Reference, and the time table will be bespoke. In simple arbitrations the Request for arbitration could stand as the claim but a full pleading out after terms of reference is also common.*] | **15.4** Within 30 days of receipt of the Statement of Defence, the Claimant shall send to the Registrar a Statement of Reply which, where there are any counterclaims, shall include a Defence to Counterclaim in the same manner as a defence is to be set out in the Statement of Defence.<br>**15.5** If the Statement of Reply contains a Defence to Counterclaim, within 30 days of its receipt the Respondent shall send to the Registrar a Statement of Reply to Counterclaim.<br>**15.6** All Statements referred to in this Article shall be accompanied by copies (or, if they are especially voluminous, lists) of all essential docu- | | **Article 41: Statement of Claim**<br>(a) Unless the Statement of Claim accompanied the Request for Arbitration, the Claimant shall, within 30 days after receipt of notification from the Center of the establishment of the Tribunal, communicate its Statement of Claim to the Respondent and to the Tribunal.<br>(b) The Statement of Claim shall contain a comprehensive statement of the facts and legal arguments supporting the claim, including a statement of the relief sought.<br>(c) The Statement of Claim shall, to as large an extent as possible, be accompanied by the documentary evidence upon which the Claimant | **Article 18:** The Respondent shall, at the latest within 60 days from the date of receipt of the Notice of Arbitration, lodge with the secretariat of the Arbitration Commission his counterclaim in writing, if any. The arbitration tribunal may extend that time limit if it deems that there are justified reasons. When lodging a counterclaim, the Respondent must state in his written statement of counterclaim his specific claim, the facts and reasons upon which his claim is based, and attach to his written statement of counterclaim the relevant documentary evidence. | **Article 21: Statement of Claim and Defence**<br>(1) The Claimant shall, within the period of time determined by the Arbitral Tribunal, submit a Statement of Claim which, unless previously provided in the case, shall include;<br>(i) the specific relief sought;<br>(ii) the material facts and circumstances on which the Claimant relies; and<br>(iii) a preliminary statement of the evidence on which the Claimant intends to rely.<br>**21(2)** The Respondent shall, within the period of time determined by the Arbitral Tribunal, submit a |

| ICC | LCIA | AAA | WIPO | CIETAC | STOCKHOLM |
|---|---|---|---|---|---|
| | ments on which the party concerned relies and which have not previously been submitted by any party, and (where appropriate) by any relevant samples and exhibits.<br>**15.7** As soon as practicable following receipt of the Statements specified in this Article, the Arbitral Tribunal shall proceed in such manner as has been agreed in writing by the parties or pursuant to its authority under these Rules.<br>**15.8** If the Respondent fails to submit a Statement of Defence or the Claimant a Statement of Defence to Counterclaim, or if at any point any party fails to avail itself of the opportunity to present its case in the manner determined by Article 15.2 to 15.6 or directed by the Arbitral Tribunal, the Arbitral Tribunal may nevertheless proceed with the arbitration and make an award. | | relies, together with a schedule of such documents. Where the documentary evidence is especially voluminous, the Claimant may add a reference to further documents it is prepared to submit.<br>**Article 42: Statement of Defense**<br>(a) The Respondent shall, within 30 days after receipt of the Statement of Claim or within 30 days after receipt of notification from the Center of the establishment of the Tribunal, whichever occurs later, communicate its Statement of Defense to the Claimant and to the Tribunal.<br>(b) The Statement of Defense shall reply to the particulars of the Statement of Claim required pursuant to Article 41(b). The Statement of Defense shall be accompanied by the corresponding documentary evidence described in Article 41(c).<br>(c) Any counterclaim or setoff by the Respondent shall be made or asserted in the Statement of Defense or, in exceptional circumstances, at a later stage in the arbitral proceedings if so determined by the Tribunal. Any such counterclaim or setoff shall contain the same particulars as those specified in Article 41(b) and (c).<br>**Article 43: Further Written Statements**<br>(a) In the event that a counterclaim or setoff has been made or asserted, the Claimant shall reply to the particulars thereof. Article 42(a) and (b) shall apply mutatis mutandis to such reply.<br>(b) The Tribunal may, in its discretion, allow or require further written statements.<br>**56(a)** If the Claimant, without showing good cause, fails to submit its Statement of Claim in accordance with Article 41, the Tribunal shall terminate the proceedings.<br>**56(b)** If the Respondent, without showing good cause, fails to submit its Statement of Defense in accordance with Article 42, the Tribunal | | Statement of Defence, which, unless previously provided in the case, shall include;<br>(i) a statement as to whether and to what extent the Respondent accepts or denies the relief sought by the Claimant;<br>(ii) the material facts and circumstances on which the Respondent relies;<br>(iii) any counterclaim or set-off claim and the grounds on which it is based; and<br>(iv) a preliminary statement of the evidence on which the Respondent intends to rely.<br>**21(3)** The Arbitral Tribunal may determine that the parties are to submit additional written statements. |

| ICC | LCIA | AAA | WIPO | CIETAC | STOCKHOLM |
|---|---|---|---|---|---|
| | | | may nevertheless proceed with the arbitration and make the award. | | |
| **16. Amendments** | | | | | |
| | **22.1(a)** to allow any party, upon such terms (as to costs and otherwise) as it shall determine, to amend any claim, counterclaim, defence and reply. | **Amendments to Claims: Article 4** During the arbitral proceedings, any party may amend or supplement its claim, counterclaim or defense, unless the tribunal considers it inappropriate to allow such amendment or supplement because of the party's delay in making it, prejudice to the other parties or any other circumstances. A party may not amend or supplement a claim or counterclaim if the amendment or supplement would fall outside the scope of the agreement to arbitrate. | **Article 44: Amendments to Claims or Defense** Subject to any contrary agreement by the parties, a party may amend or supplement its claim, counterclaim, defense or setoff during the course of the arbitral proceedings, unless the Tribunal considers it inappropriate to allow such amendment having regard to its nature or the delay in making it and to the provisions of Article 38(b) and (c). | **Article 19:** The Claimant may request to amend his claim and the Respondent may request to amend his counterclaim; but the arbitration tribunal may refuse such an amendment if it considers that it is too late to raise the request and the amendment may affect the arbitration proceedings. | **Article 22: Amendments to Claim or Defence** (1) A party may amend his claim or defence in the course of the proceedings if his case, as amended, is still comprised by the arbitration agreement, unless the Arbitral Tribunal considers it inappropriate having regard to the point of time at which the amendments are requested, the prejudice that may be caused to the other party or other circumstances. (2) The provisions of Article 10 shall not preclude the preceding paragraph from being applied with respect to the right of a party to introduce a counterclaim or a set-off claim. |
| **17. Evidence** | | | | | |
| **20(1)** The Arbitral Tribunal shall proceed within as short a time as possible to establish the facts of case by all appropriate means. | **15.6** All Statements referred to in this Article shall be accompanied by copies (or, if they are especially voluminous, lists) of all essential documents on which the party concerned relies and which have not previously been submitted by any party, and (where appropriate) by any relevant samples and exhibits. **20.1** Before any hearing, the Arbitral Tribunal may require any party to give notice of the identity of each witness that party wishes to call (including rebuttal witnesses), as well as the subject matter of that witness's testimony, its content and its relevance to the issues in the arbitration. **20.2** The Arbitral Tribunal may also determine the time, manner and form in which such materials should be exchanged between the parties | **16.3.** The tribunal may in its discretion direct the order of proof, bifurcate proceedings, exclude cumulative or irrelevant testimony or other evidence, and direct the parties to focus their presentations on issues the decision of which could dispose of all or part of the case. **19.1.** Each party shall have the burden of proving the facts relied on to support its claim or defense. **19.2.** The tribunal may order a party to deliver to the tribunal and to the other parties a summary of the documents and other evidence which that party intends to present in support of its claim, counterclaim or defense. **19.3.** At any time during the proceedings, the tribunal may order parties to produce other documents, exhibits or other evidence it deems | **48(a)** The Tribunal shall determine the admissibility, relevance, materiality and weight of evidence. **48(b)** At any time during the arbitration, the Tribunal may, at the request of a party or on its own motion, order a party to produce such documents or other evidence as it considers necessary or appropriate and may order a party to make available to the Tribunal or to an expert appointed by it or to the other party any property in its possession or control for inspection or testing. **49(a)** A party may give notice to the Tribunal and to the other party at any reasonable time before a hearing that specified experiments have been conducted on which it intends to rely. The notice shall specify the purpose of the experiment, a summary of the experiment, the method | **Article 38:** The parties shall produce evidence for the facts on which their claim, defense or counterclaim is based. The arbitration tribunal may undertake investigations and collect evidence on its own initiative, if it deems it necessary. If the arbitration tribunal investigates and collects evidence on its own initiative, it shall timely inform the parties to be present on the spot if it deems it necessary. Should one party or both parties fail to appear on the spot, the investigation and collection of evidence shall by no means be affected. **Article 41:** The evidence submitted by the parties shall be examined and decided by the arbitration tribunal. The adoption of the expert's report and the appraiser's report shall be determined by the arbitration tribunal. | **Article 26: Evidence** (1) At the request of the Arbitral Tribunal, the parties shall state the evidence on which they intend to rely, specifying what they intend to prove with each item of evidence, and present the documentary evidence on which they rely. (2) The Arbitral Tribunal may refuse to accept evidence submitted to it if it considers such evidence to be irrelevant, non-essential or if proof can be established by other means which it considers more convenient or less expensive. |

| ICC | LCIA | AAA | WIPO | CIETAC | STOCKHOLM |
|---|---|---|---|---|---|
| | and presented to the Arbitral Tribunal; and it has a discretion to allow, refuse, or limit the appearance of witnesses (whether witness of fact or expert witness).<br>**20.3** Subject to any order otherwise by the Arbitral Tribunal, the testimony of a witness may be presented by a party in written form, either as a signed statement or as a sworn affidavit.<br>**22.1(c)** to conduct such enquiries as may appear to the Arbitral Tribunal to be necessary or expedient, including whether and to what extent the Arbitral Tribunal should itself take the initiative in identifying the issues and ascertaining the relevant facts and the law(s) or rules of law applicable to the arbitration, the merits of the parties' dispute and the Arbitration Agreement;<br>**22.1(d)** to order any party to make any property, site or thing under its control and relating to the subject matter of the arbitration available for inspection by the Arbitral Tribunal, any other party, its expert or any expert to the Arbitral Tribunal;<br>**22.1(e)** to order any party to produce to the Arbitral Tribunal, and to the other parties for inspection, and to supply copies of, any documents or classes of documents in their possession, custody or power which the Arbitral Tribunal determines to be relevant;<br>**22.1(f)** to decide whether or not to apply any strict rules of evidence (or any other rules) as to the admissibility, relevance or weight of any material tendered by a party on any matter of fact or expert opinion; and to determine the time, manner and form in which such material should be exchanged between the parties and presented to the Arbitral Tribunal; | necessary or appropriate.<br>**20.2.** At least 15 days before the hearings, each party shall give the tribunal and the other parties the names and addresses of any witnesses it intends to present, the subject of their testimony and the languages in which such witnesses will give their testimony.<br>**20.6.** The tribunal shall determine the admissibility, relevance, materiality and weight of the evidence offered by any party. The tribunal shall take into account applicable principles of legal privilege, such as those involving the confidentiality of communications between a lawyer and client. | employed, the results and the conclusion. The other party may by notice to the Tribunal request that any or all such experiments be repeated in its presence. If the Tribunal considers such request justified, it shall determine the timetable for the repetition of the experiments.<br>**49(b)** For the purposes of this Article, "experiments" shall include tests or other processes of verification.<br>**50.** The Tribunal may, at the request of a party or on its own motion, inspect or require the inspection of any site, property, machinery, facility, production line, model, film, material, product or process as it deems appropriate. A party may request such an inspection at any reasonable time prior to any hearing, and the Tribunal, if it grants such a request, shall determine the timing and arrangements for the inspection.<br>**51(i)** a technical primer setting out the background of the scientific, technical or other specialized information necessary to fully understand the matters in issue; and<br>**51(ii)** models, drawings or other materials that the Tribunal or the parties require for reference purposes at any hearing. | | |

| ICC | LCIA | AAA | WIPO | CIETAC | STOCKHOLM |
|---|---|---|---|---|---|
| **18. Provision for hearings** | | | | | |
| **20(2)** After studing the written submissions of the parties and all documents relied upon, the Arbitral Tribunal shall hear the parties together in person if any of them so requests or, failing such a request, it may of its own motion decide to hear them. | **Article 19: Hearings.**<br>**19.1** Any party which expresses a desire to that effect has the right to be heard orally before the Arbitral Tribunal on the merits of the dispute, unless the parties have agreed in writing on documents-only arbitration.<br>**19.2** The Arbitral Tribunal shall fix the date, time and physical place of any meetings and hearings in the arbitration, and shall give the parties reasonable notice thereof.<br>**19.3** The Arbitral Tribunal may in advance of any hearing submit to the parties a list of questions which it wishes them to answer with special attention.<br>**19.4** All meetings and hearings shall be in private unless the parties agree otherwise in writing or the Arbitral Tribunal directs otherwise.<br>**19.5** The Arbitral Tribunal shall have the fullest authority to establish time-limits for meetings and hearings, or for any parts thereof. | | | **Article 32:** The arbitration tribunal shall hold oral hearings when examining a case. At the request of the parties or with their consent, oral hearings may be omitted if the arbitration tribunal also deems that oral hearings are unnecessary, and then the arbitration tribunal may examine the case and make an award on the basis of documents only. | |
| **19. Witnesses** | | | | | |
| | **Article 20: Witnesses.**<br>**20.1** Before any hearing, the Arbitral Tribunal may require any party to give notice of the identity of each witness that party wishes to call (including rebuttal witnesses), as well as the subject matter of that witness's testimony, its content and its relevance to the issues in the arbitration.<br>**20.2** The Arbitral Tribunal may also determine the time, manner and form in which such materials should be exchanged between the parties and presented to the Arbitral Tribunal; and it has a discretion to allow, refuse, or limit the appearance of witnesses (whether witness of fact | **20.2.** At least 15 days before the hearings, each party shall give the tribunal and the other parties the names and addresses of any witnesses it intends to present, the subject of their testimony and the languages in which such witnesses will give their testimony.<br>**20.5.** Evidence of witnesses may also be presented in the form of written statements signed by them. | **54(a)** Before any hearing, the Tribunal may require either party to give notice of the identity of witnesses it wishes to call, as well as of the subject matter of their testimony and its relevance to the issues.<br>**54(b)** The Tribunal has discretion, on the grounds of redundance and irrelevance, to limit or refuse the appearance of any witness, whether witness of fact or expert witness.<br>**54(c)** Any witness who gives oral evidence may be questioned, under the control of the Tribunal, by each of the parties. The Tribunal may put questions at any stage of the examination of the witnesses.<br>**54(d)** The testimony of witnesses | | |

| ICC | LCIA | AAA | WIPO | CIETAC | STOCKHOLM |
|---|---|---|---|---|---|
| | or expert witness).<br>**20.3** Subject to any order otherwise by the Arbitral Tribunal, the testimony of a witness may be presented by a party in written form, either as a signed statement or as a sworn affidavit.<br>**20.4** Subject to Article 14.1 and 14.2, any party may request that a witness, on whose testimony another party seeks to rely, should attend for oral questioning at a hearing before the Arbitral Tribunal. If the Arbitral Tribunal orders that other party to produce the witness and the witness fails to attend the oral hearing without good cause, the Arbitral Tribunal may place such weight on the written testimony (or exclude the same altogether) as it considers appropriate in the circumstances of the case.<br>**20.5** Any witness who gives oral evidence at a hearing before the Arbitral Tribunal may be questioned by each of the parties under the control of the Arbitral Tribunal. The Arbitral Tribunal may put questions at any stage of his evidence.<br>**20.6** Subject to the mandatory provisions of any applicable law, it shall not be improper for any party or its legal representatives to interview any witness or potential witness for the purpose of presenting his testimony in written form or producing him as an oral witness.<br>**20.7** Any individual intending to testify to the Arbitral Tribunal on any issue of fact or expertise shall be treated as a witness under these Rules notwithstanding that the individual is a party to the arbitration or was or is an officer, employee or shareholder of any party. | | may, either at the choice of a party or as directed by the Tribunal, be submitted in written form, whether by way of signed statements, sworn affidavits or otherwise, in which case the Tribunal may make the admissibility of the testimony conditional upon the witnesses being made available for oral testimony.<br>**54(e)** A party shall be responsible for the practical arrangements, cost and availability of any witness it calls.<br>**54(f)** The Tribunal shall determine whether any witness shall retire during any part of the proceedings, particularly during the testimony of other witnesses. | | |
| **20. Tribunal appointed experts** | | | | | |
| 20(3) The Arbitral Tribunal may decide to hear witnesses, experts appointed by the parties or any other | **21.1** Unless otherwise agreed by the parties in writing, the Arbitral Tribunal: | **Experts: Article 22**<br>**22.1.** The tribunal may appoint one or more independent experts to | **55(a)** The Tribunal may, after consultation with the parties, appoint one or more independent experts to | **Article 39:** The arbitration tribunal may consult an expert or appoint an appraiser for the clarification of spe- | **Article 27: Experts**<br>**27(1)** Unless otherwise agreed by the parties, the Arbitral Tribunal may |

| ICC | LCIA | AAA | WIPO | CIETAC | STOCKHOLM |
|---|---|---|---|---|---|
| person, in the presence of the parties, or in their absence provided they have been duly summoned<br>**20(4)** The Arbitral Tribunal, after having consulted the parties, may appoint one or more experts, define their terms of reference and receive their reports. At the request of a party, the parties shall be given the opportunity to question at a hearing any such expert appointed by the Tribunal. | (a) may appoint one or more experts to report to the Arbitral Tribunal on specific issues, who shall be and remain impartial and independent of the parties throughout the arbitration proceedings; and<br>(b) may require a party to give any such expert any relevant information or to provide access to any relevant documents, goods, samples, property or site for inspection by the expert.<br>**21.2** Unless otherwise agreed by the parties in writing, if a party so requests or if the Arbitral Tribunal considers it necessary, the expert shall, after delivery of his written or oral report to the Arbitral Tribunal and the parties, participate in one or more hearings at which the parties shall have the opportunity to question the expert on his report and to present expert witnesses in order to testify on the points at issue. | report to it, in writing, on specific issues designated by the tribunal and communicated to the parties.<br>**22.2.** The parties shall provide such an expert with any relevant information or produce for inspection any relevant documents or goods that the expert may require. Any dispute between a party and the expert as to the relevance of the requested information or goods shall be referred to the tribunal for decision.<br>**22.3.** Upon receipt of an expert's report, the tribunal shall send a copy of the report to all parties and shall give the parties an opportunity to express, in writing, their opinion on the report. A party may examine any document on which the expert has relied in such a report.<br>**22.4.** At the request of any party, the tribunal shall give the parties an opportunity to question the expert at a hearing. At this hearing, parties may present expert witnesses to testify on the points at issue. | report to it on specific issues designated by the Tribunal. A copy of the expert's terms of reference, established by the Tribunal, having regard to any observations of the parties, shall be communicated to the parties. Any such expert shall be required to sign an appropriate confidentiality undertaking.<br>**55(b)** Subject to Article 52, upon receipt of the expert's report, the Tribunal shall communicate a copy of the report to the parties, which shall be given the opportunity to express, in writing, their opinion on the report. A party may, subject to Article 52, examine any document on which the expert has relied in such a report.<br>**55(c)** At the request of a party, the parties shall be given the opportunity to question the expert at a hearing. At this hearing, the parties may present expert witnesses to testify on the points at issue.<br>**55(d)** The opinion of any expert on the issue or issues submitted to the expert shall be subject to the Tribunal's power of assessment of those issues in the context of all the circumstances of the case, unless the parties have agreed that the expert's determination shall be conclusive in respect of any specific issue. | cial questions relating to the case. Such an expert or appraiser can be an organization or a citizen, Chinese or foreign. The arbitration tribunal has the power to order the parties and the parties are also obliged to submit or produce to the expert or appraiser any materials, documents, properties or goods related to the case for check -up, inspection and/or appraisal.<br>**Article 40:** The expert's report and the appraiser's report shall be copied to the parties so that the parties may have the opportunity to give their opinions thereon. At the request of any party to the case and with the approval of the arbitration tribunal, the expert and appraiser may be present at the hearing and give explanations of their reports when the arbitration tribunal deems it necessary and appropriate. | appoint one or more experts to report to it on a specific issue.<br>27(2) At the request of a party, the parties shall be given the opportunity to put questions to any such expert. |

## 21. Tribunal power to call for additional evidence and to order rectification

| ICC | LCIA | AAA | WIPO | CIETAC | STOCKHOLM |
|---|---|---|---|---|---|
| **20(5)** At any time during the proceedings, the Arbitral Tribunal may summon any party to provide additional evidence. | **22.** The Arbitration shall have the power… **(c)** to conduct such enquiries as may appear to the Arbitral Tribunal to be necessary or expedient, including whether and to what extent the Arbitral Tribunal should itself take the initiative in identifying the issues and ascertaining the relevant facts and the law(s) or rules of law applicable to the arbitration, the merits of the parties' dispute and the Arbitration Agreement;<br>**22.1(d)** to order any party to make | **16.3.** The tribunal may in its discretion direct the order of proof, bifurcate proceedings, exclude cumulative or irrelevant testimony or other evidence, and direct the parties to focus their presentations on issues the decision of which could dispose of all or part of the case. | | | |

| ICC | LCIA | AAA | WIPO | CIETAC | STOCKHOLM |
|---|---|---|---|---|---|
| | any property, site or thing under its control and relating to the subject matter of the arbitration available for inspection by the Arbitral Tribunal, any other party, its expert or any expert to the Arbitral Tribunal;<br>**22.1(e)** to order any party to produce to the Arbitral Tribunal, and to the other parties for inspection, and to supply copies of, any documents or classes of documents in their possession, custody or power which the Arbitral Tribunal determines to be relevant;<br>**22.1(g)** to order the correction of any contract between the parties or the Arbitration Agreement, but only to the extent required to rectify any mistake which the Arbitral Tribunal determines to be common to the parties and then only if and to the extent to which the law(s) or rules of law applicable to the contract or Arbitration Agreement permit such correction; and | | | | |

## 22. Paper arbitrations

| ICC | LCIA | AAA | WIPO | CIETAC | STOCKHOLM |
|---|---|---|---|---|---|
| **20(6)** The Arbitral Tribunal may decide the case solely on the documents submitted by the parties unless any of the parties requests a hearing. | **19.1** Any party which expresses a desire to that effect has the right to be heard orally before the Arbitral Tribunal on the merits of the dispute, unless the parties have agreed in writing on documents-only arbitration. | | | | |

## 23. Protecting confidentiality

| ICC | LCIA | AAA | WIPO | CIETAC | STOCKHOLM |
|---|---|---|---|---|---|
| **20(7)** The Arbitral Tribunal may take measures for protecting trade secrets and confidential information. | | **Confidentiality: Article 34**<br>Confidential information disclosed during the proceedings by the parties or by witnesses shall not be divulged by an arbitrator or by the administrator. Unless otherwise agreed by the parties, or required by applicable law, the members of the tribunal and | **Article 52: Disclosure of Trade Secrets and Other Confidential Information**<br>(a) For the purposes of this Article, confidential information shall mean any information, regardless of the medium in which it is expressed, which is | | |

| ICC | LCIA | AAA | WIPO | CIETAC | STOCKHOLM |
|---|---|---|---|---|---|
| | | the administrator shall keep confidential all matters relating to the arbitration or the award. | (i) in the possession of a party,<br>(ii) not accessible to the public,<br>(iii) of commercial, financial or industrial significance, and<br>(iv) treated as confidential by the party possessing it.<br>(b) A party invoking the confidentiality of any information it wishes or is required to submit in the arbitration, including to an expert appointed by the Tribunal, shall make an application to have the information classified as confidential by notice to the Tribunal, with a copy to the other party. Without disclosing the substance of the information, the party shall give in the notice the reasons for which it considers the information confidential.<br>(c) The Tribunal shall determine whether the information is to be classified as confidential and of such a nature that the absence of special measures of protection in the proceedings would be likely to cause serious harm to the party invoking its confidentiality. If the Tribunal so determines, it shall decide under which conditions and to whom the confidential information may in part or in whole be disclosed and shall require any person to whom the confidential information is to be disclosed to sign an appropriate confidentiality undertaking.<br>(d) In exceptional circumstances, in lieu of itself determining whether the information is to be classified as confidential and of such nature that the absence of special measures of protection in the proceedings would be likely to cause serious harm to the party invoking its confidentiality, the Tribunal may, at the request of a party or on its own motion and after consultation with the parties, designate a confidentiality advisor who will determine whether the information is to be so classified, and, if so, decide under which conditions and to whom it may in part or in whole | | |

| ICC | LCIA | AAA | WIPO | CIETAC | STOCKHOLM |
|---|---|---|---|---|---|
| | | | be disclosed. Any such confidentiality advisor shall be required to sign an appropriate confidentiality undertaking.<br>(e) The Tribunal may also, at the request of a party or on its own motion, appoint the confidentiality advisor as an expert in accordance with Article 55 in order to report to it, on the basis of the confidential information, on specific issues designated by the Tribunal without disclosing the confidential information either to the party from whom the confidential information does not originate or to the Tribunal. | | |

## 24. Hearings – general

| ICC | LCIA | AAA | WIPO | CIETAC | STOCKHOLM |
|---|---|---|---|---|---|
| **Article 21: Hearings**<br>21(1) When a hearing is to be held, the Arbitral Tribunal, giving reasonable notice, shall summon the parties to appear before it on the day and at the place fixed by it. | **19.2** The Arbitral Tribunal shall fix the date, time and physical place of any meetings and hearings in the arbitration, and shall give the parties reasonable notice thereof. | **20.1.** The Tribunal shall give the parties at least 30 days' advance notice of the date, time and place of the initial oral hearing. The tribunal shall give reasonable notice of subsequent hearings. | **Article 53: Hearings**<br>(a) If either party so requests, the Tribunal shall hold a hearing for the presentation of evidence by witnesses, including expert witnesses, or for oral argument or for both. In the absence of a request, the Tribunal shall decide whether to hold such a hearing or hearings. If no hearings are held, the proceedings shall be conducted on the basis of documents and other materials alone.<br>(b) In the event of a hearing, the Tribunal shall give the parties adequate advance notice of the date, time and place thereof.<br>(c) Unless the parties agree otherwise, all hearings shall be in private.<br>(d) The Tribunal shall determine whether and, if so, in what form a record shall be made of any hearing. | **Article 32:** The arbitration tribunal shall hold oral hearings when examining a case. At the request of the parties or with their consent, oral hearings may be omitted if the arbitration tribunal also deems that oral hearings are unnecessary, and then the arbitration tribunal may examine the case and make an award on the basis of documents only.<br>**Article 33:** The date of the first oral hearing shall be fixed by the arbitration tribunal in consultation with the secretariat of the Arbitration Commission. The notice of the date of the hearing shall becommunicated by the secretariat of the Arbitration Commission to the parties 30 days before the date of the hearing. A party having justified reasons may request a postponement of the date of the hearing. His request must be communicated to the secretariat of the Arbitration Commission 12 days before the date of the hearing and the arbitration tribunal shall decide whether to postpone the hearing or not.<br>**Article 34:** The notice of the date of hearing subsequent to the first hearing is not subject to the 30-day time limit. | **25(1)** An oral hearing shall be arranged if requested by either party, or if the Arbitral Tribunal considers it appropriate. If a hearing is held, the Arbitral Tribunal, taking into account the wishes of the parties, shall determine the time for the hearing, its duration and how it is to be organised, including the manner in which evidence is to be presented. |

| ICC | LCIA | AAA | WIPO | CIETAC | STOCKHOLM |
|---|---|---|---|---|---|
| **25. Hearings in default of attendance by party; default generally (see also 2.9)** | | | | | |
| **21(2)** If any of the parties, although duly summoned, fails to appear without valid excuse, the Arbitral Tribunal shall have the power to proceed with the hearing. | | **23.2.**If a party, duly notified under these rules, fails to appear at a hearing without showing sufficient cause for such failure, as determined by the tribunal, the tribunal may proceed with the arbitration.<br>**23.3.** If a party, duly invited to produce evidence or take any other steps in the proceedings, fails to do so within the time established by the tribunal without showing sufficient cause for such failure, as determined by the tribunal, the tribunal may make the award on the evidence before it. | **56(c)** The Tribunal may also proceed with the arbitration and make the award if a party, without showing good cause, fails to avail itself of the opportunity to present its case within the period of time determined by the Tribunal.<br>**56(d)** If a party, without showing good cause, fails to comply with any provision of, or requirement under, these Rules or any direction given by the Tribunal, the Tribunal may draw the inferences therefrom that it considers appropriate. | | **Article 28: Failure of a Party to Appear**<br>If any of the parties, without showing valid cause, fails to appear at a hearing or otherwise fails to comply with an order of the Arbitral Tribunal, such failure shall not prevent the Arbitral Tribunal from proceeding with the case nor from rendering an Award. |
| **26. Privacy of hearings** | | | | | |
| **21(3)** The Arbitral Tribunal shall be in full charge of the hearings, at which all the parties shall be entitled to be present. Save with the approval of the Arbitral Tribunal and the parties, persons not involved in the proceedings shall not be admitted. | **19.4** All meetings and hearings shall be in private unless the parties agree otherwise in writing or the Arbitral Tribunal directs otherwise. | **20.4.**Hearings are private unless the parties agree otherwise or the law provides to the contrary. The Tribunal may require any witness or witnesses to retire during the testimony of other witnesses. The tribunal may determine the manner in which witnesses are examined. | | | |
| **27. Open sessions** | | | | | |
| | | | | **Article 36:** The Arbitration Tribunal shall not hear cases in open session. If both parties request a hearing to be held in open session, the arbitration tribunal shall decide whether to hold the hearing in open session or not. | |
| **28. Party representation at hearings** | | | | | |
| **21(4)** The parties may appear in person or through duly authorised representatives. In addition, they may be assisted by advisers. | **Article 18: Party Representation.**<br>**18.1** Any party may be represented by legal practitioners or any other representatives.<br>**18.2** At any time the Arbitral Tribunal may require from any party proof of authority granted to its rep- | **Representation: Article 12**<br>Any party may be represented in the arbitration. The names, addresses and telephone numbers of representatives shall be communicated in writing to the other parties and to the administrator. Once the tribunal | **Article 13: Representation**<br>(a) The parties may be represented by persons of their choice, irrespective of, in particular, nationality or professional qualification. The names, addresses and telephone, telex, telefax or other communica- | **Article 22:** The parties may authorize arbitration agents to deal with the matters relating to arbitration; the authorized attorney must produce a Power of Attorney to the Arbitration Commission. Chinese and foreign citizens can be authorized to act as | |

| ICC | LCIA | AAA | WIPO | CIETAC | STOCKHOLM |
|---|---|---|---|---|---|
| | resentative(s) in such form as the Arbitral Tribunal may determine. | has been established, the parties or their representatives may communicate in writing directly with the tribunal. | tion references of representatives shall be communicated to the Center, the other party and, after its establishment, the Tribunal.<br>(b) Each party shall ensure that its representatives have sufficient time available to enable the arbitration to proceed expeditiously.<br>(c) The parties may also be assisted by persons of their choice. | arbitration agents. | |
| **29. Transcripts** | | | | | |
| | | **20.3** At the request of the tribunal or pursuant to mutual agreement of the parties, the administrator shall make arrangements for the interpretation of oral testimony or for a record of the hearing. | | **Article 43:** During the hearing, the arbitration tribunal may make a record in writing and/or by tape-recording. The arbitration tribunal may, when it deems it necessary, make a minute stating the main points of the hearing and ask the parties and/or their attorneys, witnesses and/or other persons involved to sign their names on it and/or affix their seals to it. The record in writing or by tape-recording is only for the use and reference of the arbitration tribunal. | |
| **30. Closure of proceedings** | | | | | |
| **Article 22: Closing of the Proceedings**<br>**22(1)** When it is satisfied that the parties have had a reasonable opportunity to present their cases, the Arbitral Tribunal shall declare the proceedings closed. Thereafter, no further submissions or argument may be made, or evidence produced, unless requested or authorized by the Arbitral Tribunal.<br>**22(2)** When the Arbitral Tribunal has declared the proceedings closed, it shall indicate to the Secretariat an approximate date by which the draft Award will be submitted to the Court for approval pursuant to Article 27. Any postponement of that date shall be communicated to the Secretariat | | **Article 24: Closure of Hearing**<br>**24.1** After asking the parties if they have any further testimony or evidentiary submissions and upon receiving negative replies or if satisfied that the record is complete, the tribunal may declare the hearings closed.<br>**24.2** The tribunal in its discretion, on its own motion or upon application of a party, may reopen the hearings at any time before the award is made. | **Article 57: Closure of Proceedings**<br>(a) The Tribunal shall declare the proceedings closed when it is satisfied that the parties have had adequate opportunity to present submissions and evidence.<br>(b) The Tribunal may, if it considers it necessary owing to exceptional circumstances, decide, on its own motion or upon application of a party, to re-open the proceedings it declared to be closed at any time before the award is made. | | |

| ICC | LCIA | AAA | WIPO | CIETAC | STOCKHOLM |
|---|---|---|---|---|---|
| by the Arbitral Tribunal. | | | | | |
| **31. Interim measures** | | | | | |
| **Article 23: Conservatory and Interim Measures**<br>**23(1)** Unless the parties have otherwise agreed, as soon as the file has been transmitted to it, the Arbitral Tribunal may, at the request of a party, order any interim or conservatory measure it deems appropriate. The Arbitral Tribunal may make the granting of any such measure subject to appropriate security being furnished by the requesting party. Any such measure shall take the form of an order, giving reasons, or of an Award, as the Arbitral Tribunal considers appropriate.<br>**23(2)** Before the file is transmitted to the Arbitral Tribunal, and in appropriate circumstances even thereafter, the parties may apply to any competent judicial authority for interim or conservatory measures. The application of a party to a judicial authority for such measures or for the implementation of any such measures ordered by an Arbitral Tribunal shall not be deemed to be an infringement or a waiver of the arbitration agreement and shall not affect the relevant powers reserved to the Arbitral Tribunal. Any such application and any measures taken by the judicial authority must be notified without delay to the Secretariat. The Secretariat shall inform the Arbitral Tribunal thereof. | **Article 25: Interim and Conservatory Measures**<br>**25.1** The Arbitral Tribunal shall have the power, unless otherwise agreed by the parties in writing, on the application of any party:<br>(a) to order any respondent party to a claim or counterclaim to provide security for all or part of the amount in dispute, by way of deposit or bank guarantee or in any other manner and upon such terms as the Arbitral Tribunal considers appropriate. Such terms may include the provision by the claiming or counterclaiming party of a cross-indemnity, itself secured in such manner as the Arbitral Tribunal considers appropriate, for any costs or losses incurred by such respondent in providing security. The amount of any costs and losses payable under such cross-indemnity may be determined by the Arbitral Tribunal in one or more awards;<br>(b) to order the preservation, storage, sale or other disposal of any property or thing under the control of any party and relating to the subject matter of the arbitration; and<br>(c) to order on a provisional basis, subject to final determination in an award, any relief which the Arbitral Tribunal would have power to grant in an award, including a provisional order for the payment of money or the disposition of property as between any parties.<br>**25.2** The Arbitral Tribunal shall have the power, upon the application of a party, to order any claiming or counterclaiming party to provide security for the legal or other costs of any other party by way of deposit or bank guarantee or in any other manner and upon such terms as the | **Article 21: Interim Measures of Protection**<br>**21.1.** At the request of any party, the tribunal may take whatever interim measures it deems necessary, including injunctive relief and measures for the protection or conservation of property.<br>**21.2.** Such interim measures may take the form of an interim award, and the tribunal may require security for the costs of such measures.<br>**21.3.** A request for interim measures addressed by a party to a judicial authority shall not be deemed incompatible with the agreement to arbitrate or a waiver of the right to arbitrate. | **Article 46: Interim Measures of Protection; Security for Claims and Costs**<br>(a) At the request of a party, the Tribunal may issue any provisional orders or take other interim measures it deems necessary, including injunctions and measures for the conservation of goods which form part of the subject matter in dispute, such as an order for their deposit with a third person or for the sale of perishable goods. The Tribunal may make the granting of such measures subject to appropriate security being furnished by the requesting party.<br>(b) At the request of a party, the Tribunal may, if it considers it to be required by exceptional circumstances, order the other party to provide security, in a form to be determined by the Tribunal, for the claim or counterclaim, as well as for costs referred to in Article 72.<br>(c) Measures and orders contemplated under this Article may take the form of an interim award.<br>(d) A request addressed by a party to a judicial authority for interim measures or for security for the claim or counterclaim, or for the implementation of any such measures or orders granted by the Tribunal, shall not be deemed incompatible with the Arbitration Agreement, or deemed to be a waiver of that Agreement. | **Article 23:** When a party applies for property preservative measures, the Arbitration Commission shall transmit the party's application for a ruling to the people's court in the place where the domicile of the party against whom the property preservative measures are sought is located or in the place where the property of the said party is located. When a party applies for taking interim measures of protection of evidence, the Arbitration Commission shall transmit the party's application for a ruling to the people's court in the place where the evidence is located. | **Article 31: Interim Measures**<br>**31(1)** Unless the parties have agreed otherwise, the Arbitral Tribunal may, during the course of the proceedings and at the request of a party, order a specific performance by the opposing party for the purpose of securing the claim which is to be tried by the Arbitral Tribunal. The Arbitral Tribunal may order the requesting party to provide reasonable security for damage which may be inflicted on the opposing party as a result of the specific performance in question.<br>**31(2)** A request addressed by a party to a judicial authority for interim measures shall not be deemed to be incompatible with the arbitration agreement or these Rules. |

| ICC | LCIA | AAA | WIPO | CIETAC | STOCKHOLM |
|---|---|---|---|---|---|
| | Arbitral Tribunal considers appropriate. Such terms may include the provision by that other party of a cross-indemnity, itself secured in such manner as the Arbitral Tribunal considers appropriate, for any costs and losses incurred by such claimant or counterclaimant in providing security. The amount of any costs and losses payable under such cross-indemnity may be determined by the Arbitral Tribunal in one or more awards. In the event that a claiming or counterclaiming party does not comply with any order to provide security, the Arbitral Tribunal may stay that party's claims or counterclaims or dismiss them in an award.<br>**25.3** The power of the Arbitral Tribunal under Article 25.1 shall not prejudice howsoever any party's right to apply to any state court or other judicial authority for interim or conservatory measures before the formation of the Arbitral Tribunal and, in exceptional cases, thereafter. Any application and any order for such measures after the formation of the Arbitral Tribunal shall be promptly communicated by the applicant to the Arbitral Tribunal and all other parties. However, by agreeing to arbitration under these Rules, the parties shall be taken to have agreed not to apply to any state court or other judicial authority for any order for security for its legal or other costs available from the Arbitral Tribunal under Article 25.2. | | | | |
| **32. Summary/expedited process** | | | | | |
| **32(1)** The parties may agree to shorten the various time limits set out in these Rules. Any such agreement entered into subsequent to the constitution of an Arbitral Tribunal shall become effective only upon the approval of the Arbitral Tribunal. | **4.7** The Arbitral Tribunal may at any time extend (even where the period of time has expired) or abridge any period of time prescribed under these Rules or under the Arbitration Agreement for the conduct of the arbitration, including any notice or communication to be served by one | | [*WIPO has a comprehensive set of expedited arbitration rules.*] | **Chapter III. Summary Procedure**<br>**Article 64:** Unless otherwise agreed by the parties, this Summary Procedure shall apply to any case in dispute where the amount of the claim totals not more than RMB 500, 000 yuan, and to any case in dispute where the amount of the claim totals more than | [The SCC Institute has adopted Rules for Expedited Arbitrations, Insurance Arbitration Rules, Mediation Rules and Procedures and Services under the UNCITRAL Arbitration Rules.] |

| ICC | LCIA | AAA | WIPO | CIETAC | STOCKHOLM |
|---|---|---|---|---|---|
| | party on any other party.<br>**Article 9: Expedited Formation**<br>**9.1** In exceptional urgency, on or after the commencement of the arbitration, any party may apply to the LCIA Court for the expedited formation of the Arbitral Tribunal, including the appointment of any replacement arbitrator under Articles 10 and 11 of these Rules.<br>**9.2** Such an application shall be made in writing to the LCIA Court, copied to all other parties to the arbitration; and it shall set out the specific grounds for exceptional urgency in the formation of the Arbitral Tribunal.<br>**9.3** The LCIA Court may, in its complete discretion, abridge or curtail any time-limit under these Rules for the formation of the Arbitral Tribunal, including service of the Response and of any matters or documents adjudged to be missing from the Request. The LCIA Court shall not be entitled to abridge or curtail any other time-limit. | | | RMB 500, 000 Yuan provided that one party applies for arbitration under this Summary Procedure and the other party agrees in writing.<br>**Article 65:** When an application for arbitration is submitted to the Arbitration Commission after examination and the Summary Procedure is applicable, the Secretariat of the Arbitration Commission shall immediately send a Notice of Arbitration to the parties.<br>Unless both parties have jointly appointed one sole arbitrator from among the Panel of Arbitrators of the Arbitration Commission, they shall jointly appoint or jointly entrust the Chairman of the Arbitration Commission to appoint one sole arbitrator within 15 days from the date on which the Notice of Arbitration is received by the Respondent. Should the parties fail to make such appointment or entrustment, the Chairman of the Arbitration Commission shall immediately appoint one sole arbitrator to form an Arbitration Tribunal to hear the case.<br>**Article 66:** The Respondent shall, within 30 days from the date of receipt of the Notice of Arbitration, submit his defense and relevant documentary evidence to the secretariat of the Arbitration Commission; a counterclaim, if any, shall be filed with documentary evidence within the said time limit.<br>**Article 67:** The arbitration tribunal may hear the case in the way it deems appropriate. The arbitration tribunal has discretion to hear the case only on the basis of the written materials and evidence submitted by the parties or to hold an oral hearing as well.<br>**Article 68:** The parties must hand in written materials and evidence needed for the arbitration in compliance with the requirements of the arbitration tribunal within the time limit given by the Arbitration Tribunal. | |

| ICC | LCIA | AAA | WIPO | CIETAC | STOCKHOLM |
|---|---|---|---|---|---|
| | | | | **Article 69:** For a case which needs an oral hearing, the secretariat of the Arbitration Commission shall, after the arbitration tribunal has fixed a date for hearing, inform the parties of the date of the hearing 15 days before the date of the hearing.<br>**Article 70:** If the arbitration tribunal decides to hear the case orally, only one oral hearing shall be held. However, the arbitration tribunal may hold two oral hearings if really necessary.<br>**Article 71:** Should one of the parties fail to act in compliance with this Summary Procedure during summary proceedings, such failure shall not affect the arbitration tribunal's conduct of the proceedings and the arbitration tribunal's power to render an arbitral award.<br>**Article 72:** The conduct of the summary proceedings shall not be affected by any amendment of the claim or by the lodging of a counterclaim, except that the disputed amount of the revised arbitration claim or counterclaim is in conflict with the provision of Article 64.<br>**Article 73:** Where a case is heard orally, the arbitration tribunal shall make an arbitral award within 30 days from the date of the oral hearing if one hearing is to be held, or from the date of the second oral hearing if two oral hearings are to be held. Where a case is examined on the basis of documents only, the arbitration tribunal shall render an arbitral award within 90 days from the date on which the arbitration tribunal is formed. The Secretary-General of the Arbitration Commission may extend the said time limit if such extension is necessary and justified.<br>**Article 74:** For matters not covered in this Chapter, the relevant provisions in the other Chapters of these Rules shall apply. | |

CHAPTER 5

# Awards

All institutions provide for awards to be written, and most have an eye to the enforcement procedure in their provisions.

With the exceptions of LCIA and AAA all institutions impose a time limit for the production of the award – ICC six months from finalisation of terms of reference, CIETAC nine months from the formation of the arbitration tribunal, WIPO nine months from delivery of defence/formation of tribunal, STOCKHOLM six months from referral to the tribunal. In practice these limits are flexible, and LCIA is gaining a reputation for speed without a definite time limit.

The ICC is the only institution which reviews ("scrutinises") awards in advance of their publication. This results in a quality product, but can contribute to delay and cost.

All institutions sensibly provide for a formula for correction of slips.

AAA is alone in excluding punitive damages; various provisions exist for the currency of awards and the award of interest – in practice the currency of the award will ordinarily be the currency of the claim/loss. Interest is generally awardable and LCIA, AAA and WIPO expressly provide for compound interest. Where there is an odd number of arbitrators majority votes prevail. The ICC, LCIA and STOCKHOLM provide for an impasse, where the chairman alone makes the award (Article 25(1)). CIETAC similarly gives the task to the "presiding arbitrator" as does WIPO.

| ICC | LCIA | AAA | WIPO | CIETAC | STOCKHOLM |
|---|---|---|---|---|---|
| **1. Form of award (see also 6.3)** | | | | | |
| **25(2)** The Award shall state the reasons upon which it is based. | **26.1** The Arbitral Tribunal shall make its award in writing and, unless all parties agree in writing otherwise, shall state the reasons upon which its award is based. The award shall also state the date when the award is made and the seat of the arbitration; and it shall be signed by the Arbitral Tribunal or those of its members assenting to it. | **Article 27: Form and Effect of the Award**<br>(1) Awards shall be made in writing, promptly by the Tribunal, and shall be final and binding on the parties. The parties undertake to carry out any such award without delay.<br>(2) The Tribunal shall state the reasons upon which the award is based, unless the parties have agreed that no reasons need be given.<br>(3) The award shall contain the date and the place where the award was made, which shall be the place designated pursuant to Article 13.<br>(4) An award may be made public only with the consent of all parties or as required by law.<br>(5) Copies of the award shall be communicated to the parties by the administrator.<br>(6) If the arbitration law of the country where the award is made requires the award to be filed or registered, the tribunal shall comply with such requirement.<br>(7) In addition to making a final award, the tribunal may make interim, interlocutory, or partial orders and awards. | **Article 62: Form and Notification of Awards**<br>(a) The Tribunal may make preliminary, interim, interlocutory, partial or final awards.<br>(b) The award shall be in writing and shall state the date on which it was made, as well as the place of arbitration in accordance with Article 39(a).<br>(c) The award shall state the reasons on which it is based, unless the parties have agreed that no reasons should be stated and the law applicable to the arbitration does not require the statement of such reasons.<br>(d) The award shall be signed by the arbitrator or arbitrators. The signature of the award by a majority of the arbitrators, or, in the case of Article 61, second sentence, by the presiding arbitrator, shall be sufficient. Where an arbitrator fails to sign, the award shall state the reason for the absence of the signature.<br>(e) The Tribunal may consult the Center with regard to matters of form, particularly to ensure the enforceability of the award.<br>(f) The award shall be communicated by the Tribunal to the Center in a number of originals sufficient to provide one for each party, the arbitrator or arbitrators and the Center. The Center shall formally communicate an original of the award to each party and the arbitrator or arbitrators.<br>(g) At the request of a party, the Center shall provide it, at cost, with a copy of the award certified by the Center. A copy so certified shall be deemed to comply with the requirements of Article IV(1)(a) of the Convention on the Recognition and Enforcement of Foreign Arbitral Awards, New York, June 10, 1958. | **Article 55:** The Arbitration Tribunal shall state in the arbitral award the claims, the facts of the dispute, the reasons on which the arbitral award is based, the result of the arbitral award, the allocation of the arbitration costs, the date on which and the place at which the arbitral award is made. The facts of the dispute and the reasons on which the arbitral award is based may not be stated in the arbitral award if the parties have agreed not to state them in the arbitral award, or the arbitral award is made in accordance with the contents of the settlement agreement reached between the parties. | |

| ICC | LCIA | AAA | WIPO | CIETAC | STOCKHOLM |
|---|---|---|---|---|---|
| **2. Time limits for awards** | | | | | |
| **Article 24: Time limit for the Award**<br>24(1) The time limit within which the Arbitral Tribunal must render its final award is six months. Such time limit shall start to run from the date of the last signature by the Arbitral Tribunal or of the parties of the Terms of Reference, or, in the case of application of Article 18(3), the date of the notification to the Arbitral Tribunal by the Secretariat of the approval of the Terms of Reference by the Court.<br>24(2) The Court may extend this time limit pursuant to a reasoned request from the Arbitral Tribunal or on its own initiative if it decides it is necessary to do so. | The Arbitral Tribunal's general duties at all times [is]<br>**14.1(ii)** to adopt procedures suitable to the circumstances of the arbitration, avoiding unnecessary delay or expense, so as to provide a fair and efficient means for the final resolution of the parties' dispute. | | **Article 63: Time Period for Delivery of the Final Award**<br>(a) The arbitration should, wherever reasonably possible, be heard and the proceedings declared closed within not more than nine months after either the delivery of the Statement of Defense or the establishment of the Tribunal, whichever event occurs later. The final award should, wherever reasonably possible, be made within three months thereafter.<br>(b) If the proceedings are not declared closed within the period of time specified in paragraph (a), the Tribunal shall send the Center a status report on the arbitration, with a copy to each party. It shall send a further status report to the Center, and a copy to each party, at the end of each ensuing period of three months during which the proceedings have not been declared closed.<br>(c) If the final award is not made within three months after the closure of the proceedings, the Tribunal shall send the Center a written explanation for the delay, with a copy to each party. It shall send a further explanation, and a copy to each party, at the end of each ensuing period of one month until the final award is made. | **Article 52:** The Arbitration Tribunal shall render an arbitral award within 9 months as from the date on which the arbitration tribunal is formed. The Secretary-General of the Arbitration Commission may extend this time limit at the request of the arbitration tribunal if the Secretary-General of the Arbitration Commission considers that it is really necessary and the reasons for extension are truly justified. | **Article 33: Time for Rendering an Award**<br>An award shall be rendered not later than six months as from the date when the case was referred to the Arbitral Tribunal. The SCC Institute may extend the period of time for rendering an Award. |
| **3. Procedure for making an award** | | | | | |
| **Article 25: Making of the Award**<br>**25(1)** When the Arbitral Tribunal is composed of more than one arbitrator, an award is given by a majority decision. If there be no majority, the award shall be made by the chairman of the Arbitral Tribunal alone.<br>**25(2)** The award shall state the reasons upon which it is based.<br>**25(3)** The award shall be deemed to be made at the place of the arbitra- | **26.2** If any arbitrator fails to comply with the mandatory provisions of any applicable law relating to the making of the award, having been given a reasonable opportunity to do so, the remaining arbitrators may proceed in his absence and state in their award the circumstances of the other arbitrator's failure to participate in the making of the award.<br>**26.3** Where there are three arbitra- | **Awards, Decisions and Rulings: Article 26**<br>**26.1.** When there is more than one arbitrator, any award, decision or ruling of the arbitral tribunal shall be made by a majority of the arbitrators. If any arbitrator fails to sign the award, it shall be accompanied by a statement of the reason for the absence of such signature.<br>**26.2.** When the parties or the tribu- | **Article 62: Form and Notification of Awards**<br>(a) The Tribunal may make preliminary, interim, interlocutory, partial or final awards.<br>(b) The award shall be in writing and shall state the date on which it was made, as well as the place of arbitration in accordance with Article 39(a).<br>(c) The award shall state the reasons | **Article 54:** Where a case is heard by an Arbitration Tribunal composed of three arbitrators, the arbitral award shall be decided by the majority of the arbitrators and the minority opinion may be written in the record and docketed into the file. When the Arbitration Tribunal cannot attain a majority opinion, the arbitral award shall be decided in accordance with the presiding arbitrator's opinion. | **Article 30: Voting**<br>When a vote is taken, that opinion shall prevail which has received more votes than any other opinion. If such majority is not attained, the opinion of the Chairman shall prevail, unless otherwise agreed by the parties.<br>**32(2)** If any arbitrator fails without valid cause to participate in the deliberations of the Arbitral Tribunal on an issue, such failure will not pre- |

| ICC | LCIA | AAA | WIPO | CIETAC | STOCKHOLM |
|---|---|---|---|---|---|
| tion and on the date stated therein. | tors and the Arbitral Tribunal fails to agree on any issue, the arbitrators shall decide that issue by a majority. Failing a majority decision on any issue, the chairman of the Arbitral Tribunal shall decide that issue.<br>**26.1** The Arbitral Tribunal shall make its award in writing and, unless all parties agree in writing otherwise, shall state the reasons upon which its award is based. The award shall also state the date when the award is made and the seat of the arbitration; and it shall be signed by the Arbitral Tribunal or those of its members assenting to it.<br>**26.6** An award may be expressed in any currency. The Arbitral Tribunal may order that simple or compound interest shall be paid by any party on any sum awarded at such rates as the Arbitral Tribunal determines to be appropriate, without being bound by legal rates of interest imposed by any state court, in respect of any period which the Arbitral Tribunal determines to be appropriate ending not later than the date upon which the award is complied with. | nal so authorize, the presiding arbitrator may make decisions or rulings on questions of procedure, subject to revision by the Tribunal.<br>**27.2.** The Tribunal shall state the reasons upon which the award is based, unless the parties have agreed that no reasons need be given.<br>**27.3.** The award shall contain the date and the place where the award was made, which shall be the place designated pursuant to Article 13. | on which it is based, unless the parties have agreed that no reasons should be stated and the law applicable to the arbitration does not require the statement of such reasons.<br>(d) The award shall be signed by the arbitrator or arbitrators. The signature of the award by a majority of the arbitrators, or, in the case of Article 61, second sentence, by the presiding arbitrator, shall be sufficient. Where an arbitrator fails to sign, the award shall state the reason for the absence of the signature.<br>(e) The Tribunal may consult the Center with regard to matters of form, particularly to ensure the enforceability of the award.<br>(f) The award shall be communicated by the Tribunal to the Center in a number of originals sufficient to provide one for each party, the arbitrator or arbitrators and the Center. The Center shall formally communicate an original of the award to each party and the arbitrator or arbitrators.<br>(g) At the request of a party, the Center shall provide it, at cost, with a copy of the award certified by the Center. A copy so certified shall be deemed to comply with the requirements of Article IV(1)(a) of the Convention on the Recognition and Enforcement of Foreign Arbitral Awards, New York, June 10, 1958.<br>**Article 61:** Unless the parties have agreed otherwise, where there is more than one arbitrator, any award, order or other decision of the Tribunal shall be made by a majority. In the absence of a majority, the presiding arbitrator shall make the award, order or other decision as if acting as sole arbitrator. | | clude a decision being made by the other arbitrators.<br>**32(1)** The Award shall be deemed to have been rendered at the Place of Arbitration. It shall state the date on which it was rendered, contain an order or a declaration, as well as the reasons for it, and shall be signed by the arbitrators. In absence of the signature of an arbitrator, an Award may be rendered provided that the Award has been signed by a majority of the arbitrators with a verification to the effect that the arbitrator whose signature is missing participated in deciding the dispute.<br>**32(2)** If any arbitrator fails without valid cause to participate in the deliberations of the Arbitral Tribunal on an issue, such failure will not preclude a decision being made by the other arbitrators.<br>**32(3)** The parties may agree that the Chairman alone shall sign the Award. |

| ICC | LCIA | AAA | WIPO | CIETAC | STOCKHOLM |
|---|---|---|---|---|---|
| **4. Consent awards/awards on admissions/withdrawn claims** | | | | | |
| **Article 26: Award by Consent**<br>If the parties reach a settlement after the file has been transmitted to the Arbitral Tribunal in accordance with Article 13, the settlement shall be recorded in the form of an award made by consent of the parties if so requested by the parties and the Arbitral Tribunal agrees to do so. | **26.8** In the event of a settlement of the parties' dispute, the Arbitral Tribunal may render an award recording the settlement if the parties so request in writing (a "Consent Award"), provided always that such award contains an express statement that it is an award made by the parties' consent. A Consent Award need not contain reasons. If the parties do not require a consent award, then on written confirmation by the parties to the LCIA Court that a settlement has been reached, the Arbitral Tribunal shall be discharged and the arbitration proceedings concluded, subject to payment by the parties of any outstanding costs of the arbitration under Article 28. | **Article 29: Settlement or Other Reasons for Termination**<br>**29(1)** If the parties settle the dispute before an award is made, the tribunal shall terminate the arbitration and, if requested by all parties, may record the settlement in the form of an award on agreed terms. The Tribunal is not obliged to give reasons for such an award.<br>**29(2)** If the continuation of the proceedings becomes unnecessary or impossible for any other reason, the tribunal shall inform the parties of its intention to terminate the proceedings. The Tribunal shall thereafter issue an order terminating the arbitration, unless a party raises justifiable grounds for objection. | **65(b)** If, before the award is made, the parties agree on a settlement of the dispute, the Tribunal shall terminate the arbitration and, if requested jointly by the parties, record the settlement in the form of a consent award. The Tribunal shall not be obliged to give reasons for such an award. | **Article 44:** If the parties reach an amicable settlement agreement by themselves, they may either request the Arbitration Tribunal to make an award in accordance with the contents of their amicable settlement agreement to end the case or request a dismissal of the case. The Secretary-General of the Arbitration Commission shall decide on the dismissal of an arbitration case if the decision on dismissal is made before the formation of the Arbitration Tribunal, and the Arbitration Tribunal shall decide thereon if the decision on dismissal is made after the formation of the arbitration tribunal.<br>If the party or the parties refer the dismissed case again to the Arbitration Commission for arbitration, the Chairman of the Arbitration Commission shall decide whether to accept the reference or not. | **32(5)** If a settlement is reached, the Arbitral Tribunal may, at the request of the parties, record the settlement in the form of an Award.<br>**35(1)** If a party withdraws a claim the Arbitral Tribunal shall dismiss such part of the dispute, unless the other party requests the Arbitral Tribunal to rule on the claim. |
| **5. Scrutiny of awards** | | | | | |
| **Appendix II. Article 6: Scrutiny of Arbitral Awards**<br>When the court scrutinises draft awards in accordance with Article 27 of the Rules, it considers, to the extent practicable, the requirements of mandatory law at the place of arbitration. | | | | | |

| ICC | LCIA | AAA | WIPO | CIETAC | STOCKHOLM |
|---|---|---|---|---|---|
| **Article 27: Scrutiny of the Award by the Court**<br>Before signing any award, the Arbitral Tribunal shall submit it in draft form to the Court. The Court may lay down modifications as to the form of the award and, without affecting the Arbitral Tribunal's liberty of decision, may also draw its attention to points of substance. No award shall be rendered by the Arbitral Tribunal until it has been approved by the Court as to its form. | | | | | |
| **6. Notification of award and effect** | | | | | |
| **Article 28: Notification, Deposit and Enforceability of the Award**<br>**28(1)** Once an award has been made, the Secretariat shall notify to the parties the text signed by the Arbitral Tribunal, provided always that the costs of the arbitration have been fully paid to the ICC by the parties or by one of them.<br>**28(2)** Additional copies certified true by the Secretary General shall be made available on request and at any time to the parties, but to no one else.<br>**28(3)** By virtue of the notification made in accordance with Paragraph 1 of this Article, the parties waive any other form of notification or deposit on the part of the Arbitral Tribunal.<br>**28(4)** An original of each award made in accordance with the present Rules shall be deposited with the Secretariat.<br>**28(5)** The Arbitral Tribunal and the Secretariat shall assist the parties in complying with whatever further formalities may be necessary.<br>**28(6)** Every award shall be binding on the parties. By submitting the dispute to arbitration under these Rules, the parties undertake to carry out any award without delay and shall be deemed to have waived their right to any form of recourse insofar | **26.5** The sole arbitrator or chairman shall be responsible for delivering the award to the LCIA Court, which shall transmit certified copies to the parties provided that the costs of arbitration have been paid to the LCIA in accordance with Article 28.<br>**26.9** All awards shall be final and binding on the parties. By agreeing to arbitration under these Rules, the parties undertake to carry out any award immediately and without any delay (subject only to Article 27); and the parties also waive irrevocably their right to any form of appeal, review or recourse to any state court or other judicial authority, insofar as such waiver may be validly made.<br>**29.1** The decisions of the LCIA Court with respect to all matters relating to the arbitration shall be conclusive and binding upon the parties and the Arbitral Tribunal. Such decisions are to be treated as administrative in nature and the LCIA Court shall not be required to give any reasons.<br>**29.2** To the extent permitted by the law of the seat of the arbitration, the parties shall be taken to have waived any right of appeal or review in respect of any such decisions of the LCIA Court to any state court or other judicial authority. If such | **27.5.** Copies of the award shall be communicated to the parties by the administrator.<br>**27.6.** If the arbitration law of the country where the award is made requires the award to be filed or registered, the tribunal shall comply with such requirement. | **Article 62: Form and Notification of Awards**<br>...<br>(f) The award shall be communicated by the Tribunal to the Center in a number of originals sufficient to provide one for each party, the arbitrator or arbitrators and the Center. The Center shall formally communicate an original of the award to each party and the arbitrator or arbitrators.<br>**Article 64: Effect of Award**<br>(a) By agreeing to arbitration under these Rules, the parties undertake to carry out the award without delay, and waive their right to any form of appeal or recourse to a court of law or other judicial authority, insofar as such waiver may validly be made under the applicable law.<br>(b) The award shall be effective and binding on the parties as from the date it is communicated by the Center pursuant to Article 62(f), second sentence. | **Article 63:** The parties must automatically execute the arbitral award within the time limit specified in the arbitral award. If no time limit is specified in the arbitral award, the parties shall carry out the arbitral award immediately. In case one party fails to execute the arbitral award, the other party may apply to the Chinese court for enforcement of the arbitral award pursuant to Chinese law or apply to the competent foreign court for enforcement of the arbitral award according to the 1958 Convention on Recognition and Enforcement of Foreign Arbitral Awards or other international treaties that China has concluded or participated in.<br>**Article 60:** The arbitral award is final and binding upon both disputing parties. Neither party may bring a suit before a law court or make a request to any other organization for revising the arbitral award. | **32(7)** The Arbitral Tribunal shall immediately send the award to the parties.<br>**Article 36: Effect of an Award**<br>When rendered an award is final and binding for the parties. |

| ICC | LCIA | AAA | WIPO | CIETAC | STOCKHOLM |
|---|---|---|---|---|---|
| as such waiver can validly be made. | appeals or review remain possible due to mandatory provisions of any applicable law, the LCIA Court shall, subject to the provisions of that applicable law, decide whether the arbitral proceedings are to continue, notwithstanding an appeal or review. | | | | |
| **7. Correction of award** | | | | | |
| **Article 29: Correction and interpretation of the Award**<br>**29(1)** On its own initiative, the Arbitral Tribunal may correct a clerical, computational or typographical error, or any errors of similar nature contained in an award, provided such correction is submitted for approval to the Court within 30 days of the date of such award.<br>**29(2)** Any application of a party for the correction of an error of the kind referred to in Article 29(1), or for the interpretation of an award, must be made to the Secretariat within 30 days of the receipt of the award by such party, in a number of copies as stated in Article 3(1). After transmittal of the application to the Arbitral Tribunal it shall grant the other party a short time limit, normally not exceeding 30 days, from the receipt of the application by that party to submit any comments thereon. If the Arbitral Tribunal decides to correct or interpret the award, it shall submit its decision in draft form to the Court not later than 30 days following the expiration of the time limit for the receipt of any comments from the other party or within such other period as the Court may decide.<br>**29(3)** The decision to correct or to interpret the award shall take the form of an addendum and shall constitute part of the award. The provisions of Articles 25, 27 and 28 shall apply *mutatis mutandis.* | **27.1** Within 30 days of receipt of any award, or such lesser period as may be agreed in writing by the parties, a party may by written notice to the Registrar (copied to all other parties) request the Arbitral Tribunal to correct in the award any errors in computation, clerical or typographical errors or any errors of a similar nature. If the Arbitral Tribunal considers the request to be justified, it shall make the corrections within 30 days of receipt of the request. Any correction shall take the form of separate memorandum dated and signed by the Arbitral Tribunal or (if three arbitrators) those of its members assenting to it; and such memorandum shall become part of the award for all purposes.<br>**27.2** The Arbitral Tribunal may likewise correct any error of the nature described in Article 27.1 on its own initiative within 30 days of the date of the award, to the same effect.<br>**27.3** Within 30 days of receipt of the final award, a party may by written notice to the Registrar (copied to all other parties), request the Arbitral Tribunal to make an additional award as to claims or counterclaims presented in the arbitration but not determined in any award. If the Arbitral Tribunal considers the request to be justified, it shall make the additional award within 60 days of receipt of the request. The provisions of Article 26 shall apply to any additional award. | **Interpretation or Correction of the Award Article 30**<br>**30(1)** Within 30 days after the receipt of an award, any party, with notice to the other parties, may request the tribunal to interpret the award or correct any clerical, typographical or computation errors or make an additional award as to claims presented but omitted from the award.<br>**30(2)** If the tribunal considers such a request justified, after considering the contentions of the parties, it shall comply with such a request within 30 days after the request. | **Article 66: Correction of the Award and Additional Award**<br>(a) Within 30 days after receipt of the award, a party may, by notice to the Tribunal, with a copy to the Center and the other party, request the Tribunal to correct in the award any clerical, typographical or computational errors. If the Tribunal considers the request to be justified, it shall make the correction within 30 days after receipt of the request. Any correction, which shall take the form of a separate memorandum, signed by the Tribunal in accordance with Article 62(d), shall become part of the award.<br>(b) The Tribunal may correct any error of the type referred to in paragraph (a) on its own initiative within 30 days after the date of the award.<br>(c) A party may, within 30 days after receipt of the award, by notice to the Tribunal, with a copy to the Center and the other party, request the Tribunal to make an additional award as to claims presented in the arbitral proceedings but not dealt with in the award. Before deciding on the request, the Tribunal shall give the parties an opportunity to be heard. If the Tribunal considers the request to be justified, it shall, wherever reasonably possible, make the additional award within 60 days of receipt of the request. | **Article 61:** Either party may request in writing that a correction be made to the writing, typing, calculating and similar errors contained in the arbitral award within 30 days from the date of receipt of the arbitral award; if there is really an error in the arbitral award, the Arbitration Tribunal shall make a correction in writing within 30 days from the date on receipt of the written request for correction, and the arbitration tribunal may by itself make a correction in writing within 30 days from the date on which the arbitral award is issued. The correction in writing forms a part of the arbitral award.<br>**Article 62:** If anything that should be awarded has been omitted in the arbitral award, either of the parties may make a request in writing to the Arbitration Tribunal for an additional award within 30 days from the date on which the arbitral award is received. If something which should be awarded is really omitted, the Arbitration Tribunal shall make an additional award within 30 days from the date of receipt of the request in writing for an additional award. The Arbitration Tribunal may also by itself make an additional award within 30 days from the date on which the arbitral award is issued. The additional award forms a part of the arbitral award which has been previously issued. | **37(1)** Any obvious miscalculation or clerical error in an Award or Decision shall be corrected by the Arbitral Tribunal.<br>**37(2)** Within 30 days of receiving the Award, the Arbitral Tribunal shall, if a party so requests, decide a question which should have been decided in the Award but which was not decided therein.<br>**37(3)** Within 30 days of receiving the Award, the Arbitral Tribunal may, if a party so requests, provide an interpretation thereof in writing.<br>**37(4)** Before the Arbitral Tribunal takes any action in accordance with the second and third paragraphs, the views of the parties shall be solicited. |

| ICC | LCIA | AAA | WIPO | CIETAC | STOCKHOLM |
|---|---|---|---|---|---|
| **8. Currency of award; interest** | | | | | |
| | **26.6** An award may be expressed in any currency. The Arbitral Tribunal may order that simple or compound interest shall be paid by any party on any sum awarded at such rates as the Arbitral Tribunal determines to be appropriate, without being bound by legal rates of interest imposed by any state court, in respect of any period which the Arbitral Tribunal determines to be appropriate ending not later than the date upon which the award is complied with. | **28.4.** A monetary award shall be in the currency or currencies of the contract unless the tribunal considers another currency more appropriate, and the tribunal may award such pre-award and post-award interest, simple or compound, as it considers appropriate, taking into consideration the contract and applicable law. | **Article 60: Currency and Interest**<br>(a) Monetary amounts in the award may be expressed in any currency.<br>(b) The Tribunal may award simple or compound interest to be paid by a party on any sum awarded against that party. It shall be free to determine the interest at such rates as it considers to be appropriate, without being bound by legal rates of interest, and shall be free to determine the period for which the interest shall be paid. | | |
| **9. Punitive damages** | | | | | |
| | | **28.5.** Unless the parties agree otherwise, the parties expressly waive and forego any right to punitive, exemplary or similar damages unless a statute requires that compensatory damages be increased in a specified manner. This provision shall not apply to any award of arbitration costs to a party to compensate for dilatory or bad faith conduct in the arbitration. | | | |
| **10. Dissenting opinions/arbitrator failing to sign** | | | | | |
| | **26.4** If any arbitrator refuses or fails to sign the award, the signatures of the majority or (failing a majority) of the chairman shall be sufficient, provided that the reason for the omitted signature is stated in the award by the majority or chairman. | | | **Article 56:** Unless the arbitral award is made in accordance with the opinion of the presiding arbitrator or the sole arbitrator, the arbitral award shall be signed by all the arbitrators or the majority arbitrators sitting on the arbitration tribunal. An arbitrator who has a dissenting opinion may sign or not sign his name on the arbitral award.<br>The arbitrator shall submit his draft arbitral award to the Arbitration Commission before signing the award. The Arbitration Commission may remind the arbitrator of any issue related to the form of the arbitral award on condition that the arbi- | **32(4)** An arbitrator may attach a dissenting opinion to the Award. |

| ICC | LCIA | AAA | WIPO | CIETAC | STOCKHOLM |
|---|---|---|---|---|---|
| | | | | trator's independence of decision is not affected. The Arbitration Commission's stamp shall be affixed to the arbitral award. The date on which the arbitral award is made is the date on which the arbitral award comes into legal effect. | |
| **11. Separate awards** | | | | | |
| | | **27.7.** In addition to making a final award, the tribunal may make interim, interlocutory, or partial orders and awards. | | **Article 57:** The arbitration tribunal may, if it deems it necessary or the parties so request and the arbitration tribunal agrees, make an interlocutory award or partial award on any issue of the case at any time in the course of arbitration before the final award is made.<br>Either party's failure to perform the interlocutory award does not affect the continuation of the arbitration proceedings and the making of the final award by the arbitration tribunal. | **34(1)** At the request of a party, a separate issue or a part of the matter in dispute may be decided in a Separate Award.<br>**34(2)** Where a party has partially admitted a claim, a Separate Award, based on such admission may be rendered. |
| **12. Duties in making the award** | | | | | |
| | | | | **Article 53:** The arbitration tribunal shall independently and impartially make its arbitral award on the basis of the facts, in accordance with the law and the terms of the contracts, with reference to international practices and in compliance with the principle of fairness and reasonableness. | |

CHAPTER 6

# Costs

A comparison of the level of costs of each institution will be found in Appendix 3.

The institutions vary little in that all can (and do) require prefunding (although on differing criteria) and maintain a right of lien on the award until all fees are paid; all permit a discretion to award the successful party recovery of their legal costs, and all impose joint and several liabilities on the parties for outstanding costs of the tribunal Institution.

The English Arbitration Act also follows this uncontroversial pattern.

## 1. Advances and deposits

| ICC | LCIA | AAA | WIPO | CIETAC | STOCKHOLM |
|---|---|---|---|---|---|
| **Article 30: Advance to Cover the Costs of the Arbitration**<br>**30(1)** After receipt of the Request, the Secretary General may request the Claimant to pay a provisional advance in an amount intended to cover the costs of arbitration until the Terms of Reference have been drawn up.<br>**30(2)** As soon as practicable, the Court shall fix the advance on costs in an amount likely to cover the fees and expenses of the arbitrators and the ICC administrative costs for the claims and counterclaims which have been referred to it by the parties. This amount may be subject to readjustment at any time during the arbitration. Where, apart from the claims, counterclaims are submitted, the Court may fix separate advances on costs for the claims and the counterclaims.<br>**30(3)** The advance on costs fixed by the Court shall be payable in equal shares by the Claimant and the Respondent. Any provisional advance paid on the basis of Article 30(1) will be considered as a partial payment thereof. However, any party shall be free to pay the whole of the advance on costs in respect of the principal claim or the counterclaim, should the other party fail to pay its share. When the Court has set separate advances on costs in accordance with Article 30(2), each of the parties shall pay the advance on costs corresponding to its claims.<br>**30(5)** If one of the parties claims a right to a set-off with regard to either claims or counterclaims, such set-off shall be taken into account in determining the advance to cover the costs of arbitration in the same way as a separate claim insofar as it may require the Arbitral Tribunal to consider additional matters. | **24.1** The LCIA Court may direct the parties, in such proportions as it thinks appropriate, to make one or several interim or final payments on account of the costs of the arbitration. Such deposits shall be made to and held by the LCIA and from time to time may be released by the LCIA Court to the arbitrator(s), any expert appointed by the Arbitral Tribunal and the LCIA itself as the arbitration progresses.<br>**24.4** Failure by a Claimant or counterclaiming party to provide promptly and in full the required deposit may be treated by the LCIA Court and the Arbitral Tribunal as a withdrawal of the claim or counterclaim respectively. | **33.2** During the course of the arbitral proceedings, the Tribunal may request supplementary deposits from the parties.<br>**33.3** If the deposits requested are not paid in full within 30 days after the receipt of the request, the administrator shall so inform the parties, in order that one or the other of them may make the required payment. If such payments are not made, the tribunal may order the suspension or termination of the proceedings.<br>**33.4** After the award has been made, the administrator shall render an accounting to the parties of the deposits received and return any unexpended balance to the parties. | **Article 67: Fees of the Center**<br>(a) The Request for Arbitration shall be subject to the payment to the Center of a registration fee, which shall belong to the International Bureau of WIPO. The amount of the registration fee shall be fixed in the Schedule of Fees applicable on the date on which the Request for Arbitration is received by the Center.<br>(b) The registration fee shall not be refundable.<br>(c) No action shall be taken by the Center on a Request for Arbitration until the registration fee has been paid.<br>(d) If a Claimant fails, within 15 days after a second reminder in writing from the Center, to pay the registration fee, it shall be deemed to have withdrawn its Request for Arbitration.<br>**Article 68**<br>**68(a)** An administration fee, which shall belong to the International Bureau of WIPO, shall be payable by the Claimant to the Center within 30 days after the commencement of the arbitration. The Center shall notify the Claimant of the amount of the administration fee as soon as possible after receipt of the Request for Arbitration.<br>**68(b)** In the case of a counterclaim, an administration fee shall also be payable by the Respondent to the Center within 30 days after the date on which the counterclaim referred to in Article 42(c) is made. The Center shall notify the Respondent of the amount of the administration fee as soon as possible after receipt of notification of the counterclaim.<br>**68(d)** Where a claim or counterclaim is increased, the amount of the administration fee may be increased in accordance with the Schedule of Fees applicable under paragraph (c), | | **14(1)** The Advance on Costs shall be equivalent to the estimated amount of the Arbitration Costs pursuant to Article 39.<br>**14(2)** Each party shall contribute half of the Advance on Costs. The SCC Institute may fix separate amounts for counterclaims and set-off claims. After notification by the Arbitral Tribunal, the SCC Institute may, in the course of the proceedings, decide that additional amounts are to be paid.<br>**14(4)** The SCC Institute may during or after the proceedings draw on the Advance on Costs to cover the fees of the arbitrator(s) and other arbitration costs.<br>**14(5)** The SCC Institute may decide that the Advance on Costs may partly consist of a bank guarantee or other form of security. |

| ICC | LCIA | AAA | WIPO | CIETAC | STOCKHOLM |
|---|---|---|---|---|---|
| | | | and the increased amount shall be payable by the Claimant or the Respondent, as the case may be.<br>**Article 69: Fees of the Arbitrators**<br>(a) The amount and currency of the fees of the arbitrators and the modalities and timing of their payment shall be fixed, in accordance with the provisions of this Article, by the Center, after consultation with the arbitrators and the parties.<br>(b) The amount of the fees of the arbitrators shall, unless the parties and arbitrators agree otherwise, be determined within the range of minimum and maximum fees set out in the Schedule of Fees applicable on the date of the commencement of the arbitration, taking into account the estimated time needed by the arbitrators for conducting the arbitration, the amount in dispute, the complexity of the subject matter of the dispute, the urgency of the case and any other relevant circumstances of the case.<br>**Article 70: Deposits**<br>(a) Upon receipt of notification from the Center of the establishment of the Tribunal, the Claimant and the Respondent shall each deposit an equal amount as an advance for the costs of arbitration referred to in Article 71. The amount of the deposit shall be determined by the Center.<br>(b) In the course of the arbitration, the Center may require that the parties make supplementary deposits.<br>(c) If the required deposits are not paid in full within 30 days after receipt of the corresponding notification, the Center shall so inform the parties in order that one or other of them may make the required payment.<br>(d) Where the amount of the counterclaim greatly exceeds the amount of the claim or involves the examination of significantly different matters, or where it otherwise appears | | |

| ICC | LCIA | AAA | WIPO | CIETAC | STOCKHOLM |
|---|---|---|---|---|---|
| | | | appropriate in the circumstances, the Center in its discretion may establish two separate deposits on account of claim and counterclaim. If separate deposits are established, the totality of the deposit on account of claim shall be paid by the Claimant and the totality of the deposit on account of counterclaim shall be paid by the Respondent.<br>(e) If a party fails, within 15 days after a second reminder in writing from the Center, to pay the required deposit, it shall be deemed to have withdrawn the relevant claim or counterclaim.<br>(f) After the award has been made, the Center shall, in accordance with the award, render an accounting to the parties of the deposits received and return any unexpended balance to the parties or require the payment of any amount owing from the parties. | | |
| **2. Method of determination of costs; recoverability of costs** | | | | | |
| **Article 31: The Costs of the Arbitration**<br>**31(1)** The costs of the arbitration shall include the fees and expenses of the arbitrators and the ICC administrative costs fixed by the Court, in accordance with the scale in force at the time of the commencement of the arbitral proceedings, as well as the fees and expenses of any experts appointed by the Arbitral Tribunal and the reasonable legal and other costs incurred by the parties for the arbitration.<br>**31(2)** The Court may fix the fees of the arbitrators at a figure higher or lower than that which would result from the application of the relevant scale should this be deemed necessary due to the exceptional circumstances of the case. Decisions on costs other than those fixed by the Court may be taken by the Arbitral | **Article 28: Arbitration and Legal Costs.**<br>**28.1** The costs of the arbitration (other than the legal or other costs incurred by the parties themselves) shall be determined by the LCIA Court in accordance with the Schedule of Costs. The parties shall be jointly and severally liable to the Arbitral Tribunal and the LCIA for such arbitration costs.<br>**28.2** The Arbitral Tribunal shall specify in the award the total amount of the costs of the arbitration as determined by the LCIA Court. Unless the parties agree otherwise in writing, the Arbitral Tribunal shall determine the proportions in which the parties shall bear all or part of such arbitration costs. If the Arbitral Tribunal has determined that all or any part of the arbitration costs shall be borne by a party other than a | **Article 31: Costs**<br>The Tribunal shall fix the costs of arbitration in its award. The Tribunal may apportion such costs among the parties if it determines that such apportionment is reasonable, taking into account the circumstances of the case Such costs may include:<br>(a) the fees and expenses of the arbitrators;<br>(b) the costs of assistance required by the Tribunal, including its experts;<br>(c) the fees and expenses of the administrator;<br>(d) the reasonable costs for legal representation of a successful party; and<br>(e) any such costs incurred in connection with an application for interim or emergency relief pursuant to Article 21. | **68(c)** The amount of the administration fee shall be calculated in accordance with the Schedule of Fees applicable on the date of commencement of the arbitration.<br>**70(a)** Upon receipt of notification from the Center of the establishment of the Tribunal, the Claimant and the Respondent shall each deposit an equal amount as an advance for the costs of arbitration referred to in Article 71. The amount of the deposit shall be determined by the Center.<br>**70(d)** Where the amount of the counterclaim greatly exceeds the amount of the claim or involves the examination of significantly different matters, or where it otherwise appears appropriate in the circumstances, the Center in its discretion may establish two separate deposits on account of claim and counter- | **Article 51:** A party who knows or should have known that any provision or equirement of these Rules has not been complied with and yet proceeds with the arbitration proceedings without explicitly raising in writing his objection to non-compliance in a timely manner shall be deemed to have waived his right to object. | **39(1)** The Arbitration Costs consist of<br>(i) the arbitrator's fee;<br>(ii) the Administrative Fee of the SCC Institute;<br>(iii) compensation due to the arbitrator and the SCC Institute to cover their expenses during the proceedings; and<br>(iv) the fees and expenses of any expert appointed by the Arbitral Tribunal pursuant to Article 27.<br>**39(2)** Amounts referred to in sections (i) through (iii) above shall be finally fixed by the SCC Institute in accordance with the Regulations for Arbitration Costs in force at the time of the commencement of the arbitration. The amounts in section (iv) shall be finally fixed by the Arbitral Tribunal.<br>**Article 41: Costs Incurred by a Party**<br>Unless the parties have agreed other- |

| ICC | LCIA | AAA | WIPO | CIETAC | STOCKHOLM |
|---|---|---|---|---|---|
| Tribunal at any time during the proceedings.<br>**31(3)** The final award shall fix the costs of the arbitration and decide which of the parties shall bear them or in what proportions they shall be borne by the parties. | party which has already paid them to the LCIA, the latter party shall have the right to recover the appropriate amount from the former party. | | claim. If separate deposits are established, the totality of the deposit on account of claim shall be paid by the Claimant and the totality of the deposit on account of counterclaim shall be paid by the Respondent.<br>**Article 72: Award of Costs Incurred by a Party**<br>In its award, the Tribunal may, subject to any contrary agreement by the parties and in the light of all the circumstances and the outcome of the arbitration, order a party to pay the whole or part of reasonable expenses incurred by the other party in presenting its case, including those incurred for legal representatives and witnesses. | | wise, the Arbitral Tribunal may, at the request of a party, in an Award or other order by which the arbitral proceedings are terminated order the losing party to compensate the other party for legal representation and other expenses for presenting its case. |
| **3. Form of award of costs** | | | | | |
| **31(3)** The final award shall fix the costs of the arbitration and decide which of the parties shall bear them or in what proportions they shall be borne by the parties. | **28.2** The Arbitral Tribunal shall specify in the award the total amount of the costs of the arbitration as determined by the LCIA Court. Unless the parties agree otherwise in writing, the Arbitral Tribunal shall determine the proportions in which the parties shall bear all or part of such arbitration costs. If the Arbitral Tribunal has determined that all or any part of the arbitration costs shall be borne by a party other than a party which has already paid them to the LCIA, the latter party shall have the right to recover the appropriate amount from the former party.<br>**28.3** The Arbitral Tribunal shall also have the power to order in its award that all or part of the legal or other costs incurred by a party be paid by another party, unless the parties agree otherwise in writing. The Arbitral Tribunal shall determine and fix the amount of each item comprising such costs on such reasonable basis as it thinks fit. | **Article 31: Costs**<br>The Tribunal shall fix the costs of arbitration in its award. The Tribunal may apportion such costs among the parties if it determines that such apportionment is reasonable, taking into account the circumstances of the case. Such costs may include:<br>(a) the fees and expenses of the arbitrators;<br>(b) the costs of assistance required by the Tribunal, including its experts;<br>(c) the fees and expenses of the administrator;<br>(d) the reasonable costs for legal representation of a successful party; and<br>(e) any such costs incurred in connection with an application for interim or emergency relief pursuant to Article 21. | **Article 71: Award of Costs of Arbitration**<br>(a) In its award, the Tribunal shall fix the costs of arbitration, which shall consist of:<br>(i) the arbitrators' fees,<br>(ii) the properly incurred travel, communication and other expenses of the arbitrators,<br>(iii) the costs of expert advice and such other assistance required by the Tribunal pursuant to these Rules, and<br>(iv) such other expenses as are necessary for the conduct of the arbitration proceedings, such as the cost of meeting and hearing facilities.<br>(b) The aforementioned costs shall, as far as possible, be debited from the deposits required under Article 70.<br>(c) The Tribunal shall, subject to any agreement of the parties, apportion the costs of arbitration and the registration and administration fees of the Center between the parties in the light of all the circumstances and the outcome of the arbitration. | **Article 58:** The arbitration tribunal has the power to determine in the arbitral award the arbitration fee and other expenses to be eventually paid by the parties to the Arbitration Commission. | **32(6)** The Arbitration Costs, in accordance with Article 39, and its apportionment between the parties shall be fixed in the Award or other order by which the arbitral proceedings are terminated. An Award may be rendered solely for costs.<br>**39(2)** Amounts referred to in sections (i) through (iii) above shall be finally fixed by the SCC Institute in accordance with the Regulations for Arbitration Costs in force at the time of the commencement of the arbitration. The amounts in section (iv) shall be finally fixed by the Arbitral Tribunal.<br>**40(2)** The Arbitral Tribunal decides on the apportionment of the arbitration costs as between the parties with regard to the outcome of the case and other circumstances. |

| ICC | LCIA | AAA | WIPO | CIETAC | STOCKHOLM |
|---|---|---|---|---|---|
| **4. Criteria for the award of costs** | | | | | |
| | **28.4** Unless the parties otherwise agree in writing, the Arbitral Tribunal shall make its orders on both arbitration and legal costs on the general principle that costs should reflect the parties' relative success and failure in the award or arbitration, except where it appears to the Arbitral Tribunal that in the particular circumstances this general approach is inappropriate. Any order for costs shall be made with reasons in the award containing such order. | **Article 31: Costs**<br>The Tribunal shall fix the costs of arbitration in its award. The Tribunal may apportion such costs among the parties if it determines that such apportionment is reasonable, taking into account the circumstances of the case. Such costs may include:<br>(a) the fees and expenses of the arbitrators;<br>(b) the costs of assistance required by the Tribunal, including its experts;<br>(c) the fees and expenses of the administrator;<br>(d) the reasonable costs for legal representation of a successful party; and<br>(e) any such costs incurred in connection with an application for interim or emergency relief pursuant to Article 21. | **Article 72: Award of Costs Incurred by a Party**<br>In its award, the Tribunal may, subject to any contrary agreement by the parties and in the light of all the circumstances and the outcome of the arbitration, order a party to pay the whole or part of reasonable expenses incurred by the other party in presenting its case, including those incurred for legal representatives and witnesses. | **Article 59:** The arbitration tribunal has the power to decide in the arbitral award that the losing party shall pay the winning party as compensation a proportion of the expenses reasonably incurred by the winning party in dealing with the case. The amount of such compensation shall not in any case exceed 10% of the total amount awarded to the winning party. | **Article 41: Costs Incurred by a Party**<br>Unless the parties have agreed otherwise, the Arbitral Tribunal may, at the request of a party, in an Award or other order by which the arbitral proceedings are terminated order the losing party to compensate the other party for legal representation and other expenses for presenting its case. |
| **5. Costs in the case of abandonment or discontinuation** | | | | | |
| | **28.5** If the arbitration is abandoned, suspended or concluded, by agreement or otherwise, before the final award is made, the parties shall remain jointly and severally liable to pay to the LCIA and the Arbitral Tribunal the costs of the arbitration as determined by the LCIA Court in accordance with the Schedule of Costs. In the event that such arbitration costs are less than the deposits made by the parties, there shall be a refund by the LCIA in such proportion as the parties may agree in writing, or failing such agreement, in the same proportions as the deposits were made by the parties to the LCIA. | **21.4.** The Tribunal may in its discretion apportion costs associated with applications for interim relief in any interim award or in the final award.<br>**Article 32: Compensation of Arbitrators**<br>Arbitrators shall be compensated based upon their amount of service, taking into account their stated rate of compensation and the size and complexity of the case. The administrator shall arrange an appropriate daily or hourly rate, based on such considerations, with the parties and with each of the arbitrators as soon as practicable after the commencement of the arbitration. If the parties fail to agree on the terms of compensation, the administrator shall establish an appropriate rate and communicate it in writing to the parties. | | **Article 78:** If a case is withdrawn after the parties have reached between themselves an amicable settlement, the Arbitration Commission may charge a certain amount of fees from the parties in consideration of the quantity of work and the amount of the actual expenses incurred by the Arbitration Commission. | |

| ICC | LCIA | AAA | WIPO | CIETAC | STOCKHOLM |
|---|---|---|---|---|---|
| **6. Failures to pay advances; consequences** | | | | | |
| **30(4)** When a request for an advance on costs has not been complied with, and after consultation with the Arbitral Tribunal, the Secretary General may direct the Arbitral Tribunal to suspend its work and set a time limit, which must be not less than 15 days, on the expiry of which the relevant claims, or counterclaims shall be considered as withdrawn. Should the party in question wish to object to this measure it must make a request within the aforementioned period for the matter to be decided by the Court. Such party shall not be prevented on the ground of such withdrawal from reintroducing the same claims or counterclaims at a later date in another proceeding. | **24.3** In the event that a party fails or refuses to provide any deposit as directed by the LCIA Court, the LCIA Court may direct the other party or parties to effect a substitute payment to allow the arbitration to proceed (subject to any award on costs). In such circumstances, the party paying the substitute payment shall be entitled to recover that amount as a debt immediately due from the defaulting party.<br>**24.4** Failure by a claimant or counterclaiming party to provide promptly and in full the required deposit may be treated by the LCIA Court and the Arbitral Tribunal as a withdrawal of the claim or counterclaim respectively. | **33.1** When a party files claims, the administrator may request the filing party to deposit appropriate amounts as an advance for the costs referred to in Article 31, paragraphs (a), (b) and (c).<br>**33.2** During the course of the arbitral proceedings, the tribunal may request supplementary deposits from the parties.<br>**33.3** If the deposits requested are not paid in full within 30 days after the receipt of the request, the administrator shall so inform the parties, in order that one or the other of them may make the required payment. If such payments are not made, the tribunal may order the suspension or termination of the proceedings.<br>33.4 After the award has been made, the administrator shall render an accounting to the parties of the deposits received and return any unexpended balance to the parties. | **68(e)** If a party fails, within 15 days after a second reminder in writing from the Center, to pay any administration fee due, it shall be deemed to have withdrawn its claim or counterclaim, or its increase in claim or counterclaim, as the case may be.<br>**68(f)** The Tribunal shall, in a timely manner, inform the Center of the amount of the claim and any counterclaim, as well as any increase thereof. | | **14(3)** If a party fails to make a required payment, the SCC Institute shall afford the other party an opportunity to do so within a specified period of time. If the required payment is not made, the case shall be dismissed either wholly or partly to such extent as is attributable to the missing payment.<br>**35(2)** If a party, who has not paid an Advance on Costs, requests the Arbitral Tribunal to rule on a withdrawn claim, the SCC Institute may, as a condition for such ruling, order the requesting party to pay an Advance on Costs. |
| **7. Costs of experts retained by the Tribunal** | | | | | |
| | **21.3** The fees and expenses of any expert appointed by the Arbitral Tribunal under this Article shall be paid out of the deposits payable by the parties under Article 24 and shall form part of the costs of the arbitration. | **Article 31: Costs**<br>The Tribunal shall fix the costs of arbitration in its award. The Tribunal may apportion such costs among the parties if it determines that such apportionment is reasonable, taking into account the circumstances of the case. Such costs may include:<br>(a) the fees and expenses of the arbitrators;<br>(b) the costs of assistance required by the Tribunal, including its experts;<br>(c) the fees and expenses of the administrator;<br>(d) the reasonable costs for legal representation of a successful party; and<br>(e) any such costs incurred in connection with an application for interim or emergency relief pursuant to Article 21. | | | |

| ICC | LCIA | AAA | WIPO | CIETAC | STOCKHOLM |
|---|---|---|---|---|---|
| **8. Responsibility for costs** | | | | | |
| | **Article 28: Arbitration and Legal Costs.**<br>**28.1** The costs of the arbitration (other than the legal or other costs incurred by the parties themselves) shall be determined by the LCIA Court in accordance with the Schedule of Costs. The parties shall be jointly and severally liable to the Arbitral Tribunal and the LCIA for such arbitration costs.<br>**28.5** If the arbitration is abandoned, suspended or concluded, by agreement or otherwise, before the final award is made, the parties shall remain jointly and severally liable to pay to the LCIA and the Arbitral Tribunal the costs of the arbitration as determined by the LCIA Court in accordance with the Schedule of Costs. In the event that such arbitration costs are less than the deposits made by the parties, there shall be a refund by the LCIA in such proportion as the parties may agree in writing, or failing such agreement, in the same proportions as the deposits were made by the parties to the LCIA. | | | **Article 78:** Apart from charging arbitration fees from the parties according to the Arbitration Fee Schedule of the Arbitration Commission, the Arbitration Commission may collect from the parties other extra, reasonable and actual expenses including arbitrators' special remuneration and their travel and boarding expenses for dealing with the case and the fees and expenses for experts, appraisers and interpreters appointed by the Arbitration Tribunal, etc. | **40(1)** The parties are jointly and severally liable for all payments of all costs mentioned in Article 39. |
| **9. Costs in interim awards** | | | | | |
| | | **21.4** The Tribunal may in its discretion apportion costs associated with applications for interim relief in any interim award or in the final award. | | | |
| **10. Arbitrator's compensation** | | | | | |
| *[The ICC Rules (their Appendix 3 on Costs) can be found in Appendix 3 to this book.]* | | **Article 32: Compensation of Arbitrators**<br>Arbitrators shall be compensated based upon their amount of service, taking into account their stated rate of compensation and the size and complexity of the case. The adminis- | **Article 69: Fees of the Arbitrators**<br>**69(a)** The amount and currency of the fees of the arbitrators and the modalities and timing of their payment shall be fixed, in accordance with the provisions of this Article, by the Center, after consultation with | | |

| ICC | LCIA | AAA | WIPO | CIETAC | STOCKHOLM |
|---|---|---|---|---|---|
| | | trator shall arrange an appropriate daily or hourly rate, based on such considerations, with the parties and with each of the arbitrators as soon as practicable after the commencement of the arbitration. If the parties fail to agree on the terms of compensation, the administrator shall establish an appropriate rate and communicate it in writing to the parties. | the arbitrators and the parties.<br>69(b) The amount of the fees of the arbitrators shall, unless the parties and arbitrators agree otherwise, be determined within the range of minimum and maximum fees set out in the Schedule of Fees applicable on the date of the commencement of the arbitration, taking into account the estimated time needed by the arbitrators for conducting the arbitration, the amount in dispute, the complexity of the subject matter of the dispute, the urgency of the case and any other relevant circumstances of the case. | | |

CHAPTER 7

# Miscellaneous

This sweep up section covers Articles which do not readily fit into the previous categories, although there is some overlap. Worthy of particular note are the following.

The organisation of the Institutions. Various of the institutions are set out in some detail according to particulars of their administration and how it may impact on the arbitration: ICC is prominent here, AAA probably has the lowest profile. It is certainly the case that the ICC has a formidable administration and probably, of all the institutions, plays the most active role in arbitration. After the appointment of a tribunal in LCIA and Stockholm, by contrast, the involvement of the institution is largely formal.

With the exception of WIPO, who are obviously and determinedly specialist, the ambit of business covered by each institution is similar. ICC "business disputes of an international character" (or not); CIETAC (Article 2) "disputes arising from economic and trade transactions, contractual or non-contractual" but see also the regional disputes listed further in Article 2; Stockholm "domestic and international disputes".

All the rules are modern, Stockholm being the most recent (as is the Swedish Arbitration Act). All contain waiver provisions intended to forestall complaint or appeal for irregularity if the point is not taken in the arbitration at an early time.

The 1990's climate of compromise finds itself reflected in all the institutions offering mediation/conciliation services. It is suggested that any set of rules that offers the tribunal as mediators with a residual role thereafter of arbitrators, carries with it a risk that the free flow of candid interchange between party and neutral associated with mediation may either be impossible if that mediator may thereafter revert to arbitrator, or may make it impossible for the arbitrator to proceed impartially thereafter if he has been privy to confidential information not shared with the other side. The CIETAC rules (Article 48) propose such a mediator/arbitrator formula and are included in the-body of their arbitration rules. WIPO keeps a greater distance. LCIA's arbitrators may offer to assist to resolve disputes probably with a mind to the backdrop of English legislation which promotes wide dispute resolution procedures.

All the institutions clothe proceedings with confidentiality. CIETAC is the institution where, for example for certain measures, recourse to the local (public) courts is most likely (and is indeed provided for in their rules).

| ICC | LCIA | AAA | WIPO | CIETAC | STOCKHOLM |
|---|---|---|---|---|---|
| **1. Constitution of courts/institutions** | | | | | |
| **INTRODUCTORY PROVISIONS**<br>**Article 1: International Court of Arbitration**<br>**1(1)** The International Court of Arbitration (the "Court") of the International Chamber of Commerce (the "ICC") is the arbitration body attached to the ICC. The statutes of the Court are set forth in Appendix 1. Members of the Court are appointed by the Council of the ICC. The function of the Court is to provide for the settlement by arbitration of business disputes of an international character in accordance with these Rules of Arbitration of the International Chamber of Commerce (the "Rules"). If so empowered by an arbitration agreement, the Court shall also provide for the settlement by arbitration in accordance with these Rules of business disputes not of an international character.<br>**1(2)** The Court does not itself settle disputes. It has the function of ensuring the application of these Rules. It draws up its own Internal Rules (Appendix II).<br>**1(3)** The Chairman of the Court, or in the Chairman's absence or otherwise at his request, one of its Vice-Chairmen shall have the power to take urgent decisions on behalf of the Court, provided that any such decision shall be reported to the Court at its next session.<br>**1(4)** As provided for in its Internal Rules, the Court may delegate to one or more committees composed of its members the power to take certain decisions, provided that any such decision is reported to the Court at its next session.<br>**Appendix 1 – statutes of the international court of arbitration of the ICC**<br>**1. Function**<br>1(1) The function of the Inter- | **Article 3 The LCIA Court and Registrar**<br>**3.1** The functions of the LCIA Court under these Rules shall be performed in its name by the President or a Vice-President of the LCIA Court or by a division of three or five members of the LCIA Court appointed by the President or a Vice-President of the LCIA Court, as determined by the President.<br>**3.2** The functions of the Registrar under these Rules shall be performed by the Registrar or any deputy Registrar of the LCIA Court under the supervision of the LCIA Court.<br>**3.3** All communications from any party or arbitrator to the LCIA Court shall be addressed to the Registrar. | | | **Article 1:** These Rules are formulated in accordance with the Arbitration Law of the People's Republic of China and the provisions of the relevant laws and pursuant to the "Decision" of the former Government Administration Council of the Central People's Government and the "Notice" and "Official Reply" of the State Council.<br>**Article 2:** China International Economic and Trade Arbitration Commission (originally named Foreign Trade Arbitration Commission of the China Council for the Promotion of International Trade, later renamed as Foreign Economic and Trade Arbitration Commission of the China Council for the Promotion of International Trade, and presently called China International Economic and Trade Arbitration Commission, hereinafter referred to as the Arbitration Commission) independently and impartially resolves, by means of arbitration, disputes arising from economic and trade transactions, contractual or non-contractual.<br>The disputes stated in the preceding paragraph include: (1) international or foreign-related disputes; (2) disputes related to the Hong Kong SAR, Macao or Taiwan regions; (3) disputes between the enterprises with foreign investment and disputes between an enterprise with foreign investment and another Chinese legal person, physical person and/or economic organization; (4) disputes arising from project financing, invitation for tender, bidding, construction and other activities conducted by Chinese legal persons, physical persons and/or other economic organizations through utilizing the capital, technology or service from foreign countries, international | **Article 1: The SCC Institute**<br>The Arbitration Institute of the Stockholm Chamber of Commerce (hereinafter referred to as "the SCC Institute") is a body for dealing with matters of dispute resolution. The SCC Institute is part of but independent from the Stockholm Chamber of Commerce. The SCC Institute does not itself settle disputes. Its objectives are:<br>– to assist in the settlement of domestic and international disputes in accordance with the Rules of the Arbitration Institute of the Stockholm Chamber of Commerce (hereinafter referred to as "the SCC Rules");<br>– to assist in the settlement of disputes in accordance with other rules which have been adopted by the SCC Institute 1;<br>– to assist, as determined by the SCC Institute, in proceedings which are conducted in a manner which differs, either in part or in whole, from that anticipated by the SCC rules, to provide guidelines concerning settlement of disputes under the SCC Institute's rules; and<br>– to provide information concerning arbitration and mediation matters.<br>**Article 2: The Board**<br>(1) The SCC Institute shall have a Board composed of six members who shall be appointed for a period of three years by the Board of Directors of the Chamber. The Board of Directors of the Chamber shall appoint a Chairman and a Vice Chairman from among the members of the Board of the SCC Institute. The Chairman and the Vice Chairman shall be lawyers.<br>(2) The Board of Directors of the Chamber may, if there are extraordi- |

| ICC | LCIA | AAA | WIPO | CIETAC | STOCKHOLM |
|---|---|---|---|---|---|
| national Court of Arbitration of the International Chamber of Commerce (the Court) is to ensure the application of the Rules of Arbitration and of the Rules of Conciliation of the International Chamber of Commerce and it has all the necessary powers for that purpose.<br>1(2) As an autonomous body, it carries out these functions in complete independence from the ICC and its organs.<br>1(3) Its members are independent from the ICC National Committee.<br>**2. Composition of the Court**<br>The Court shall consist of a Chairman, Vice-Chairman and members and alternate members (collectively designated as members). In its work it is assisted by its Secretariat (Secretariat of the Court).<br>**3. Appointment**<br>1. The Chairman is elected by the ICC Council upon recommendation of the Executive Board of the ICC.<br>2. The ICC Council appoints the Vice-Chairman of the Court from among the members of the Court or otherwise.<br>3. Its members are appointed by the ICC Council on the proposal of National Committees, one member for each Committee.<br>4. On the proposal of the Chairman of the Court, the Council may appoint alternate members.<br>5. The terms of office of all members is three years. If a member is no longer in a position to exercise his functions, his successor is appointed by the Council for the remainder of the term.<br>**4. Plenary Session of the Court**<br>The Plenary Sessions of the Court are presided by the Chairman, in his absence by one of the Vice-Chairmen designated by him. The deliberations shall be valid when at least six members are present. Decisions are taken by a majority vote, the Chairman | | | | organizations or from the Hong Kong SAR, Macao and Taiwan regions; and (5) disputes that may be taken cognizance of by the Arbitration Commission in accordance with special provisions of or upon special authorization from the law or administrative regulations of the People's Republic of China.<br>**Article 8:** The Arbitration Commission has one honorary Chairman and several advisers.<br>**Article 9:** The Arbitration Commission is composed of one Chairman, several Vice-Chairmen and a number of Commission members. The Chairman performs the functions and duties vested in him by these Rules and the Vice-Chairmen may perform the Chairman's functions and duties with the Chairman's authorization.<br>The Arbitration Commission has a secretariat to handle its day-to-day work under the leadership of the Secretary-General of the Arbitration Commission.<br>**Article 10:** The Arbitration Commission maintains a Panel of Arbitrators. The arbitrators are selected and appointed by the Arbitration Commission from among Chinese and foreign personages with special knowledge and practical experience in the fields of law, economics and trade, science and technology, and other fields.<br>**Article 11:** The Arbitration Commission is located in Beijing. The Arbitration Commission has a Shenzhen Sub-Commission in Shenzhen Special Economic Zone and a Shanghai Sub-Commission in Shanghai. The Sub-Commissions are an integral part of the Arbitration Commission. The Sub-Commissions have their own Secretariats to handle their day-to-day work under the leadership of the Secretaries-General of the Sub-Commissions. These Rules uniformly apply to the | nary reasons for doing so, remove a member of the Board of the SCC Institute. If a member resigns or is removed during his term of office, the Board of Directors of the Chamber will appoint a new member for the remainder of his term.<br>**Article 3: Decisions by the Board**<br>Two members of the Board shall form a *quorum*. If no majority is attained, the Chairman shall cast the deciding vote. The Chairman or the Vice Chairman shall have the power to take decisions on behalf of the Board in urgent matters. Decisions of the Board are final and cannot be reviewed by the Chamber. |

| ICC | LCIA | AAA | WIPO | CIETAC | STOCKHOLM |
|---|---|---|---|---|---|
| having a casting vote in the event of a tie.<br>**5. Committees**<br>The Court may set up one or more Committees and lay down the functions and organisation of such Committees.<br>**6. Confidentiality**<br>The work of the Court is of a confidential nature and must be respected by everyone who participates in that work in whatever capacity. The Court lays down the rules regarding the persons who can attend the meetings of the Court and its Committees and who are entitled to have access to the material submitted to the Court and its Secretariat.<br>**7. Modification of the Rules of Arbitration**<br>Any proposal of the Court for a modification of the Rules is laid before the Commission on International Arbitration before submission to the Executive Board and the Council of the ICC for approval.<br>**Appendix II**<br>**Article 3: Relations between the Members of the court and the ICC National Committee**<br>1. By virtue of their capacity, the members of the Court are independent of the ICC National Committees which proposed them for appointment by the ICC Council.<br>2. Furthermore, they must regard as confidential, *vis-à-vis* the said National Committees, any information concerning individual cases with which they have become acquainted in their capacity as members of the Court except when they have been requested by the Chairman of the Court, or by its Secretary-General to communicate specific information to their respective National Committee.<br>**Article 4: Committee of the Court**<br>1. In accordance with the provisions of Article 1(4) of the Rules and | | | | Arbitration Commission and its Sub-Commissions. When arbitration proceedings are conducted in the Sub-Commissions, the functions and duties under these Rules to be carried out by the Chairman, the secretariat and the Secretary-General of the Arbitration Commission shall be performed by the Vice-Chairmen authorized by the Chairman, the secretariats and the Secretaries-General of the Sub-Commissions respectively and accordingly. | |

| ICC | LCIA | AAA | WIPO | CIETAC | STOCKHOLM |
|---|---|---|---|---|---|
| Article 5 of its Statutes (Appendix I), the Court hereby establishes a Committee of the Court.<br>2. The members of the Committee consist of a Chairman and at least two other members. The Chairman of the Court acts as the Chairman of the Committee. If absent, the Chairman may designate a Vice-Chairman of the Court or, in exceptional circumstances, another member of the Court as Chairman of the Committee.<br>3. The other two members of the Committee are appointed by the Court from among the Vice-Chairmen or the other members of the Court. At each Plenary Session the Court appoints the members who are to attend the meetings of the Committee to be held before the next Plenary Session.<br>4. The Committee meets when convened by its Chairman. Two members constitute a *quorum*.<br>5(a) The Court shall issue directions determining the decisions that may be taken by the Committee.<br>(b) The decisions of the Committee are taken unanimously.<br>(c) When the Committee cannot reach a decision or deems it preferable to abstain, it transfers the case to the next Plenary Session, making any suggestions it deems appropriate.<br>(d) The Committee's decisions are brought to the notice of the Court at its next Plenary Session. | | | | | |

| ICC | LCIA | AAA | WIPO | CIETAC | STOCKHOLM |
|---|---|---|---|---|---|
| **2. Effective date of rules** | | | | | |
| 1 January 1998 | (Adopted to take effect for arbitrations commencing on or after 1 January 1998.) | 1 April 1997 | | **Article 80:** These Rules shall come into force as from May 10, 1998. For cases which have been taken cognizance of by the Arbitration Commission or by its Sub-Commissions before the date on which these Rules become effective, the Rules of Arbitration effective on the date when the cases were taken cognizance of shall apply. However, these Rules shall be applied if the parties so agree. | 1 April 1999 |
| **3. Submission by the parties to the rules/exclusion of local courts** | | | | | |
| | **Preamble**<br>Where any agreement, submission or reference provides in writing and in whatsoever manner for arbitration under the rules of the LCIA or by the Court of the LCIA ("the LCIA Court"), the parties shall be taken to have agreed in writing that the arbitration shall be conducted in accordance with the following rules ("the Rules") or such amended rules as the LCIA may have adopted hereafter to take effect before the commencement of the arbitration. The Rules include the Schedule of Costs in effect at the commencement of the arbitration, as separately amended from time to time by the LCIA Court.<br>**Article 22**<br>22.2 By agreeing to arbitration under these Rules, the parties shall be treated as having agreed not to apply to any state court or other judicial authority for any order available from the Arbitral Tribunal under Article 22.1, except with the agreement in writing of all parties.<br>**Article 26**<br>26.9 All awards shall be final and binding on the parties. By agreeing to arbitration under these Rules, the | **Article 1**<br>**1.1** Where parties have agreed in writing to arbitrate disputes under these International Arbitration Rules or have provided for arbitration of an international dispute by the American Arbitration Association without designating particular rules, the arbitration shall take place in accordance with these rules, as in effect at the date of commencement of the arbitration, subject to whatever modifications the parties may adopt in writing.<br>**1.2** These rules govern the arbitration, except that, where any such rule is in conflict with any provision of the law applicable to the arbitration from which the parties cannot derogate, that provision shall prevail.<br>**1.3** These rules specify the duties and responsibilities of the administrator, the American Arbitration Association. The administrator may provide services through its own facilities or through the facilities of arbitral institutions with whom it has agreements of cooperation | **Article 2**<br>Where an Arbitration Agreement provides for arbitration under the WIPO Arbitration Rules, these Rules shall be deemed to form part of that Arbitration Agreement and the dispute shall be settled in accordance with these Rules, as in effect on the date of the commencement of the arbitration, unless the parties have agreed otherwise. | **Article 79:** Where an arbitration agreement or an arbitration clause contained in the contract provides for arbitration to be conducted by China International Economic and Trade Arbitration Commission or its Sub-Commissions or by the formerly named Foreign Trade Arbitration Commission or Foreign Economic and Trade Arbitration Commission of the China Council for the Promotion of International Trade, it shall be deemed that the parties have unanimously agreed that the arbitration shall be conducted by China International Economic and Trade Arbitration Commission or by its Sub-Commissions. Where an arbitration agreement or an arbitration clause contained in the contract provides for arbitration by China Council for the Promotion of International Trade/China Chamber of International Commerce or by the arbitration commission of China Council for the Promotion of International Trade/China Chamber of International Commerce, it shall be deemed that the parties have unanimously agreed that the arbitration shall be conducted by China International Economic and Trade Arbitration Commission. | **Regulations for arbitration costs:**<br>**IV. Effectiveness**<br>These Regulations enter into force on 1 April 1999 and will replace the former Regulations. The Regulations will be applied to any arbitration commenced on this date or thereafter. |

| ICC | LCIA | AAA | WIPO | CIETAC | STOCKHOLM |
|---|---|---|---|---|---|
| | parties undertake to carry out any award immediately and without any delay (subject only to Article 27); and the parties also waive irrevocably their right to any form of appeal, review or recourse to any state court or other judicial authority, insofar as such waiver may be validly made. | | | | |
| **4. Definitions** | | | | | |
| **Article 2: Definitions**<br>In these Rules<br>(i) "Arbitral Tribunal" includes one or more arbitrators.<br>(ii) "Claimant" includes one or more Claimants and "Respondent" includes one or more respondents.<br>(iii) "Award" includes, *inter alia*, an interim, partial or final Award. | **5.1** The expression "the Arbitral Tribunal" in these Rules includes a sole arbitrator or all the arbitrators where more than one. All references to an arbitrator shall include the masculine and feminine. ( References to the President, Vice-President and members of the LCIA Court, the Registrar or deputy Registrar, expert, witness, party and legal representative shall be similarly understood.) | | **Article 1: Abbreviated Expressions**<br>In these Rules:<br>"Arbitration Agreement" means an agreement by the parties to submit to arbitration all or certain disputes which have arisen or which may arise between them; an Arbitration Agreement may be in the form of an arbitration clause in a contract or in the form of a separate contract;<br>"Claimant" means the party initiating an arbitration;<br>"Respondent" means the party against which the arbitration is initiated, as named in the Request for Arbitration;<br>"Tribunal" includes a sole arbitrator or all the arbitrators where more than one is appointed;<br>"WIPO" means the World Intellectual Property Organization;<br>"Center" means the WIPO Arbitration Center, a unit of the International Bureau of WIPO;<br>Words used in the singular include the plural and vice versa, as the context may require. | | |
| **5. Secretariat** | | | | | |
| **Article 1(5):** The Secretariat of the Court (the "Secretariat") under the direction of its Secretary General (the "Secretary General") shall have its seat at the headquarters of the ICC. | | | | | **Article 4: The Secretariat**<br>The SCC Institute shall have a Secretariat under the direction of a Secretary General who shall be a lawyer. |

| ICC | LCIA | AAA | WIPO | CIETAC | STOCKHOLM |
|---|---|---|---|---|---|
| **Appendix II. Article 5**<br>**Court Secretariat**<br>**1.** In case of absence, the Secretary-General may delegate to the General Counsel and Deputy Secretary-General the authority to confirm arbitrators, to certify true copies of awards and to request the payment of a provisional advance respectively provided for in Articles 9(2), 28(2) and 30(1) of the ICC Rules.<br>**2.** The Secretariat may, with the approval of the Court, issue notes and other documents for the information of the parties and the arbitrators or necessary for the proper conduct of the arbitral proceedings. | | | | | |

## 6. Procedural matters. circulation of correspondence, time limits, extensions

| ICC | LCIA | AAA | WIPO | CIETAC | STOCKHOLM |
|---|---|---|---|---|---|
| | **Article 13: Communications between Parties and the Arbitral Tribunal.**<br>**13.1** Until the Arbitral Tribunal is formed, all communications between parties and arbitrators shall be made through the Registrar.<br>**13.2** Thereafter, unless and until the Arbitral Tribunal directs that communications shall take place directly between the Arbitral Tribunal and the parties (with simultaneous copies to the Registrar), all written communications between the parties and the Arbitral Tribunal shall continue to be made through the Registrar.<br>**13.3** Where the Registrar sends any written communication to one party on behalf of the Arbitral Tribunal, he shall send a copy to each of the other parties. Where any party sends to the Registrar any communication (including Written Statements and Documents under Article 15), it shall include a copy for each arbitrator; and it shall also send copies direct to all other parties and confirm to the Registrar in writing that it has done or is doing so. | **16.4.** Documents or information supplied to the tribunal by one party shall at the same time be communicated by that party to the other party or parties. | | | |

| ICC | LCIA | AAA | WIPO | CIETAC | STOCKHOLM |
|---|---|---|---|---|---|
| **Article 3: Written Notifications or Communications; Time Limits**<br>**3(1)** All pleadings and other written communications submitted by any party, as well as all documents annexed thereto, shall be supplied in a number of copies sufficient to provide one copy for each party, plus one for each arbitrator, and one for the Secretariat. A copy of any communication from the Arbitral Tribunal to the parties shall be sent to the Secretariat.<br>**3(2)** All notifications or communications from the Secretariat and the Arbitral Tribunal shall be made to the last address of the party or its representatives for whom the same or are intended, as notified either by the party in question or by the other party. Such notification or communication may be made by delivery against receipt, registered post, courier, facsimile transmission, telex, telegram or any other means of telecommunication that provides a record of the sending thereof.<br>**3(3)** A notification or communication shall be deemed to have been effected on the day it was received by the party itself or by its representative, or would have been received if made in accordance with the preceding paragraph.<br>**3(4)** Periods of time specified in or fixed under the present Rules, shall start to run on the day following the date of notification or communication is deemed to have been made in accordance with the preceding paragraph. When the day next following such date is an official holiday, or a non business day in the country where the notification or communication is deemed to have been made, the period of time shall commence on the first following business day. Official holidays and non-business days are included in the calculation of the period of time. If the last day of the relevant period of time grant- | **Article 4: Notices and Periods of Time**<br>**4.1** Any notice or other communication that may be or is required to be given by a party under these Rules shall be in writing and shall be delivered by registered postal or courier service or transmitted by facsimile, telex, e-mail or any other means of telecommunication that provides a record of its transmission.<br>**4.2** A party's last-known residence or place of business during the arbitration shall be a valid address for the purpose of any notice or other communication in the absence of any notification of a change to such address by that party to the other parties, the Arbitral Tribunal and the Registrar.<br>**4.3** For the purpose of determining the date of commencement of a time limit, a notice or other communication shall be treated as having been received on the day it is delivered or, in the case of telecommunications, transmitted in accordance with Articles 4.1 and 4.2.<br>**4.4** For the purpose of determining compliance with a time limit, a notice or other communication shall be treated as having been sent, made or transmitted if it is dispatched in accordance with Articles 4.1 and 4.2 prior to or on the date of the expiration of the time-limit.<br>**4.5** Notwithstanding the above, any notice or communication by one party may be addressed to another party in the manner agreed in writing between them or, failing such agreement, according to the practice followed in the course of their previous dealings or in whatever manner ordered by the Arbitral Tribunal.<br>**4.6** For the purpose of calculating a period of time under these Rules, such period shall begin to run on the day following the day when a notice or other communication is received. If the last day of such period is an | **Notices: Article 18**<br>**18.1.** Unless otherwise agreed by the parties or ordered by the Tribunal, all notices, statements and written communications may be served on a party by air mail, air courier, facsimile transmission, telex, telegram, or other written forms of electronic communication addressed to the party or its representative at its last known address or by personal service.<br>**18.2.** For the purpose of calculating a period of time under these rules, such period shall begin to run on the day following the day when a notice, statement or written communication is received. If the last day of such period is an official holiday at the place received, the period is extended until the first business day which follows. Official holidays occurring during the running of the period of time are included in calculating the period. | **4(a)** Any notice or other communication that may or is required to be given under these Rules shall be in writing and shall be delivered by expedited postal or courier service, or transmitted by telex, telefax or other means of telecommunication that provide a record thereof.<br>**4(c)** For the purpose of determining the date of commencement of a time limit, a notice or other communication shall be deemed to have been received on the day it is delivered or, in the case of telecommunications, transmitted in accordance with paragraphs (a) and (b) of this Article.<br>**4(d)** For the purpose of determining compliance with a time limit, a notice or other communication shall be deemed to have been sent, made or transmitted if it is dispatched, in accordance with paragraphs (a) and (b) of this Article, prior to or on the day of the expiration of the time limit.<br>**4(e)** For the purpose of calculating a period of time under these Rules, such period shall begin to run on the day following the day when a notice or other communication is received. If the last day of such period is an official holiday or a non-business day at the residence or place of business of the addressee, the period is extended until the first business day which follows. Official holidays or non-business days occurring during the running of the period of time are included in calculating the period.<br>**4(f)** The parties may agree to reduce or extend the periods of time referred to in Articles 11, 15(b), 16(b), 17(b), 17(c), 18(b), 19(b)(iii), 41(a) and 42(a).<br>**4(g)** The Center may, at the request of a party or on its own motion, extend the periods of time referred to in Articles 11, 15(b), 16(b), 17(b), 17(c), 18(b), 19(b)(iii), 67(d), 68(e) and 70(e). | **Article 76:** All the arbitration documents, notices and materials may be sent to the parties and/or their attorneys in person, or by registered letter or express airmail, telefax, telex, cable or by any other means which are deemed proper by the secretariat of the Arbitration Commission.<br>**Article 77:** Any written communication to the parties is deemed to have been properly served if it is delivered to the addressee or delivered at his place of business, habitual residence or mailing address; or if none of these can be found after making a reasonable inquiry, a written communication is deemed to have been properly served if it is sent to the addressee's last known place of business, habitual residence or mailing address by registered letter or by any other means which provides a record of the attempt to deliver it. | **12(1)** Any notice or other communication from the SCC Institute shall be delivered to the last known address of the addressee.<br>**12(2)** Any notice or other communication shall be delivered by courier or registered mail, facsimile transmission, e-mail or by any other means of communication that provides a record of the sending thereof.<br>**12(3)** A notice or communication sent in accordance with paragraph two shall be deemed to have been received, by the addressee, at the latest on the date it would normally have been received given the chosen means of communication. |

| ICC | LCIA | AAA | WIPO | CIETAC | STOCKHOLM |
|---|---|---|---|---|---|
| ed is an official holiday or a non-business day in the country where the notification or communication is deemed to have been made, the period of time shall expire at the end of the first following business day.<br>**Article 32: Modified Time Limits**<br>**32(1)** The parties may agree to shorten the various time limits set out in these Rules. Any such agreement entered into subsequent to the constitution of an Arbitral Tribunal shall become effective only upon the approval of the Arbitral Tribunal.<br>**32(2)** The Court, on its own initiative, may extend any time-limit which has been modified pursuant to Article 32(1) on its own initiative if it decides that it is necessary to do so in order that the Arbitral Tribunal or the Court may fulfil their responsibilities in accordance with these Rules. | official holiday or a non-business day at the residence or place of business of the addressee, the period is extended until the first business day which follows. Official holidays or non-business days occurring during the running of the period of time are included in calculating that period.<br>**4.7** The Arbitral Tribunal may at any time extend (even where the period of time has expired) or abridge any period of time prescribed under these Rules or under the Arbitration Agreement for the conduct of the arbitration, including any notice or communication to be served by one party on any other party.<br>**22.1(b)** to extend or abbreviate any time-limit provided by the Arbitration Agreement or these Rules for the conduct of the arbitration or by the Arbitral Tribunal's own orders; | | | | |
| | | | **4(b)** A party's last known residence or place of business shall be a valid address for the purpose of any notice or other communication in the absence of any notification of a change by that party. Communications may in any event be addressed to a party in the manner stipulated or, failing such a stipulation, according to the practice followed in the course of the dealings between the parties. | | |
| | | | | **Article 20:** When submitting application for arbitration, written defense, statement of counterclaim, documentary evidence and other documents, the party/parties shall submit them in quintuplicate. If the number of the parties exceeds two, additional copies shall be submitted accordingly; if the number of arbitrator of the arbitration tribunal is one, two copies may be reduced. | |

| ICC | LCIA | AAA | WIPO | CIETAC | STOCKHOLM |
|---|---|---|---|---|---|
| **7. Waiver** | | | | | |
| **Article 33: Waiver**<br>A party which proceeds with the arbitration without raising its objection to a failure to comply with any provisions of these Rules or any other rules applicable to the proceedings, any direction given by the Arbitral Tribunal or any requirement under the arbitration agreement relating to the constitution of the Arbitral Tribunal, or to the conduct of the proceedings, shall be deemed to have waived its right to object. | **32.1** A party who knows that any provision of the Arbitration Agreement (including these Rules) has not been complied with and yet proceeds with the arbitration without promptly stating its objection to such non-compliance, shall be treated as having irrevocably waived its right to object. | **Waiver of Rules: Article 25**<br>A party who knows that any provision of the rules or requirement under the rules has not been complied with, but proceeds with the arbitration without promptly stating an objection in writing thereto, shall be deemed to have waived the right to object. | **Article 58: Waiver**<br>A party who knows or should have known that any provision or requirement of these Rules has not been complied with and yet proceeds with the arbitration proceedings without explicitly raising in writing his objection to non-compliance in a timely manner shall be deemed to have waived his right to object. | | **Article 29: Failure to Object to Procedural Irregularities**<br>A party, who during the proceedings fails to object within a reasonable time to any deviation from provisions of the arbitration agreement, these Rules or other rules applicable to the proceedings, shall be deemed to have waived his right to invoke such irregularity. |
| **8. Conciliation** | | | | | |
| [*ICC has separate rules.*] | [*LCIA has separate rules.*] | [*AAA state that mediation or conciliation can be discussed with AAA, either when the contract is being written or after a dispute arises and that the AAA is prepared to arrange for mediation or conciliation anywhere in the world.*] | **65(a)** The Tribunal may suggest that the parties explore settlement at such times as the Tribunal may deem appropriate. | **Article 46:** If both parties have a desire for conciliation or one party so desires and the other party agrees to it when consulted by the Arbitration Tribunal, the Arbitration Tribunal may conciliate the case under its cognizance in the process of arbitration.<br>**Article 47:** The Arbitration Tribunal may conciliate cases in the manner it deems appropriate.<br>**Article 48:** The Arbitration Tribunal shall terminate conciliation and continue the arbitration proceedings when one of the parties requests a termination of conciliation or when the Arbitration Tribunal believes that further efforts to conciliate will be futile.<br>**Article 49:** If the parties have reached an amicable settlement outside the Arbitration Tribunal in the course of conciliation conducted by the Arbitration Tribunal, such settlement shall be deemed as one which has been reached through the Arbitration Tribunal's conciliation.<br>**Article 50:** The parties shall sign a settlement agreement in writing when an amicable settlement is reached through conciliation conducted by the Arbitration Tribunal, | [*The SCC Institute has adopted Rules for Expedited Arbitrations, Insurance Arbitration Rules, Mediation Rules and Procedures and Services under the UNCITRAL Arbitration Rules.*] |

| ICC | LCIA | AAA | WIPO | CIETAC | STOCKHOLM |
|---|---|---|---|---|---|
| | | | | and the Arbitration Tribunal shall end the case by making an arbitration award in accordance with the contents of the settlement agreement unless otherwise agreed by the parties.<br>**Article 51:** Should conciliation fail, any statement, opinion, view or proposal which has been made, raised, put forward, acknowledged, accepted or rejected by either party or by the arbitration tribunal in the process of conciliation shall not be invoked as grounds for any claim, defense and/or counterclaim in the subsequent arbitration proceedings, judicial proceedings or any other proceedings. | |
| **9. Exclusion of liability** | | | | | |
| **Article 34: Exclusion of Liability**<br>Neither the arbitrators, nor the Court and its members, nor the ICC and its employees, nor the ICC National Committees shall be liable to any person for any act or omission in connection with the arbitration. | **Article 31: Exclusion of Liability**<br>**31.1** None of the LCIA, the LCIA Court (including its President, Vice-Presidents and individual members), the Registrar, any deputy Registrar, any arbitrator and any expert to the Arbitral Tribunal shall be liable to any party howsoever for any act or omission in connection with any arbitration conducted by reference to these Rules, save where the act or omission is shown by that party to constitute conscious and deliberate wrongdoing committed by the body or person alleged to be liable to that party.<br>**31.2** After the award has been made and the possibilities of correction and additional awards referred to in Article 27 have lapsed or been exhausted, neither the LCIA, the LCIA Court (including its President, Vice-Presidents and individual members), the Registrar, any deputy Registrar, any arbitrator or expert to the Arbitral Tribunal shall be under any legal obligation to make any statement to any person about any matter concerning the arbitration, nor shall any party seek to make any | **Article 35: Exclusion of Liability**<br>The members of the Tribunal and the administrator shall not be liable to any party for any act or omission in connection with any arbitration conducted under these rules, except that they may be liable for the consequences of conscious and deliberate wrongdoing. | **Article 77: Exclusion of Liability**<br>Except in respect of deliberate wrongdoing, the arbitrator or arbitrators, WIPO and the Center shall not be liable to a party for any act or omission in connection with the arbitration. | | **Article 42: Exclusion of Liability**<br>The SCC Institute is not liable to any party for any act or omission in connection with the arbitration unless such act or omission is shown to constitute wilful misconduct or gross negligence by the SCC Institute. An arbitrator is liable only if shown to have caused damage by wilful misconduct or gross negligence. |

| ICC | LCIA | AAA | WIPO | CIETAC | STOCKHOLM |
|---|---|---|---|---|---|
| | of these persons a witness in any legal or other proceedings arising out of the arbitration.<br>**32.2** In all matters not expressly provided for in these Rules, the LCIA Court, the Arbitral Tribunal and the parties shall act in the spirit of these Rules and shall make every reasonable effort to ensure that an award is legally enforceable. | | | | |
| **10. Defamation release** | | | | | |
| | | | **Article 78: Waiver of Defamation**<br>The parties and, by acceptance of appointment, the arbitrator agree that any statements or comments, whether written or oral, made or used by them or their representatives in preparation for or in the course of the arbitration shall not be relied upon to found or maintain any action for defamation, libel, slander or any related complaint, and this Article may be pleaded as a bar to any such action. | | |
| **11. Jurisdiction to interpret rules** | | | | | |
| **Article 35 General rule**<br>In all matters not expressly provided for in these Rules, the Court and the Arbitral Tribunal shall act in the spirit of these Rules and shall make every effort to make sure that the award is enforceable in law. | | | **Article 3**<br>(a) These Rules shall govern the arbitration, except that, where any of these Rules is in conflict with a provision of the law applicable to the arbitration from which the parties cannot derogate, that provision shall prevail.<br>(b) The law applicable to the arbitration shall be determined in accordance with Article 59(b). | **Article 81:** The power to interpret these Rules is vested in the Arbitration Commission. | |
| **12. Confidentiality** | | | | | |
| **Appendix I. Article 6. Confidentiality**<br>The work of the Court is of a confidential character which must be respected by everyone who participates in that work in whatever capacity. The Court lays down the rules | **Article 30: Confidentiality.**<br>30.1 Unless the parties expressly agree in writing to the contrary, the parties undertake as a general principle to keep confidential all awards in their arbitration, together with all materials | **27.4.** An award may be made public only with the consent of all parties or as required by law.<br>**Confidentiality: Article 34**<br>Confidential information disclosed during the proceedings by the parties | **Article 73: Confidentiality of the Existence of the Arbitration**<br>(a) Except to the extent necessary in connection with a court challenge to the arbitration or an action for enforcement of an award, no infor- | **Article 37:** When a case is heard in closed session, the parties, their attorneys, witnesses, arbitrators, experts consulted by the Arbitration Tribunal, appraisers appointed by the Arbitration Tribunal and the relevant | **Article 9: Procedures of the SCC Institute**<br>The SCC Institute shall maintain the confidentiality of the arbitration and shall deal with the arbitration in an impartial, practical and expeditious |

| ICC | LCIA | AAA | WIPO | CIETAC | STOCKHOLM |
|---|---|---|---|---|---|
| regarding the persons who can attend the meetings of the Court and its Committees and who are entitled to have access to the material submitted to the Court and its Secretariat.<br>**Appendix II – Internal Rules of the International Court of Arbitration.**<br>**Confidential character of the work of the International Court of Arbitration**<br>1. The sessions of the Court, whether international or plenary or those of a Committee of the Court, are open only to its members and to the Secretariat.<br>2. However, in exceptional circumstances the Chairman of the Court may invite the other persons to attend. Such persons must respect the confidential character of the work of the Court.<br>3. The documents submitted to the Court or drawn up by it in the course of its proceedings are communicated only to the members of the Court and to the Secretariat and to persons authorised by the Chairman to attend Court sessions.<br>4. The Chairman or the Secretary-General of the Court may authorise researchers undertaking work of a scientific nature on international trade law to acquaint themselves with awards and other documents of general interest, with the exception of memoranda, notes, statements and documents remitted by the parties within the framework of arbitration proceedings.<br>5. Such authorisation shall not be given unless the beneficiary has undertaken to respect the confidential character of the documents made available and to refrain from any publication in their respect without having previously submitted the text for approval to the Secretary-General of the Court.<br>6. The Secretariat will in each case submitted to arbitration under the | in the proceedings created for the purpose of the arbitration and all other documents produced by another party in the proceedings not otherwise in the public domain - save and to the extent that disclosure may be required of a party by legal duty, to protect or pursue a legal right or to enforce or challenge an award in bona fide legal proceedings before a state court or other judicial authority.<br>**30.2** The deliberations of the Arbitral Tribunal are likewise confidential to its members, save and to the extent that disclosure of an arbitrator's refusal to participate in the arbitration is required of the other members of the Arbitral Tribunal under Articles 10, 12 and 26.<br>**30.3** The LCIA Court does not publish any award or any part of an award without the prior written consent of all parties and the Arbitral Tribunal. | or by witnesses shall not be divulged by an arbitrator or by the administrator. Unless otherwise agreed by the parties, or required by applicable law, the members of the tribunal and the administrator shall keep confidential all matters relating to the arbitration or the award. | mation concerning the existence of an arbitration may be unilaterally disclosed by a party to any third party unless it is required to do so by law or by a competent regulatory body, and then only<br>(i) by disclosing no more than what is legally required, and<br>(ii) by furnishing to the Tribunal and to the other party, if the disclosure takes place during the arbitration, or to the other party alone, if the disclosure takes place after the termination of the arbitration, details of the disclosure and an explanation of the reason for it.<br>(b) Notwithstanding paragraph (a), a party may disclose to a third party the names of the parties to the arbitration and the relief requested for the purpose of satisfying any obligation of good faith or candor owed to that third party.<br>**Article 74: Confidentiality of Disclosures Made During the Arbitration**<br>(a) In addition to any specific measures that may be available under Article 52, any documentary or other evidence given by a party or a witness in the arbitration shall be treated as confidential and, to the extent that such evidence describes information that is not in the public domain, shall not be used or disclosed to any third party by a party whose access to that information arises exclusively as a result of its participation in the arbitration for any purpose without the consent of the parties or order of a court having jurisdiction.<br>(b) For the purposes of this Article, a witness called by a party shall not be considered to be a third party. To the extent that a witness is given access to evidence or other information obtained in the arbitration in order to prepare the witness's testimony, the party calling such witness shall be responsible for the mainte- | staff-members of the secretariat of the Arbitration Commission shall not disclose to outsiders the substantive or procedural matters of the case. | manner. |

| ICC | LCIA | AAA | WIPO | CIETAC | STOCKHOLM |
|---|---|---|---|---|---|
| Rules of Arbitration of the International Chamber of Commerce ("the ICC Rules") retain in the archives of the Court all awards, terms of reference, decisions of the Court as well as copies of the pertinent correspondence of the Secretariat.<br>7. Any documents, communications or correspondence submitted by the parties or the arbitrators may be destroyed unless a party or an arbitrator requests in writing within a period fixed by the Secretariat the return of such documents. All related costs and expenses shall be borne by such party or arbitrator. | | | nance by the witness of the same degree of confidentiality as that required of the party.<br>**Article 75: Confidentiality of the Award**<br>The award shall be treated as confidential by the parties and may only be disclosed to a third party if and to the extent that<br>(i) the parties consent, or<br>(ii) it falls into the public domain as a result of an action before a national court or other competent authority, or<br>(iii) it must be disclosed in order to comply with a legal requirement imposed on a party or in order to establish or protect a party's legal rights against a third party.<br>**Article 76: Maintenance of Confidentiality by the Center and Arbitrator**<br>(a) Unless the parties agree otherwise, the Center and the arbitrator shall maintain the confidentiality of the arbitration, the award and, to the extent that they describe information that is not in the public domain, any documentary or other evidence disclosed during the arbitration, except to the extent necessary in connection with a court action relating to the award, or as otherwise required by law.<br>(b) Notwithstanding paragraph (a), the Center may include information concerning the arbitration in any aggregate statistical data that it publishes concerning its activities, provided that such information does not enable the parties or the particular circumstances of the dispute to be identified. | | |
| **13. Variation of rules** | | | | | |
| **Appendix I. Article 7: Modification of the Rules of Arbitration**<br>Any proposals of the Court for a modification of the Rules are laid before the Commission on Inter- | | | | | |

| ICC | LCIA | AAA | WIPO | CIETAC | STOCKHOLM |
|---|---|---|---|---|---|
| national Arbitration before submission to the Executive Board and the Council of the ICC for approval. | | | | | |
| **14. Filing awards** | | | | | |
| | | | | | **Article 38: Filing of Awards**<br>An Arbitral Tribunal shall, after the close of the proceedings, submit to the SCC Institute one copy of every Award and written order issued in the case, as well as of all recorded minutes therein. The above mentioned documents shall be kept on file by the SCC Institute. |
| **15. Restriction of eligibility of institution officials to participate in arbitration** | | | | | |
| **Appendix II. Article 2: Participation of members of the International Court of Arbitration in ICC arbitration**<br>1. The Chairman and the members of the Secretariat of the Court may not act as arbitrators or as counsel in cases submitted to ICC arbitration.<br>2. The Court shall not appoint Vice-Chairmen or members of the Court as arbitration. They may, however, be proposed for such duties by one or more of the parties or pursuant to any other procedure agreed upon by the parties, subject to confirmation by the Court.<br>3. When the Chairman, a Vice-Chairman or a member of the Court or of the Secretariat is involved, in any capacity whatsoever, in proceedings pending before the Court, such person must inform the Secretary-General of the Court upon becoming aware of such involvement.<br>4. Such person must refrain from participating in the discussions or in the decisions of the Court concerning the proceedings and must be absent from the courtroom whenever the matter is considered.<br>5. Such person will not receive any material documentation or information pertaining to such proceedings. | | | | | |

APPENDIX 1

# Arbitration Institutions

### Argentina

Argentina National Office of the ICC
c/o Camara Argentina de Comercio
Avenida Leandro N Alem 36
1003 - Buenos Aires
Tel: (54-1) 331 8051/343 9423
Fax: (54-1) 331 8055

### Australia

The Institute of Arbitrators and Mediators Australia
22 William Street Level 1
Melbourne
Victoria 3000
Australia
Tel: (03) 9629 6799
Fax: (03) 9629 5250

Australian Centre for International Commercial Arbitration
ACN 006 404 664
Level 1 22 William Street
Melbourne
Victoria 3000
Australia
Tel: (+61 3) 9629 6799
Fax: (+61 3) 9629 5250

Australia National Office of the ICC
P O Box E 188
Kingston
Canberra ACT 2604
Tel: (61-6) 295 1961
Fax: (61-6) 295 0170

The Australian Chamber of Commerce and Industry
(ACCI)
Commerce House
Level 3 24 Brisbane Avenue
Sydney
Tel: (612) 6273 2311
Fax: (612) 6273 3286

### Austria

Aussenwirtschaftsorganisation der Wirtschaftkammer
Osterreich
(Austria National office of ICC)
Wiedner Haupstrasse 63
Postfach 150
A-1045 Wien
Fax: 43 1502 063702

Federal Economic Chamber, Vienna
Wiedner Haupstrasse 63 (Schaum)
P O B 319
A-1045 Vienna
Tel: (43-1) 50105 4397
Fax: (43-1) 5020 6216

### Bangaladesh

Bangladesh National Office of the ICC
Dhaka Chamber Building (Ground Floor)
65-66 Motijheel Commercial Area
GPO Box 858 - Dhaka 1000
Tel: (880-2) 955 5239/7478
Fax: (880-2) 973 214500

### Bahrain

GCC Commercial Arbitration Centre
P O Box 2338 Manama
Bahrain
Tel: 973-214800/211827
Fax: 973-214500

### Belgium

Belgium National Office of the ICC
c/o FEB 8 rue des Sols
B-1000
Brussels
Tel: (32-2) 515 08 35
Fax: (32-2) 515 08 75

Centre Belge Pour L'Etude et la Pratique de L'Arbitrage
National et International (CEPANI)
rue des Sols
8-B 1000
Brussels
Tel: (32-2) 515 0835
Fax: (32-2) 515 0875

Institut vor Arbitrage - Institut D'Arbitrage
(Belgian Institute for Arbitration)
Dreve Ste Anne 68b
B-1020 Brussels
Tel: 32 0 70 233 6209
Fax: 32 0 70 233 62024

### Brazil

Arbitration Commission of the Canadian Chamber
of Commerce for Brazil
Avenida Brigadeiro Faria Lime
1058-4 andar
01452-000 Sau Paulo - SP
Tel: (55-11) 815-6420/8226
Fax: (55-11) 814-8226

### Bulgaria

Bulgarian Chamber of Commerce and Industry
42 Parchevich Street
1000 Sofia
Bulgaria
Tel: 359 2 987 2631
Fax: 359 2 987 3209

Court of Arbitration at the Bulgarian Chamber of Commerce and Industry
42 Parchevich Street
1000 Sofia
Bulgaria
Tel: 359 2 987 2631
Fax: 349 2 987 3209

**Burkina Faso**

Burkina Faso National Office of the ICC
c/o Chambre de Commerce d'Industrie et d'Artisanat du Burkina Faso
Bolte Postale 502 - Ouagadougou 01
Tel: (226) 30 61 14 / 15 or 31 1266 / 67
Fax: (226) 30 61 16

**Canada**

British Columbia International Commercial Arbitration Centre
P O Box 27 Suite 1140
1090 West Georgia Street
Vancouver BC
Canada V6E 3V7
Tel: (604) 684 2821
Fax: (604) 684 2825

Canada National Office of the ICC
55 Metcalfe Street
Suite 1160
Ottawa
Ontario K1P 6N4
Tel: (1-613) 230 54 62
Fax: (1-613) 230 7087

Quebec National and International Commercial Arbitration Centre
295 Boulevard Charest Est
Bureau 090
Quebec
G1K 3G8
Tel: (418) 649 1374
Fax: (418) 649 0845

**Chile**

Chile National Office of the ICC
Camara Nacional de Comercio de Chile
Santa Lucia no. 302
Pisa 5
Santiago
Tel: (56-2) 639 6639
Fax: (56-2) 639 7859

**China**

China National Office of the ICC
c/o China Chamber of International Commerce (CCOIC)
1 Fu Xing Men Wai Street
Beijing 100860
Tel: (86-10) 6851 3344
Fax: (86-10) 6857 3554 / 7851 1370

**Colombia**

Colombia National office of the ICC
c/o Camara de Comercio de Bogota
Santafe de Bogota
Tel: (57-1) 284 82 68 / 281 91 64
Fax: (57-1) 284 77 35

**Croatia**

Croatian Chamber of Commerce
Rooseveltov trg 2
41000 Zagreb
Croatia
Tel: ( 385) 1-453422
Fax: (385) 1-448618

**Cyprus**

Cyprus National office of the ICC
c/o Cyprus Chamber of Commerce and Industry
(Chamber Building)
38 Grivas Dhigenis Avenue
3 Deligiorgis Street
P O Box 1455
Nicosia CY 1509
Tel: (357-2) 44 95 00 / 46 23 12
Fax: (357-2) 44 90 48 / 45 86 30

**Czech Republic**

Arbitration Court of the Economic Chamber of the Czech Republic
Diouda 13
11000 Prague

**Denmark**

Danish Institute of Arbitration
Frederiksborggade 1, 3
DK-1360 Copenhagen K
Tel: (+45) 33 13 37 00
Fax: (+45) 33 13 04 03

Denmark National Office of the ICC
Borsen
DK-1217 Kobenhavn K
Tel: (45-33) 95 05 99
Fax: (45-33) 15 22 66

**Ecuador**

Ecuador National Office of the ICC
Avenida Olmedo 414 y Boyaca
Piso 1
Casilla P O Box 09 001 7515 Guayaquil
Tel: (593-4) 32 59 64 / 32 50 66
Fax: (593-4) 32 59 66

**Egypt**

Cairo Regional Centre for International Commercial Arbitration
Al-Saleh Ayoub St
Zamalek
Cairo
Tel: (202) 340 1333 / 340 1335 / 340 1337 / 342 3691 / 342 3693
Fax: (202) 340 1336

Egypt National Office of the ICC
c/o Federation of Egyptian Chambers of Commerce
4 Midan El Falaki (Bab El Louk)
Cairo
Tel: (20-2) 355 11 64 / 354 29 43
Fax: (20-2) 355 70 40

**Finland**

Board of Arbitration of the Central Chamber of Commerce of Finland
Fabianinkatu 14
P O Box 1000
00100 Helsinki
Tel: 358 0 650 133
Fax: 358 0 650 303

Finland National Office of the ICC
Aleksanterinkatu 17
FIN 00100 Helsinki
Tel: (358-0) 660 459 (standard)
Fax: (358-9) 6969 6647

**France**

Association Francaise d'Arbitrage
8 Avenue Bertie Albrecht
75008 Paris
Tel: (33-1) 53 77 24 31
Fax: (33-1) 45 63 93 92

France National Office of the ICC
9 Boulevard Malesherbes
75008 Paris
Tel: (33-1) 42 65 12 66
Fax: (33-1) 49 24 06 39

ICC International Court of Arbitration
38 Cours Albert 1er
75008 Paris
France
Tel: 39 1 4953 2829
Fax: 39 1 4953 2933
www.iccwbo.org
ab@iccwbo.org

Cabinet International de Mediation Economique
33 rue Galilee
75111 Paris
Tel: 33 1 34 80 17 18
Fax: 33 1 34 80 17 64

Centre de Mediation et d'Arbitrage de Paris (CMAP)
7 rue Balzac
Paris 75008
Tel: 33 1 42 89 74 98
Fax: 33 1 42 89 74 99

Centre National de la Meditation
127 rue Notre Dame des Champs
75006 Paris
Tel: 33 1 44 09 03 53

**Germany**

German Institution of Arbitration
(Deutsche Institution fuer Schiedsgerichtsbarkeit)
Schedestrabe 13
53113 Bonn
Tel: (49) 228/210023-24
Fax: (49) 228/212275

DIS-Geschaftsstelle Berlin
Fasanenstr 85
10623 Berlin
Tel: (49) 30 / 31510-589
Fax: (49) 30/31510-120

DIS-Geschaftsstelle Munchen
Max-Joseph Str 2
80333 Munchen
Tel: (49) 89/5116-258
Fax: (49) 89/5116-8258

Germany National Office of the ICC
Duetsche Gruppe der Internationalen Handelskammer
Mittelstrasse 12-14
D-506 72 Koln
Postfach 10 08 26
D-50448 Koln
Tel: (49-221) 257 5571
Fax: (49-221) 257 5593

**Greece**

Greece National Office of the ICC
27 Kaningos Street
Athens 10683
Tel: (30 1) 38 10 879
Fax: (30 1) 38 31 189

**Hong Kong**

Hong Kong International Arbitration Centre
38th Floor 2 Exchange Square
8 Connaught Place
Tel: 852 2525 2381
Fax: 852 2524 2171

**Hungary**

Court of Arbitration Attached to the Hungarian Chamber of Commerce and Industry
Kossuth Lajos ter
6-8 H 1055 Budapest
Tel: (36-1) 153 24 25
Fax: (36-1) 153 34 96

Hungary National Office of the ICC
Kossuth Lajos ter
6-8 H 1055 Budapest
Tel: (36-1) 132 1195
Fax: (36-1) 153 34 96

**Iceland**

Iceland National Office of the ICC
House of Commerce
103 Reykjavik
Tel: (354) 588 6666
Fax: (354) 568 6564

**India**

Bengal National Chamber of Commerce and Industry
23 R N Mukherjee Road
Calcutta 700 001
West Bengal
Tel: 91 33 248 2951
Fax: 91 33 248 7058 / 7668

Indian Council of Arbitration
Federation House
Tangsen Marg
New Delhi 11001
Tel: 91 11 3738 760 / 91 11 331 9251
Fax: 91 11 3320 714

**Indonesia**

Indonesia National Office of the ICC
c/o P T Prima Comexindo
BR1 11 Building 24th Floor
JL Jend Sudirman 44-46
Jakarta 10210
Tel: (62-21) 5707434 / 5713415
Fax: (62-21) 5719008 / 5719009

**Iran**

Iran National Office of the ICC
254 Taleghani Avenue
Tehran 15814
Tel: (98-21) 836 127
Fax: (98-21) 838 330

**Ireland**

Ireland National Office of the ICC
22 Merrion Square
Dublin 2
Tel: (353-1) 661 2888
Fax: (353-1) 661 2811

**Israel**

Israel National Office of the ICC
84 Hahashmonaim Street
P O Box 20027
Tel Aviv 61200
Tel: (972-3) 673 10 48 / 10 49
Fax: (972-3) 562 32 74

**Italy**

Chamber of Arbitration of Milan (Chamber of National & International Arbitration in Milan)
Palazzo Mezzanotte
Piazza Affari
6-20123 Milan
Tel: 39 2 8515 4536
Fax: 39 2 8515 4384

Associazione Italiana per L'Arbitrato
Via XX Settembre 5
00187 Rome
Tel: (39 6) 488 2518 / 488 2438 / 474 3594
Fax: (39 6) 488 2677

Italy National Office of the ICC
Via XX Settembre No. 5
IT 00187 Rome
Tel: (39 6) 48 82 438 / 48 82 575
Fax: (39 6) 48 82 6 77

Swiss Chamber of Commerce in Italy (CCSI)
Via Palestro 2
20121 Milan
Tel: (39 2) 7600 3606
Fax: (39 2) 781 084

**Japan**

Japan National office of the ICC
P O Box 7029
Amman 111 18
Tel: (962-6) 566 5942
Fax: (962-6) 568 5997

Japan Commercial Arbitration Association
Taishoseimei Hibiya Building
9-1 Yurakucho 1 Chome
Chiyoda-ku
Tokyo
Tel: (813) 3287 3061
Fax: (813) 3287 3064

**Jordan**

Jordan National Office of the ICC
P O Box 7029
Amman 111 18
Tel: (962-6) 566 5942
Fax: (962-6) 568 5997

**Korea**

Korean Commercial Arbitration Board
World Trade Centre 43rd Floor
159 Samsung-Dong
Kangnam-Ku
Seoul 135 729
Tel: (82 2) 551 2000
Fax: (822) 551 2020

Korea National Office of the IC
45 Namdaemun-ro 4-ga
Chung-gu
(CPO Box 25)
Seoul
Tel: (82-2) 316 3536/8
Fax: (82-2) 757 9475

**Kuwait**

Kuwait National Office of the ICC
Ali Al-Salem Street

KCCI Building
P O Box 775 Safat
Kuwait 13008
Tel: (241) 7285/241 6391
Fax: (965) 240 4110 / 243 3858

**Lebanon**

Lebanon National Office of the ICC
Georges Haimari Street
Elias Abdel-Nour Building
Achrafieh - Sassine
P O Box 11 - 1801 Beirut
Tel: (961-1) 200 437 / 438
Fax: (961-1) 321 220

**Lithuania**

Lithuania National Office of the ICC
c/o Lithuanian Chamber of Commerce and Industry Association
18 V. Kudirkos Street
2600 Vilnius
Tel: (370-2) 222 630
Fax: (370-2) 222 621

**Luxembourg**

Luxembourg National Office of the ICC
7 rue Alcide de Gasperi
L-2981 Luxembourg
Tel: (352) 42 39 39 303
Fax: (352) 43 83 26

**Malaysia**

Regional Centre for Arbitration Kuala Lumpur
12 Jalan Conlay
50450 Kuala Lumpur
Tel: (603) 2420103 and 2420702
Fax: (603) 2424513

**Mexico**

Arbitraje Corporativo SC
Privada Topacio 3505-302
Col Residencial Esmeralda
Puebla
Tel: 22 31 48 20
Fax: 22 49 54 10

Commission to Protect Mexico's Foreign Trade (COMPROMEX)
Camino a Santa Teresa No. 1679
70 Piso
Colonia Jardines del Pedregal
01900 DF

Mexico City National Chamber of Commerce
Paseo de la Reforma No. 42
Col Centro
Delagacion Cuauhtemoc
06048 Mexico DF
Tel: (52-5) 669 22 09 /26 09
Fax: (52-5) 669 2928

**Morocco**

Morocco National Office of the ICC
201 Boulevard de Bordeaux
Apartement 505 (5e etage)
Tel: (212-2) 2251 11 / 47 39 003
Fax: (212-2) 2251 19

**Nepal**

Nepal Council of Arbitration
Ramshah Path
Kathmandu
GPO Box 4865
Tel: 215725

**Netherlands**

Netherlands Arbitration Institue
P O Box 22105
3003 DC Rotterdam
Tel: (+31) (10) 400 82 00
Fax: (+31) (10) 400 83 33

T M C Asser Institute
P O Box 30461
2500 GL The Hague
Tel: 31 70 342 0300
Fax: 31 70 342 0359

Netherlands National Office of the ICC
Bezuidenhoutseweg 12
PO Box 95309
2509-AV Den Haag
Te: (31-70) 383 6646
Fax: (31-70) 381 9563

**Norway**

Arbitration and Dispute Resolution Institute of the Oslo Chamber of Commerce
P O Box 2874 Solli
N-0230 Oslo
Tel: (47 22) 55 74 00
Fax: (47 22) 55 89 53

Norway National Office of the ICC
Drammensvn 30
P O Box 2483
Solli - 0202 Oslo
Tel: (47) 22 54 17 00
Fax: (47) 22 56 17 00

**Pakistan**

Lahore Chamber of Commerce and Industry
11 Shara-e-Aiwan-e-Tijarat
PO Box 597
54000 Lahore
Pakistan
Tel: 92-42-630 5538
Fax: 92-42-636 8854
library@chmbrs.lcci.org.pk

**Peru**

Peru National Office of the ICC
Avenida Gregorio Escobedo 396
Oficina 301 - Lima 11
Tel: (51-1) 463 4263
Fax: (51-1) 463 9629

**Philippines**

Philippine Dispute Centre Inc of the Philippine Chamber of Commerce and Industry (PDDRCI)
G/F /East Wing Secretariat Building
Philippine International Convention Centre (PICC)
CCP Complex
Roxas Boulevard
Pasay City
Tel: (63-2) 833 8591 / 92 / 95
Fax: (63-2) 833 88 95 or (63-2) 551 02 55

**Poland**

Court of Arbitration at the Polish Chamber of Foreign Trade
Trebacka Str 4
00 074 Warsaw
Tel: (48 22) 27 47 54
Fax: (48 22) 27 47 54

**Portugal**

Commercial Arbitration Centre of the Portuguese Chamber of Commerce and Industry
Rua das Portas de Sto Antao 89
1194 Lisboa Codex
Tel: (351-1) 322 4053
Fax: (351-1) 322 4052

Portugal National Office of the ICC
Rua Portas de Santo Antao 90
1194 Lisboa Codex
Tel: (351-1) 357 2561
Fax: (351-1) 357 2580

**Russia**

International Commercial Arbitration Court at the Chamber of Commerce and Industry of the Russian Federation
6 Ilynka Street
Moscow 103012
Tel: +7 (095) 929 0193
Fax: +7 (095) 929 0334

St Petersburg International Commercial Arbitration Court
Admiralteiski pr 12
St Petersburg 190000
Russian Federation
Tel: +7 (812) 219 1233
Fax: +7 (812) 219 1484

**Saudi Arabia**

Saudi Arabia National Office of the ICC
c/o Council of Saudi Chambers of Commerce and Industry
PO Box 16683
Riyadh 11474
Tel: (966-1) 405 32 00 # 148
Fax: (966-1) 402 47 47

**Singapore**

Singapore National Office of the ICC
Chamber of Commerce Building
47 Hill Street
No. 03-01 Chinese
Singapore 179365
Tel: (65) 338 97 61
Fax: (65) 229 56 20
Singapore International Arbitration Centre
1 Coleman Street #05-08
The Adelphi
Singapore 179803
Tel: (65) 334 1277
Fax: (65) 334 2942

**South Africa**

South Africa National Office of the ICC
3rd Floor JCC House
Cnr Empire and Owl Streets Milpark
P O Box 91267
Auckland Park
Johannesburg 2006
Tel: (27-11) 483 25 24
Fax: (27-11) 726 13 44

Association of Arbitrators (Southern Africa)
146 Arbitration House
4 Protea Place
Benmore 2010
Tel: (27 11) 320 0591/2
Fax: (27 11) 320 0593

**South Korea**

*See* address for Korean Commercial Arbitration Board under **Korea**

**Spain**

Spain National Office of the ICC
Avinguda Diagonal
452 454
08006 Barcelona
Tel: (34-3) 416 93 00
Fax: (34-3) 416 93 01

**Sri Lanka**

Sri Lanka National Office of the ICC
1st Floor CNAPT Centre No. 51
Sir Marcus Fernando Mawatha
P O Box 1733
Colombo 7
Tel: (94-1) 69 12 90
Fax: (94-1) 69 12 90

**Sweden**

Arbitration Institute of the Stockholm Chamber of Commerce
PO Box 160 50

S-103 121 Stockholm
Tel: +46 8 613 1800
Fax: + 46 8 7230 176

Sweden National Office of the ICC
Vastra Tradgardsgatan 9
PO Box 16050
S-103 21 Stockholm
Tel: (46-8) 440 8920
Fax: (46-8) 411 31 15

**Switzerland**

Chamber of Commerce and Industry of Geneva (CCIG)
4 bd du Theatre
1204 Geneva
Tel: +41 22 / 819 91 11
Fax: +41 22 / 819 91 00

Switzerland National Office of the ICC
CCI/ICC Chambre de Commerce
Internationale - Internationale
Handelskammer c/op Vorort
Mainaustrasse 49
Case Postale 690 CH 8034 Zurich
Tel: (41-1) 382 23 40
Fax: (41-1) 382 23 32

World Intellectual Property Organisation
Arbitration & Mediation Centre
34 Chenin des Colombettes
PO Box 18
1211 Geneva 20
Switzerland

Zurich Chamber of Commerce
Bleicherweg 5
Postfach 4031
8022 Zurich
Tel: (41-1) 211 0742
Fax: (41-1) 211 7615

ASA Secretariat (ASA)
Dr Rainer Gueg
St Allan-Graben 8
P O Box 1548
CH 4001 Basle

**Syria**

Syria National Office of the ICC
Federation of Syrian Chambers of Commerce
Moosa Bin Nusair Street
P O Box 2908 Damascus
Tel: (963-11) 333 59 20
Fax: (963-11) 333 11 27

**Taiwan**

Chinese Taipei Business Council of the ICC
13th Floor
390 Fu Hsing South Road
Section 1
Taipei 10640
Taiwan
Tel: (886-2) 707 01 11
Fax: (886-2) 701 76 01

Commercial Arbitration Association of the Republic of China
Suite 803 8th Floor Lotus Building
136 Jen-ai Road
Sec 3
Taipei
Taiwan
ROC
Tel: (886-2) 270 78672
Fax: (886-2) 270 78462

**Thailand**

Thai Arbitration Institute Ministry of Justice
Arbitration Office
Ministry of Justice
Criminal Court Building 5th Floor
Ratchadaphisake Road
Bangkok 10900
Tel: (66 2) 541 2298 / 541 2299 / 541 2284
Fax: (66 2) 541 2298 / 541 2299

**Togo**

Togo National Office of the ICC
c/o Chambre de Commerce d'Agriculture et d'Industrie de Togo
Angle av de la Presidence et
Av Georges Pompidou
BP 360 Lome
Tel: (228) 21 2o 65 / 21 7065
Fax: (228) 21 47 30

**Tunisia**

Tunisia National Office of the ICC
1 rue des Entrepreneurs - 100 Tunis
Tel: (216-1) 341 607 / 242 810
Fax: (216-1) 332 968

**Turkey**

Turkey National Office of the ICC
Ataturk Bulvari No. 149
06640 Bakanliklar
Ankara
Tel: (90-312) 417 87 33
Fax: (90-312) 417 1483

**United Kingdom**

London Court of International Arbitration
The International Dispute Resolution Centre
8 Breams Buildings
London EC4A 1HP
Tel: 020 7405 8008
http://www.lcia-arbitration.com

The Chartered Institute of Arbitrators
International Arbitration Centre
24 Angel Gate
City Road
London EC1V 2RS
Tel: +44 (020) 7837 4483
Fax: +44 (020) 7837 4185

United Kingdom National Office of the ICC
14-15 Belgrave Square
London SW1X 8PS
Tel: +44 (020) 7823 2811
Fax: +44 (020) 7235 5447

**United States**

American Arbitration Association
335 Madison Avenue
10th Floor, New York
New York 10017-4605
Tel: 001 212 716 5800
Fax: 001 212 716 5901

CPR Institute for Dispute Resolution
366 Madison Avenue
New York
NY 10017-3122
Tel: (1-212) 949 6490
Fax: (1-212) 949 8859

National Arbitration Forum
P O Box 50191 Minneapolis
MN 55405
Tel: 001 800 474 2371
Fax: 001 651 631 0802

United States National Office of the ICC
(United States Council for International Business)
1212 Avenue of the Americas
New York
NY 10036
Tel: (1-212) 354 4480
Fax: (1-212) 575 0327

United States National Office of the ICC
(United States Council for International Business, Washington)
1015 15th Street
NW Suite 975
Washington
DC 20005
Tel: (1-202) 371 1316
Fax: (1-202) 371 8249

International Centre for Settlement of Investment Disputes
1818 H Street, NW
Washington DC 20433
USA
Tel: 001 202 458 1534
Fax: 001 202 522 2615

**Uruguay**

Uruguay National Office of the ICC
c/o Camara Nacional de Comercio
Misiones 1400 .2 Casilla de Correo
1000 Montevideo
Tel: (598-2) 96 12 77
Fax: (598-2) 96 12 43

**Vietnam**

Vietnam International Arbitration Centre
33 Ba Trieu Street
Ha Noi
Tel: (84-4) 8250875, 8266230
Fax: (84-4) 8256446, 8244617

**Yugoslavia**

Yugoslav Chamber of Commerce and Industry
Foreign Trade Court of Arbitration
Terazije 23
11000 Belgrade
Yugoslavia
Tel: (+381) 11 3248 123; 3248 042
Fax: (+381) 11 3248 754; 3225 903

Yugoslavia National Office of the ICC
Knez Mihajlova
10-1100 Beograd
Tel: (381-11) 633 14
Fax: (381-11) 4238 754 / 3225 903

## SPECIALIST ARBITRATION ORGANISATIONS

**Marine**

- LMAA (London Maritime Arbitrators Association)
  Rodwell House
  100 Middlesex Street
  London E1 7HD
- Society of Maritime Arbitrators Inc, New York
  14 Wall Street
  Suite 8A15
  New York
  NY 10005-2101
  USA
- Chambre Arbitrale Maritime de Paris
- Miami Maritime Arbitration Council
- TAMARA: Transport and Maritime Arbitration – Rotterdam – Amsterdam
  P O Box 30025
  3001 DA Rotterdam
  The Netherlands
- The Association of Maritime Arbitrators of Canada
  801 Chemin St Louis
  Suite 160
  Quebec
  G1S ICI
  Canada
- Lloyds – Salvage Arbitrations

**Soft Commodities**

- Refined Sugar Association (RSA)
- Grain and Feed Trade Association (GAFTA)
  Gafta House
  6 Chapel Place
  Rivington Street
  London EC2A 3SH
  Tel: +44 (020) 7814 9666
  Arbitration@gafta.com
- FOSFA International
  (the international trade association supporting the world trade of oilseeds, oils, fats and edible groundnuts/peanuts.
  20 St Dunstan's Hill
  London EC3R 8NQ
  Tel: +44 (020) 7283 5511/2707
  Fax: +44 (020) 7663 1310
  E-mail: contact@fosfa.org

**Other commodities**

- Stock Exchange
- London Metal Exchange
  56 Leadenhall Street
  London EC3A 2DX
  Tel: +44 (020) 7264 5555
  Fax: +44 (020) 7680 0505
  info@lme.co.uk

**Insurance**

- ARIAS (UK)
  (the reinsurance and insurance arbitration society of the International Association for Insurance Law) (or AIDA from its French title Association Internationale de Droit des Assurances)
- In Sweden with effect from 1 April 1999 special "Insurance Arbitration Rules" are administered by the Stockholm Chamber.

APPENDIX 2

# Arbitration Clauses

The following are the currently recommended model arbitration clauses from each institution:

## 1. ICC

All disputes arising out of or in connection with the present contract shall be finally settled under the Rules of Arbitration of the International Chamber of Commerce by one or more arbitrators appointed in accordance with the said Rules.

## 2. LCIA

*Future disputes:*

For contracting parties who wish to have future disputes referred to arbitration under the LCIA Rules, the following clause is recommended. Words/spaces in square brackets should be deleted/completed as appropriate.

Any dispute arising out of or in connection with the contract including any question regarding its existence, validity or termination, shall be referred to and finally resolved by arbitration under the LCIA Rules, which Rules are deemed to be incorporated into this clause.

The number of arbitrators shall be [one/three].

The place of arbitration shall be used in the arbitral proceedings shall be [ ].

The language to be used in the arbitral proceedings shall be [ ].

The governing law of the contract shall be the substantive law of [ ].

*Existing disputes*

If a dispute has arisen, but there is no agreement between the parties to arbitrate, or if the parties wish to vary a dispute resolution clause to provide for LCIA arbitration, the following clause is recommended. Words/spaces in square brackets should be deleted/completed as appropriate.

A dispute having arisen between the parties concerning [ ], the parties hereby agree that the dispute shall be referred to and finally resolved by arbitration under the LCIA Rules.

The number of arbitrators shall be [one/three].

The place of arbitration shall be [City and/or Country].

The language to be used in the arbitral proceedings shall be [ ].

The governing law of the contract is/shall be the substantive law of [ ].

The arbitral tribunal may hold hearings, meetings and deliberations at any convenient geographical place in its discretion, and if elsewhere than the seat of the arbitration, the arbitration shall be treated as an arbitration conducted at the seat of the arbitration and any award as an award made at the seat of an arbitration for all purposes.

## 3. AAA

Any controversy or claim arising out of or relating to this contract shall be determined by arbitration in accordance with the International Arbitration Rules of the American Arbitration Association.

The parties may wish to consider adding:

A: The number of arbitrators shall be (one or three);

B. The place of arbitration shall be (city and/or country), or

C. The language(s) of the arbitration shall be [ ].

## 4. WIPO

"Any dispute, controversy or claim arising under, out of or relating to this contract and any subsequent amendments of this contract, including, without iimitation, its formation, validity, binding effect, interpretation, performance, breach or termination, as well as non-contractual claims, shall be referred to and finally determined by arbitration in accordance with the WIPO Arbitration Rules. The arbitral tribunal shall consist of [three arbitrators][a sole arbitrator]. The place of arbitration shall be ... The language to be used in the arbitral proceedings shall be ... The dispute, controversy or claim shall be decided in accordance with the law of ..."

**Recommended WIPO Expedited Arbitration Clause**

"Any dispute, controversy or claim arising under, out of or relating to this contract and any subsequent amendments of this contract, including, without limitation, its formation, validity, binding effect, interpretation, performance, breach or termination, as well as non-contractual claims, shall be referred to and finally determined by arbitration in accordance with the WIPO Expedited Arbitration Rules. The place of arbitration shall be ... The language to be used in the arbitral proceedings shall be ... The dispute, controversy or claim shall be decided in accordance with the law of ..."

Recommended Clause for WIPO Mediation Followed, in the Absence of a Settlement, by Arbitration:
"Any dispute, controversy or claim arising under, out of or relating to this contract and any subsequent amendments of this contract, including, without limitation, its formation, validity, binding effect, interpretation, performance, breach or termination, as well as non-contractual claims, shall be submitted to mediation in accordance with the WIPO Mediation Rules. The place of mediation shall be ... The language to be used in the mediation shail be ... "
If, and to the extent that, any such dispute, controversy or claim has not been settled pursuant to the mediation within [60][90] days of the commencement of the mediation, it shall, upon the filing of a Request for Arbitration by either party, be referred to and finally determined by arbitration in accordance with the WIPO Arbitration Rules. Alternatively if, before the expiration of the said period of [60] [90] days, either party fails to participate or to continue to participate in the mediation, the dispute, controversy or claim shall, upon the filing of a Request for Arbitration by the other party, be referred to and finally determined by arbitration in accordance with the WIPO Arbitration Rules. The arbitral tribunal shall consist of [three arbitrators] [a sole arbitrator]. The place of arbitration shall be ... The language to be used in the arbitral proceedings shall be ... The dispute, controversy or claim referred to arbitration shall be decided in accordance with the law of ..."

*Existing disputes*

**Recommended Submission Agreement for WIPO Arbitration**
"We, the undersigned parties hereby agree that the following dispute shall be referred to and finally determined by arbitration in accordance with the WIPO Arbitration Rules:

[Brief description of the dispute]

"The arbitral tribunal shall consist of [three arbitrators] [a sole arbitrator]. The place of arbitration shall be ... The language to be used in the arbitral proceedings shall be ... The dispute shall be decided in accordance with the law of ...

Recommended Submission Agreement for WIPO Expedited Arbitration
"We, the undersigned parties, hereby agree that the following dispute shall be referred to and finally determined by arbitration in accordance with the WiPO Expedited Arbitration Rules:

[Brief description of the dispute]

"The place of arbitration shall be ... The language to be used in the arbitral proceedings shall be ... The dispute shall be decided in accordance with the iaw of ...

Recommended Submission Agreement for WIPO Mediation Followed, in the Absence of a Settlement, by Arbitration
"We, the undersigned parties, hereby agree to submit to mediation in accordance with the WIPO Mediation Rules the following dispute:

[Brief description of the dispute]

"The place of mediation shall be ... The language to be used in the mediation shall be... "
We further agree that, if, and to the extent that, the dispute has not been settled pursuant to the mediation within [60][90] days of the commencement of the mediation, it shall, upon the filing of a Request for Arbitration by either party, be referred to and finally determined by arbitration in accordance with the WIPO Arbitration Rules. Alternatively, if, before the expiration of the said period of [60] [90] days, either party fails to participate or to continue to participate in the mediation, the dispute shall, upon the filing of a Request for Arbitration by the other party, be referred to and finally determined by arbitration in accordance with the WIPO Arbitration Rules. The arbitral tribunal shall consist of [three arbitrators][a sole arbitrator]. The place of arbitration shall be ... The language to be used in the arbitral proceedings shall be ... The dispute referred to arbitration shall be decided in accordance with the law of ..."

## 5. CIETAC

"Any dispute arising from or in connection with this contract shall be submitted to China International Economic any Trade Arbitration Commission for arbitration which shall be conducted in accordance with the Commission's arbitration rules in effect at the time of applying for arbitration. The arbitral award is final and binding upon both parties."

## 6. STOCKHOLM

Any dispute, controversy or claim arising out of or in connection with this contract, or the breach, termination or invalidity thereof, shall be settled by arbitration in accordance with the Rules of the Arbitration Institute of the Stockholm Chamber of Commerce.

The parties are advised to make the following additions to the clause, as required:

The Arbitral tribunal shall be composed of [ ] arbitrators (a sole arbitrator).

The place of arbitration shall be [ ].

The language to be used in the arbitral proceedings shall be [ ].

This contract shall be governed by the law of [ ] (insert jurisdiction).

APPENDIX 3

# Institutions' Fees (current at August 1999)

How much is it going to cost? – is an enquiry raised at the outset of an arbitration. It would be better raised in advance of deciding what form of dispute resolution is to be negotiated. Most national courts impose a series of relatively modest flat fees for access to their services. Arbitration tribunals typically charge by the hour, and may require significant prefunding for the arbitration to start. Without access to this type of early cashflow nascent claims may be stifled at birth. Add to this the cost of legal fees (regularly recoverable at the completion of the arbitration by the successful party) and the financial requirements merely to get an arbitration up and running can be acute.

Take by way of example a claim for US$80million. The ICC would require a US$2,500 payment on filing of the request towards administrative expenses. That is non-refundable. In the early stages of the arbitration – leading up to the terms of reference being finalised – it may further require the administrative expense advance to be increased to US$75,800. It will also seek an advance on arbitrator's fees which will be a maximum of US$240,000 (per arbitrator – rising to a ceiling of US$720,000 for a tribunal of three), or US$795,800 in total.

This figure is there to be drawn against by the tribunal and any surplus is returned; equally in matters of extreme complexity there may be calls for a top-up. The rates the ICC pays its arbitrators are fixed subject to some flexibility and are in line with rates for other institutions so the ultimate cost should not be particularly different, save that the ICC imposes an additional tier of "terms of reference" which may increase (or possibly decrease if issues are agreed) the tribunal's work. The ICC court/administration probably assumes the greatest workload of all the institutions (e.g., the scrutiny of the award stage) which explains the higher provisions for administrative costs.

The "front loading" of fees by the ICC is a factor worth taking into account in selection of forum. Major international disputes are regularly adjudicated upon by the ICC with great expertise, but smaller organisations should consider carefully if they would be able to commence arbitration and pays its lawyers without hardship. Failure to pay fees will result in the arbitration ending. Whilst there is no bar to fresh proceedings (for example if cash flow improves) if a time bar is approaching and the original date is important, this will not assist.

The LCIA adopts a different approach. A non-refundable registration fee of £1,500 (about US$$2,400 – so similar to ICC) is payable upon registration of a Request for arbitration. Thereafter the time of the Registrar and his staff and expenses are charged at modest rates (currently £150/hour for the Registrar, who is a qualified solicitor, and £75 for the Secretariat). These tend not to be extensive as, with the formation of the tribunal, the LCIA's role is largely formal. The tribunal's fees are fixed and are presently £100–£200 an hour per member, or £800–£2,000 a working day. Exceptionally they may exceed these bands. The practice of the LCIA is to ask for a series of advances to cover the anticipated work going forward to successive stages of the arbitration so that the tribunal is always prefunded, but the cash flow requirement is spread over time. This may well result in the same ultimate "bill" as for the ICC. It is fair to say however – and this may equally be a factor of the type of claim submitted to the LCIA – that generally the ultimate costs are lower. As with the ICC failure to pay will result in the deemed withdrawal of a claim. Also in common with the ICC, a default of payment by one party may be remedied by payment from the other – unlike the ICC, however, if that happens "the party paying the substitute payment shall be entitled to recover that amount as a debt immediately due from the defaulting party – which, subject to collection procedures, may well ease cash flow.

AAA. The filing fees (fee payable to commence arbitration) are calculated on a sliding scale depending on the value of the claim. The scale stops at US$5,000,000 claims, for which a fee of $7,000 is payable. A claim for US$80,000,000 would be negotiated with AAA and would exceed US$7,000. Thereafter administrative fees are payable to the AAA based on the tasks it performs. These tend to be modest. Arbitration compensation is dealt with separately. There is liberty to call for advances, but for smaller claims, the arbitrator's fees will be calculated in the award and payable at that time and prior to the release of the award. They are likely to be in line with the rates of other institutions. Whilst appeals (save for irregularity, waiver provisions notwithstanding) are increasingly infrequent, the traditional lien on the award pending release can cause problems avoided by for example the ICC practice of ensuring prefunding. Typically in most jurisdictions, time for appealing is restricted and runs from the date of signing of the award, not the date of collection. If cash flow is restricted and there is a lapse of time before collection can be effected against full payment of arbitrator's fees (when the outcome will be unknown) the time available to settle papers for any appeal may be eroded or extinguished.

WIPO. WIPO's rules are clearly and comprehensively set out in the body of their arbitration rules (Articles 67, 68, 69 and 70) and in the Schedule of Fees (see below). A non-refundable registration fee must be paid on a shallow sliding scale (maximum US$3,000 for claims in excess of US$10,000,000). If not paid, the claim is deemed withdrawn. Shortly thereafter an administration fee is payable calculated, again, on a sliding scale, up to a maximum of US$35,000 which applies for all claims of more than about US$25,000,000. Then there is a formula for agreeing arbitrator's fees, against which figure there will be (joint) calls for deposits. If at the end of the arbitration these are, on the basis of the actual fees of the tribunal, inadequate or too much, a top-up will be requested of the balance refunded. The calculation is once again made on the basis of a tabulated sliding scale, and for a US$80m claim before a three-man tribunal the maximum would be US$2,146,250 making it the most expensive of all the institutions on the schedules, although by way of comparison, if the matter went to a sole arbitrator and the minimum figures were used the fee would be US$257,500. The WIPO calculation tables are very well set out and probably the easiest to use.

CIETAC. To understand if CIETAC is expensive or not, it is necessary to take a broad conversion figure for the Yuan, the Centre's fees being expressed in that currency. For illustrative purposes the rate of Yuan 8:US$1 is used. On this basis a registration fee of 10,000 Yuan (US$1,250) is charged on a non-refundable basis. There is a general liberty to call for additional costs and disbursements to be paid, and a fee, again calculated on a sliding scale, is also payable. There is no process to increase this fee should more than one arbitrator be used. For a US$80,000,000 claim the fee would be Yuan 3,610,000 (US$451,250) (US$80million treated as Yuan 640,000,000; Y660,000 payable for first Y50,000,000, and thereafter 0.5% of the balance over Y50,000,000).

Stockholm. The Stockholm Arbitration Institute performs all its currency calculations in Euros. Artificially, at the time of writing, parity has been assumed between US$ and Euro for the purposes of comparison.

The fees are set out in a series of sliding scale tables again calculated by reference to the size of the claim. A non-refundable registration fee of Euro 1,000 is payable for a US$80,000,000 (Euro 80,000,000) claim. An advance for arbitration fees would be a maximum (for a three-man tribunal) of US$/Euro 379,280 (chairman Euro 172,400, two others 60% each of this); the administration fee would be Euro 31,000. Expenses and other costs are payable. There is flexibility with the amounts if the circumstances of the case dictate. The registration fee is payable on commencement of arbitration. The other fees payable are also fixed by the SCC Institute (Article 39). The arbitrator's advance is payable after exchange of written submission (see Article 13) and is payable by the parties jointly (Article 14) or in default of one side, by the other, and in default by both the case will be dismissed.

Cost comparison: This table is based on the maximum fees chargeable under each institution's rules for a US$80m claim. As the general rule is, however, that fees are charged on an hourly basis, there may be substantial rebates given or top-ups sought from these figures on completion of the arbitration.

| | **Registration fee US$** | **Administration costs US$** | **Arbitration fees US$** | **Total US$** |
|---|---|---|---|---|
| ICC | 2,500<br>No refund | 73,300 | 720,000 | 795,800 |
| LCIA | 2,400 | hourly rate called for at intervals | hourly rate called for at intervals | |
| AAA | 7,000* | ditto | ditto | |
| WIPO | 3,000 | 35,000 | 2,146,250 | 2,181,250 |
| CIETAC | 1,250 | | 451,250 | 452,500 |
| Stockholm | 1,000 | 31,000 | 379,280 | 411,280 |

All institutions also provide for recovery of miscellaneous costs and disbursements and for payment of any fees incurred by the tribunal in the retention of an expert.

By way of final comparison, the cost of a London ad hoc or trade association arbitration is worth review. Whilst many professional arbitrators in London are members of trade associations and, in concluding a contyract with parties to arbitrate, incorporate those association's rules (e.g., LMAA – London Maritime Arbitrator's Association), in reality the association may have almost nothing to do with the arbitration, and will not levy a fee from the parties. The arbitrator will maintain a file and negotiate terms with the parties. He may or may not charge an appointment fee. If he does, it is unlikely to exceed £100. He will thereafter charge an hourly rate, likely to be in the region off £200 an hour – in line with the rates of the major institutions. There will be no administration fee for professional parties, especially those with smaller claims. Experience shows that with co-operation from all sides, and given the provisions of the 1996 Act exhorting, in effect, proportionality and cost effectiveness, this can produce a less costly award. Certainly the provisions of the 1996 Act provide an effective backdrop for functions which might otherwise be performed by an institution or included within their rules (e.g., appointment of a sole arbitrator if parties cannot agree, subpoenas, security for costs). Ad hoc appointments may not always be appropriate for the largest of disputes, but are always worth considering.

# Arbitration Costs and Fees

## 1. CURRENT ICC COSTS

**Article 1: Advance on Costs**

1. Each request to commence an arbitration pursuant to the Rules must be accompanied by an advance payment of US$2,500 on the administrative expenses. Such payment is non-refundable, and shall be credited to the Claimant's portion of the advance on costs,

2. The provisional advance on costs fixed by the Secretary General according to Article 30(1) of the Rules shall normally not exceed the amount obtained by adding together the administrative expenses, the minimum of the fees (as set out in the scale hereinafter) based upon the amount of the claim and the expected reimbursable expenses of the Arbitral Tribunal incurred with respect to the drafting of the Terms of Reference. If such amount is not quantified, the provisional advance shall be fixed at the discretion of the Secretary General. Payment by the Claimant shall be credited to its share of the advance on costs fixed by the Court.

3. In general, after the Terms of Reference have been signed or approved by the Court and the provisional timetable has been established, the Arbitral Tribunal shall, in accordance with Article 30(4) of the Rules, proceed only with respect to those claims or counterclaims in regard to which the whole of the advance on costs has been paid.

4. The advance on costs fixed by the Court according to Article 30(2) of the Rules comprises the fees of the arbitrator or arbitrators (hereinafter referred to as "arbitrator"), any arbitration-related expenses of the arbitrator and the administrative expenses.

5. Each party shall pay in cash its share of the total advance on costs. However, if its share exceeds an amount fixed from time to time by the Court, a party may post a bank guarantee for this additional amount.

6. A party that has already paid in full its share of the advance on costs fixed by the Court may, in accordance with Article 30(3) of the Rules, pay the unpaid portion of the advance owed by the defaulting party by posting a bank guarantee.

7. When the Court has fixed separate advances on costs pursuant to Article 30(2) of the Rules, the Secretariat shall invite each party to pay the amount of the advance corresponding to its respective claims.

8. When, as a result of the fixing of separate advances on costs, the separate advance fixed for the claim of either party exceeding one-half of such global advance as was previously fixed (in respect of the same claims and counterclaims that are the object of separate advances), a bank guarantee may be posted to cover any such excess amount. In the event that the amount of the separate advance is subsequently increased. at least one-half of the increase shall be paid in cash.

9. The Secretariat shall establish the terms governing all bank guarantees which the parties may post pursuant to the above provisions.

10. As provided in Article 30(2) of the Rules, the advance on costs may be subject to readjustment at any time during the arbitration, in particular to take into account fluctuations in the amount in dispute, changes in the amount of the estimated expenses of the arbitrator or the evolving difficulty or complexity of arbitration proceedings

11. Before any expertise ordered by the Arbitral Tribunal can be commenced, the parties, or one of them, shall pay an advance on costs fixed by the Arbitral Tribunal sufficient to cover the expected fees and expenses of the expert as determined by the Arbitral Tribunal. The Arbitral Tribunal shall be responsible for ensuring the payment by the parties of such fees and expenses.

**Article 2: Costs and Fees**

1. Subject to Article 31(2) of the Rules, the Court shall fix the fees of the arbitrator in accordance with the scale hereinafter set out or, where the sum in dispute is not stated, at its discretion.

2. In setting the Arbitrator's fees, the Court shall take into consideration the diligence of the arbitrator, the time spent, the rapidity of the proceedings, and the complexity of the dispute so as to arrive at a figure within the limits specified, or, in exceptional circumstances (Article 31(2) of the Rules), at a figure higher or lower than those limits.

3. When a case is submitted to more than one arbitrator, the Court, at its discretion, shall have the right to increase the total fees up to a maximum which shall normally not exceed three times the fee of one arbitrator.

4. The Arbitrator's fees and expenses shall be fixed exclusively by the Court as required by the Rules, Separate fee arrangements between the parties and the arbitrators are contrary to the Rules.

5. The Court shall fix the administrative expenses of each arbitration in accordance with the scale hereinafter set out, or, where the sum in dispute is not stated, at its discretion. In exceptional circumstances, the Court may fix the administrative expenses at a lower or higher figure than that which would result from the application of such scale, provided that such expenses shall normally not exceed the maximum amount of the scale. Further, the Court may require the payment of administrative expenses in addition to those provided in the scale of administrative expenses as a condition to holding an arbitration in abeyance at the request of the parties or of one of them with the acquiescence of the other.

6. If an arbitration terminates before the rendering of a final award, the Court shall fix the costs of the arbitration at its discretion, taking into account the stage attained by the arbitral proceedings and any other relevent circumstances.

7. In the case of an application under Article 29(2) of the Rules, the Court may fix an advance to cover additional fees and expenses of the Arbitral Tribunal and may subordinate the transmission of such application to the Arbitral Tribunal to the prior cash payment in full to the ICC of such advance. The Court shall fix at its discretion any possible fees of the arbitrator when approving the decision of the Arbitral Tribunal.

8. When an arbitration is preceded by attempted conciliatian, one-half of the administrative expenses paid for such conciliation shall be credited to the administrative expenses of the arbitration.

9. Amounts paid to the arbitrator do not include any possible value-added taxes (VAT) or other taxes or charges and imposts applicable to arbitrator's fees. Parties are expected to pay any such taxes or charges; however, the recovery of any such charges or taxes is a matter solely between the arbitrator and the parties.

**Article 3: Appointment of Arbitrators**

1. A registration fee normally not exceeding US $2,500 is payable by the requesting party in respect of each request made to the ICC to appoint an arbitrator for any arbitration not conducted under the Rules. No request for appointment of an arbitrator will be considered unless accompanied by the said fee, which is not recoverable and becomes the property of the ICC.

2. The said fee shall cover any additional services rendered by the ICC regarding the appointment, such as decisions on a challenge of an arbitrator and the appointment of a substitute arbitrator.

**Article 4: Scales of Administrative Expenses and of Arbitrator's Fees**

1. The Scales of Administrative Expenses and Arbitrator's Fees set out below shall be effective as of 1 January 1998 in respect of all arbitrations commenced on or after such date, irrespective of the version of the Rules applying to such.

2. To calculate the administrative expense and the arbitrator's fees, the amounts calculated for each successive slice of the sum in dispute must be added together, except that where the sum in dispute is over US$80 million. A flat amount of US$75,800 shall constitute the entirety of the administrative expenses.

## A. Administrative Expenses

| | Sum in dispute (in US Dollars) | | | Administrative expenses (*) |
|---|---|---|---|---|
| up to | 50 000 | | | $2 500 |
| from | 50 001 | to | 100 000 | 3.50% |
| from | 1 00 001 | to | 500 000 | 1.70% |
| from | 500 000 | to | 1 000 000 | 1.15% |
| from | 1 000 001 | to | 2 000 000 | .60% |
| from | 2 000 001 | to | 5 000 000 | .20% |
| from | 5 000 001 | to | 10 000 000 | .10% |
| from | 10 000 001 | to | 50 000 000 | .06% |
| from | 50 000 001 | to | 80 000 000 | .06% |
| from | 80 000 000 | | | $75 800 |

(*) For illustrative purposes only, the table on the following page indicates the resulting administrative expenses in US$ when the proper calculations have been made.

## B. Arbitrator's Fees

| | Sum in dispute (in US Dollars) | | | Fees (**) | |
|---|---|---|---|---|---|
| | | | | minimum | maximum |
| up to | 50 000 | | | $2 500 | 17.00% |
| from | 50 001 | to | 100 000 | 2.00% | 11.00% |
| from | 100 001 | to | 500 000 | 1.00% | 5.50% |
| from | 500 001 | to | 1 000 000 | 0.75% | 3.50% |
| from | 1 000 001 | to | 2 000 000 | 0.50% | 2.50% |
| from | 2 000 001 | to | 5 000 000 | 0.25% | 1.00% |
| from | 5 000 001 | to | 10 000 000 | .10% | 0.55% |
| from | 10 000 001 | to | 50 000 000 | .05% | 0.17% |
| from | 50 000 001 | to | 80 000 000 | .03% | 0.12% |
| from | 80 000 001 | to | 100 000 000 | .02% | 0.10% |
| from | 100 000 000 | | | .01% | 0.05% |

(*) For illustrative purposes only, the table on the following page indicates the resulting range of fees when the proper calculations have been made.

## Illustrative Calculation of Administrative Expenses and Arbitrator's Fees

| | Sum in dispute (US$) | A. Administrative Expenses (*) (US$) | | B. Arbitrator's Fees (**) (US$) minimum | | maximum | |
|---|---|---|---|---|---|---|---|
| Up to | 50,000 | 2,500 | | 2,500 | | 17.00% of amount in dispute | |
| from | 50,000 to 100,000 | 2,500 + 3.5% of amount over | 50,000 | 2,500 + 2.00% of amount over | 50,000 | 8,500 + 11.00% of amount over | 50,000 |
| from | 100,001 to 500,000 | 4,250 + 1.70% of amount over | 100,000 | 3,500 + 1.00% of amount over | 100,000 | 14,000 + 5.50% of amount over | 100,000 |
| from | 500,001 to 1,000,000 | 11,050 + 1.15% of amount over | 500,000 | 7,500 + 0.75% of amount over | 500,000 | 36,000 + 3.50% of amount over | 500,000 |
| from | 1,000,001 to 2,000,000 | 16,800 + 0.60% of amount over | 1,000,000 | 11,250 + 0.50% of amount over | 1,000,000 | 53,500 + 2.50% of amount over | 1,000,000 |
| from | 2,000,001 to 5,000,000 | 22,800 + 0.20% of amount over | 2,000,000 | 16,250 + 0.25% of amount over | 2,000,000 | 78,500 + 1.00% of amount over | 2,000,000 |
| from | 5,000,001 to 10,000,000 | 28,800 + 0.10% of amount over | 5,000,000 | 23,750 + 0.10% of amount over | 5,000,000 | 108,500 + 0.55% of amount over | 5,000,000 |
| from | 10,000,001 to 50,000,000 | 33,800 + 0.06% of amount over | 10,000,000 | 28,750 + 0.05% of amount over | 10,000,000 | 136,000 + 0.17% of amount over | 10,000,000 |
| from | 50,000,001 to 80,000,000 | 57,800 + 0.60% of amount over | 50,000,000 | 48,750 + 0.03% of amount over | 50,000,000 | 204,000 + 0.12% of amount over | 50,000,000 |
| from | 80,000,001 to 100,000,000 | 75,800 | | 57,750 + 0.02% | | 240,000 + 0.10% | 80,000,000 |
| over | 100,000,000 | 75,800 | | 61,750 + 0.01% of amount over | | 260,000 + 0.05% of amount over | 100,000,000 |

(*) (**) See preceding page.

## 2. LCIA SCHEDULE OF COSTS AND FEES

Effective 1 January 1998

***For arbitrations under the LCIA Rules; under UNCITRAL Rules when administered by the LCIA; when the LCIA acts as Appointing Authority only; and when the LCIA is appointed to decide challenges.***

**1. Administrative Charges under LCIA and UNCITRAL Rules**

1(a) Registration Fee (payable in advance with Request for Arbitration – non-refundable). **£1,500**

1(b) 5% applied to the fees of the Tribunal (excluding expenses). *

1(c) Time spent** by the Registrar and his/her deputy, and by the Secretariat of the LCIA in the administration of the arbitration.*

Registrar and his/her deputy **£150 per hour**
Secretariat **£75 per hour**

1(d) Expenses incurred by the Secretariat in connection with the arbitration (such as postage, telephone, facsimile, travel etc.), and additional arbitration support services, whether provided by the Secretariat from its own resources or otherwise.* **At applicable hourly rates or at cost**

*Items 1(b), 1(c),and 1(d) above, are payable on interim invoice; with the award, or as directed by the LCIA Court under Article 24.1 of the Rules.

** Minimum unit of time in all cases: 15 minutes.

**2. Request to Act as Appointing Authority only**

2(a) Appointment Fee (payable in advance with request - non-refundable). **£1,000**

2(b) As for 1(c) and 1(d)- above.

3. Request to Act in Deciding Challenges to Arbitrators in non-LCIA arbitrations.

3(a) As for 2(a) and 2(b), above; plus

3(b) Time spent by members of the LCIA Court in carrying out their functions in deciding the challenges.

**At hourly rates advised by members of the LCIA Court**

**4. Fees and Expenses of the Tribunal**

4(a) The Tribunal's fees will be calculated by reference to work done by its members in connection with the arbitration and will be charged at rates appropriate to the particular circumstances of the case, including its complexity and the special qualifications of the arbitrators. The Tribunal shall agree in writing upon fee rates conforming to this Schedule of Fees and Costs prior to its appointment by the LCIA Court. The rates will be advised by the Registrar to the parties at the time of the appointment of the Tribunal, but may be reviewed annually if the duration of the arbitration requires.

The fee rates shall be within the following bands: **£800 to £2,000**

**per normal working day**

***and***

**£100 to £250**

**per hour for periods less than**

**or in addition to a normal working day**

However, in exceptional cases, the rates may be higher or lower, provided that, in such cases, (a) the fees of the Tribunal shall be fixed by the LCIA Court on the recommendation of the Registrar, following consultations with the arbitrator(s), and (b) the fees shall be agreed expressly by all parties.

4(b) The Tribunal's fees may include a charge for time spent travelling.

4(c) The Tribunal's fees may also include a charge for time reserved but not used as a result of late postponement or cancellation, provided that the basis for such charge shall be advised in writing to, and approved by, the LCIA Court.

4(d) Expenses incurred by the Tribunal in connection with the arbitration will be charged at cost

4(e) In the event of the revocation of the appointment of any arbitrator, pursuant to the provisions of Article 10 of the LCIA Rules, the LCIA Court shall decide upon the amount of fees and expenses to be paid for the former arbitrator's services (if any) as it may consider appropriate in all the circumstances.

**5. Deposits**

5(a) The LCIA Court may direct the parties, in such proportions as it thinks appropriate, to make one or several interim or final payments on account of the costs of the arbitration. The LCIA Court may limit such payments to a sum sufficient to cover fees, expenses and costs for the next stage of the arbitration.

5(b) The Tribunal shall not proceed with the arbitration without ascertaining at all times from the Registrar or any deputy Registrar that the LCIA is in requisite funds

5(c) In the event that a party fails or refuses to provide any deposit as directed by the LCIA Court, the LCIA Court may direct the other party or parties to effect a substitute payment to allow the arbitration to proceed (subject to any award on costs). In such circumstances, the party paying the substitute payment shall be entitled to recover that amount as a debt immediately due from the defaulting party.

5(d) Failure by a claimant or counterclaiming party to provide promptly and in full the required deposit may be treated by the LCIA Court and the Arbitral Tribunal as a withdrawal of the claim or counterclaim respectively.

**6. Interest on Deposits**

Interest on sums deposited shall be credited to the benefit of the parties depositing them, at a rate applicable to the amount of the deposit, as advised by the LCIA's bank from time to time.

**7. Interim Payments**

7(a) When interim payments are required to cover the LCIA's administrative costs or the Tribunal's fees or expenses, including the fees or expenses of any expert appointed by the Tribunal, such payments rnay be made out of deposits held, upon the approval of the LCIA Court.

7(b) The LCIA may, in any event, submit interim invoices in respect of all current arbitrations, in March, June, September and December of each year, for payment direct by the parties or from funds held on deposit.

**8. Notes**

8(a) The costs of the arbitration (other than the legal or other costs incurred by the parties themselves) shall be determined by the LCIA Court in accordance with the Schedule of Fees and Costs.

8(b) The parties shall be jointly and severally liable to the Arbitral Tribunal and the LCIA for such arbitration costs, until all such costs have been paid in full.

8(c) The Tribunal's Award(s) shall not be transmitted to the parties unless and until the costs of the arbitration have been fully paid to date.

8(d) Value Added Tax will be added to all charges at the appropriate rate.

8(e) The LCIA's fees and expenses will be invoiced in sterling but may be paid in other convertible currencies at rates prevailing at the time of payment, provided that any transfer and/or currency exchange charges shall be borne by the payer.

8(f) The Tribunal's fees may be invoiced either in the currency of account between the Tribunal and the parties or in sterling; the Tribunal's expenses may be invoiced in the currency in which they were incurred, or in sterling.

8(g) The rates quoted in this Schedule may be reviewed from time to time.

8(h) Any dispute regarding administration costs or the fees and expenses of the Tribunal shall be determined by the LCIA Court.

## 3. AAA SCHEDULE OF COSTS AND FEES

**Administrative Fees**

The administrative fees of the AAA are based on the amount of the claim or counterclaim. Arbitrator compensation is not included in this schedule. Unless the parties agree otherwise, arbitrator compensation and administrative fees are subject to allocation by the arbitrator in the award.

**Filing Fees**

A nonrefundable filing fee is payable in full by a filing party when a claim, counterclaim or additional claim is filed, as provided below.

| Amount of Claim | Filing Fee |
|---|---|
| Up to $10,000 | $500 |
| Above $10,000 to $50,000 | $750 |
| Above $50,000 to $100,000 | $1,250 |
| Above $100,000 to $250,000 | $2,000 |
| Above $250,000 to $500,000 | $3,500 |
| Above $500,000 to $1,000,000 | $5,000 |
| Above $1,000,000 to $5,000,000 | $7,000 |

When no amount can be stated at the time of filing, the minimum filing fee is $2,000, subject to increase when the claim or counterclaim is disclosed.

When a claim or counterclaim is not for a monetary amount, an appropriate filing fee will be determined by the AAA.

The minimum filing fee for any case having three or more arbitrators is $2,000.

The administrative fee for claims in excess of $5,000,000 will be negotiated.

**Hearing Fees**

For each day of hearing held before a single arbitrator, an administrative fee of $150 is payable by each party.

For each day of hearing held before a multi-arbitrator panel, an administrative fee of $250 is payable by each party.

There is no AAA hearing fee for the initial Procedural Hearing.

**Postponement/Cancellation Fees**

A fee of $150 is payable by a party causing a postponement of any hearing scheduled before a single arbitrator.

A fee of $250 is payable by a party causing a postponement of any hearing scheduled before a multi-arbitrator panel.

**Suspension for Nonpayment**

If arbitrator compensation or administrative charges have not been paid in full, the administrator may so inform the parties in order that one of them may advance the required payment. If such payments are not made, the tribunal may order the suspension or termination of the proceedings. If no arbitrator has yet been appointed, the AAA may suspend the proceedings.

**Hearing Room Rental**

The Hearing Fees described above do not cover the rental of hearing rooms, which are available on a rental basis. Check with the administrator for availability and rates.

## 4. WIPO SCHEDULE OF FEES

(All amounts are in United States dollars)

*Fees of the Centre*

I. REGISTRATION FEE (ARTICLE 67, WIPO ARBITRATION RULES)

| **Amount of Claim** | **Registration Fee** |
|---|---|
| Up to $1,000,000 | $1,000 |
| $1,000,001 to $10,000,000 | $2,000 |
| Over $10,000,000 | $3,000 |

NOTES:

1. Where the amount of the claim is not specified at the time of submitting the Request for Arbitration, a registration fee of $1,000 shall be payable, subject to adjustment when the Statement of Claim is filed.
2. Here a claim is not for a monetary amount, a registration fee of $1,000 shall be payable, subject to adjustment. The adjustment shall be made by reference to the registration fee that the Centre, upon examination of the Request for Arbitration or the Statement of Claim, determines to be appropriate in the circumstances.
3. The amount of claims expressed in currencies other than United States Dollars shall, for the purposes of calculating the registration fee, be converted to amounts expressed in United States Dollars on the basis of the official United Nations exchange rate prevailing on the date of submission of the Request for Arbitration.

II. ADMINISTRATION FEE (ARTICLE 68, WIPO ARBITRATION RULES)

| **Amount of Claim or Counter-Claim** | **Administration Fee** |
|---|---|
| Up to $100,000 | $1,000 |
| $100,001 to $1,000,000 | $1,000 + 0.4% (of the amount above $100,000) |
| $1,000,001 to $5,000,000 | $4,600 + 0.2% (of the amount above $1,000,000) |
| $5,000,001 to $20,000,000 | $12,600 + 0.10% (of the amount above $5,000,000) |
| Over $20,000,000 | $27,600 + 0.05% (of the amount above $20,000,000 up to a maximum administration fee of $35,000) |

NOTES:

1. Where a claim or counterclaim is not for a monetary amount, the Centre shall determine an appropriate administration fee.
2. For the purpose of calculating the administration fee, the percentage figures are applied to each successive part of the claim or counterclaim. For example, if the amount of claim is $5,000,000 the administration fee would be calculated as follows:

| | | |
|---|---|---|
| $100,000 | | $1,000 |
| $900,000 (difference between $100,000 and $1,000,000 | 0.4% | $3,600 |
| $4,000,000 (difference between $1,000,000 and $5,000,000) | 0.20% | $8,000 |
| $5,000,000 | | $12,600 |

1. The maximum administration fee payable is $35,000.
2. The amounts of claims or counterclaims expressed in currencies other than United States Dollars shall, for the purposes of calculating the administration fee, be converted to amounts expressed in United States Dollars on the basis of the official United Nations exchange rate prevailing on the date of submission of the claim or of the counterclaim, respectively.

ARBITRATOR'S FEES

| Amount of claims | Fees | | | |
|---|---|---|---|---|
| | Minimum | | Maximum | |
| | Sole Arbitrator | Three-person Tribunal | Sole Arbitrator | Three-person Tribunal |
| Up to $100,000 | $2,000 | $5,000 | 10.00% | 25.00% |
| $100,001 to $500,000 | $2,000 + 2.00% (of the amount above $100,000) | $5,000 + 5.00% (of the amount above $100,000) | $10,000 + 4.00% (of the amount above $100,000) | $25,000 + 10.00% (of the amount above $100,000) |
| $500,001 to $1,000,000 | $10,000 + 1.50% (of the amount above $500,000) | $25,000 + 3.75% (of the amount above $500,000) | $26,000 + 3.50% (of the amount above $500,000) | $65,000 + 8.75% (of the amount above $500,000) |
| $1,000,001 to $2,000,000 | $17,500 + 1.00% (of the amount above $1,000,000) | $43,750 + 2.50% (of the amount above $1,000,000) | $43,500 + 2.00% (of the amount above $1,000,000) | $108,750 + 5.00% (of the amount above $1,000,000) |
| $2,000,001 to $5,000,000 | $27,500 + 0.75% (of the amount above $2,000,000) | $68,750 + 1.90% (of the amount above $2,000,000) | $63,500 + 1.50% (of the amount above $2,000,000) | $158,750 + 3.75% (of the amount above $2,000,000) |
| $5,000,001 to $10,000,000 | $50,000 + 0.50% (of the amount above $5,000,000) | $125,750 + 1.25% (of the amount above $5,000,000) | $108,500 + 1.00% (of the amount above $5,000,000) | $271,250+ 2.50% (of the amount above $5,000,000) |
| $10,000,001 to $25,000,000 | $75,000 + 0.30% (of the amount above $10,000,000) | $188,250 + 0.75% (of the amount above $10,000,000) | $158,500 + 1.00% (of the amount above $10,000,000) | $396,250 + 2.5% (of the amount above $10,000,000) |
| Over | $120,000 + 0.25% (of the amount above $25,000,000) | $300,750 + 0.65% (of the amount above $25,000,000) | $308,500+ 1.00% (of the amount above $25,000,000) | $771,250 + 2.50% (of the amount above $25,000,000) |

NOTES:

1. For the purpose of calculating the amount of claims, the value of any counterclaim is added to the amount of the claim.
2. For the purpose of calculating the minimum and maximum amounts of the arbitrator's fees, the percentage figures are applied to each successive part of the whole amount of claims. For example, if the amount of claim is $1,500,000,the minimum fee for a sole arbitrator would be calculated as follows:

| | | |
|---|---|---|
| $100,000 | | $2,000 |
| $400,000 (difference between $100,000 and $500,000) | 2.00% | $8,000 |
| $500,000 (difference between $500,000 and $1,000,000) | 1.50% | $7,500 |
| $500,000 (difference between $1,000,000 and $1,500,000) | 1.00% | $5,000 |
| $1,500,000 | | $22,500 |

3. Where a claim or counterclaim is not a monetary amount, the Centre shall, in consultation with the arbitrators and the parties, determine an appropriate value for the claim or counterclaim for the purpose of determining the arbitrator's fees.
4. The amounts of claims or counterclaims expressed in currencies other than United States Dollars shall, for the purpose of determining the arbitrator's fees, be converted to amounts expressed in United States Dollars on the basis of the official United Nations exchange rate prevailing on the date of submission of the claim or of the counterclaim, respectively.
5. The amounts and percentage figures specified in the Table for a three-person Tribunal represent the total fees payable to such a Tribunal, and not the fees payable to each arbitrator. Such fees shall be distributed between the three persons in accordance with the unanimous decision of those three persons. In the absence of such a decision, the distribution shall

be 40 per cent for the presiding arbitrator, and 30 per cent for each of the other two arbitrators.
6. Where, by the agreement of the parties, a number of arbitrators other than one or three is appointed to a Tribunal, the scale of minimum and maximum fees for the Tribunal in question shall be determined by the Centre. That scale shall be so determined by multiplying the scale for a sole arbitrator by the number of arbitrators reduced by a factor that takes into account of the sharing of work and responsibility among the arbitrators.

## 4. CHINA INTERNATIONAL ECONOMIC AND TRADE ARBITRATION COMMISSION ARBITRATION FEE SCHEDULE

*(Effective as from May 10, 1998)*

| **Amount of claim** | **Amount of Fee (RMB)** |
|---|---|
| 1,000,000 Yuan or less | 4% of the Claimed Amount, minimum 20,000 Yuan |
| 1,000,000 Yuan to 5,000,000 Yuan | 40,000 Yuan Plus 3% of the excess over 1,000,000 Yuan |
| 5,000,000 Yuan to 10,000,000 Yuan | 160,000 Yuan Plus 2% of the excess over 5,000,000 Yuan |
| 10,000,000 Yuan to 50,000,000 Yuan | 260,000 Yuan Plus 1% of the excess over 10,000,000 Yuan |
| 50,000,000 Yuan or more | 660,000 Yuan Plus 0.5% of the excess over 50,000,000 Yuan |

When applying for arbitration, each case shall be charged an additional amount of RMB 10,000 Yuan as a Registration Fee which includes the expenses for examining the application for arbitration, accepting the case, computerized management and filing the documents.

Where the amount of the claim is not ascertained at the time when application for arbitration is handed in, or there exists special circumstance, the amount of arbitration fee shall be determined by the Secretariat of the Arbitration Commission or the secretariats of the Sub-Commissions of the Arbitration Commission.

If the arbitration fee is charged in foreign currency, an amount of foreign currency equivalent to the corresponding RMB value specified in this schedule shall be paid.

Apart from charging arbitration according to this Arbitration Fee Schedule, the Arbitration Commission may collect other extra, reasonable and actual expenses pursuant to the relevant provisions of the Arbitration Rules.
For arbitration cases taken cognizance of by the Arbitration Commission in accordance with Paragraph 2(3), (4) and (5) of Article 2 of the Arbitration Rules, the arbitration fees shall be charged pursuant to The Methods of Charging Fees by the Arbitration Commissions formulated by the General Office of the State Council.

## 5. STOCKHOLM

### Regulations for Arbitration Costs

#### *I. Registration Fee*

The Registration Fee in Article 6 of the Rules of the Arbitration Institute of the Stockholm Chamber of Commerce (hereinafter referred to as "the SCC Rules") is EUR 1000.

The registration fee is non-refundable and shall constitute a part of the Administrative Fee due to the SCC Institute under Section III Article 2 below and shall be deducted from the Advance on Costs to be paid by the Claimant pursuant to Article 14 of the SCC Rules.

#### *II. Advance on costs*

According to Article 13 of the SCC Rules, the SCC Institute shall fix an amount which, together with the accrued interest, shall constitute an advance on the Arbitration Costs. The amount shall cover the estimated Arbitration Costs pursuant to Article 39 of the Rules and, if required, value added tax. Amounts referred to in the first paragraph, sections (i) through (iii) in Article 39 of the Rules are to be determined pursuant to these Regulations.

#### *III. Arbitration costs*

ARTICLE 1 – ARBITRATOR'S FEE

(1) Unless otherwise agreed by the parties, the SCC Institute shall decide the fees of the arbitrator in accordance with the table below, based on the amount in dispute. If so required by law, value added tax shall be added to such fees.

(2) For the purpose of calculating the amount in dispute, the value of any counterclaim or set-off claim is to be added to the amount of the claim with the exception of interest claims. Where the amount in dispute is not speci-

fied, the SCC Institute will fix the fees on the basis of an assessment of the size of the case. Each party must provide the SCC Institute with the information deemed necessary for such assessment.

(3) If a case has required substantially more or less work than is considered normal, the SCC Institute may deviate from the amounts stated in the table.

(4) The fee due to the co-arbitrator is fixed per person to 60 per cent of the total fee paid to the Chairman, unless the SCC Institute decides otherwise in view of any special circumstances of the case.

| **Amount in dispute (EUR)** | **Chairman of the Tribunal /Sole Arbitrator (EUR)** | |
|---|---|---|
| | **Minimum** | **Maximum** |
| Up to 25,001 to 50,000 | 2,500 | 5,000 |
| From 25,001 to 50,000 | 2,500 + 2% on the amount above 25,000 | 5,000 + 10% on the amount above 25,000 |
| From 50,000 to 100,000 | 3,000 + 2% on the amount above 50,000 | 7,500 + 5% on the amount above 50,000 |
| From100,001 to 500,000 | 4,000 + 1% on the amount above 100,000 | 10,000 + 3% on the amount above 100,000 |
| From 500,001 to 1,000,000 | 8,000 + 0.8% on the amount above 500,000 | 22,000 + 2.4% on the amount above 500,000 |
| From 1,000,001 to 2,000,000 | 12,000 + 0.5% on the amount above 1,000,000 | 34,000 + 2% on the amount above 1,000,000 |
| From 2,000,000 to 5,000,000 | 17,000 + 0.2% on the amount above 2,000,000 | 54,000 + 1% on the amount above 2,000,000 |
| From 5,000,001 to 10,000,000 | 23,000 + 0.1% on the amount above 5,000,000 | 84,000 + 0.52% on the amount above 5,000,000 |
| From 10,000,001 to 50,000,000 | 28,000 + 0.03% on the amount above 10,000,000 | 110,000 + 0.1% on the amount above 10,000,000 |
| From 50,000,001 to 75,000,000 | 40,000 + 0.02% on the amount above 50,000,000 | 150,000 + 0.048% on the amount above 75,000,000 |
| From 75,000,000 to 100,000,000 | 45,000 + 0.012% on the amount above 75,000,000 | 170,000 + 0.048% on the amount above 75,000,000 |
| From 100,000,001 | 48,000 + 0.01% on the amount above 100,000,000 | 182,000 + 0.045% on the amount above 100,000,000 |

ARTICLE 2 – ADMINISTRATIVE FEE OF THE SCC INSTITUTE

(1) The SCC Institute shall decide the Administrative Fee due to it. The decision is based on the amount in dispute in accordance with the table below. If so required by law, value added tax shall be added to the Administrative Fee.

(2) For the purpose of calculating the amount in dispute, the value of any counterclaim or set-off claim is to be added to the amount of the claim, with the exemption of interest claims. Where the amount in dispute is not specified, the SCC Institute will fix the Administrative Fee on the basis of an assessment of the size of the case. Each party must provide the SCC Institute with the information deemed necessary for such assessment.

(3) If a case has required substantially more or less work than is considered normal, the SCC Institute may deviate from the amounts stated in the table.

| **Amount in dispute (EUR)** | **Administrative Fee for the SCC Institute (EUR)** |
|---|---|
| Up to 25,000 | 1,000 |
| From 25,001 to 50,000 | 1,000 + 4% on the amount above 25,000 |
| From 50,001 to 100,000 | 2,000 + 2% on the amount above 50,000 |
| From 100,001 to 500,000 | 3,000 + 1% on the amount above 100,000 |
| From 500,001 to 1,000,000 | 7,000 + 0.8% on the amount above 500,000 |
| From 1,000,001 to 2,000,000 | 11,000 + 0.3% on the amount above 1,000,000 |
| From 2,000,001 to 5,000,000 | 14,000 + 0.1% on the amount above 2,000,000 |
| From 5,000,001 to 10,000,000 | 17,000 + 0.06% on the amount above 5,000,000 |
| From 10,000,001 to 50,000,000 | 20,000 + 0.02% on the amount above 10,000,000 |
| From 50,000,001 to 75,000,000 | 28,000 + 0.01% on the amount above 50,000,000 |
| From 75,000,001 | 30,500 + 0.01% on the amount above 75,000,000<br>Maximum 60,000 |

ARTICLE 3 – EXPENSES

In addition to the fee(s) of the arbitrator(s) and the Administrative Fee of the SCC Institute, the SCC Institute shall fix an amount, to be provided by the parties, to cover reasonable expenses for the arbitrator(s) and to the SCC Institute.

**1. Effectiveness**

These Regulations enter into force on 1 April 1999 and will replace the former Regulations. The Regulations will be applied to any arbitration commenced on this date or thereafter.

# Index